i386/i486

ADVANCED PROGRAMMING

i386/i486

ADVANCED PROGRAMMING

REAL MODE
PROTECTED MODE
VIRTUAL 8086 MODE

Sen-Cuo Ro

Nexgen Microsystems

Sheau-Chuen Her

Nexgen Microsystems

Consulting Editor: Rajvir Singh

Automata Publishing Company, San Jose, CA 95129

 VAN NOSTRAND REINHOLD
_____ New York

Automata Publishing Company, San Jose, CA 95129

To our families and friends

who make this, and all things, possible.

Copyright © 1993 by Van Nostrand Reinhold

Library of Congress Catalog Card Nnmber
ISBN 0-442-01377-9

Printed in the United States of America.

Van Nostrand Reinhold
115 Fifth Avenue
New York, New York 10003

Chapman and Hall
2-6 Boundary Row
London, SEI 8HN, England

Thomas Nelson Australia
102 Dodds Street
South Melbourne 3205
Victoria, Australia

Nelson Canada
1120 Birchmount Road
Scarborough, Ontario MIK 5G4, Canada

16 15 14 13 12 11 10 9 8 7 6 5 4 3 2 1

Library of Congress Cataloging-in-Publication Data

Ro, Sen-Cuo.
        i386/i486 advanced programming: real mode, protected mode,
virtual 8086 mode / Sen-Cuo Ro, Sheau-chuen Her.
        p.   cm.
        Includes index.
        ISBN 0-442-01377-9
        1. Intel 80386 (microprocessor)--programming.
2. Intel 80486 (microprocessor)--programming.
3. Assembler language (computer program language)
I. Her, Sheau-Chuen. II. Title.
QA76.8.12684R6   1992
005.265--dc20   92-30338
                                                                    CIP

Contents

SECTION IV VIRTUAL-8086 MODE   **167**

SECTION V APPENDICES   **197**

PREFACE

This book gives x86 assembly language programmers a view about how to use the resources and features provided by the i386/i486 processor, the newest and most advanced microprocessor from the Intel x86 family. Because the i386/i486 processor is entirely compatible with its predecessor, the 8086/88 processor, this book concentrates on the enhanced features compared to its predecessor. We assume the reader is already familiar with the concepts of 8086/88 assembly language programming.

Our goal is to show you the programming methods that apply to powerful features of the i386/i486. The i387 math coprocessor is not discussed in this book. A detailed explanation about how to use each i386/i486 instruction is not covered in this book. However, we list the complete i386/i486 instruction set in Appendix B.

Organization of the Book

This book is divided into sections to help readers start learning from the concepts that are similar to the 8086/8088 processor. Then, the discussion shifts to the resources and environment of the i386/i486 processor. Throughout the book, real-life program examples are used to illustrate in detail how you can use the enhanced features or functions of the processor.

Chapter 1 introduces the i386/i486 architecture and its enhanced features. The discussion includes the operation mode, general registers, segment registers, system registers, and system data structures.

Chapter 2 discusses the method that the i386/i486 processor uses to make itself fully compatible with the 8086/88 processor and to define the interrupt vector table address, which is different from the 8086/88 processor.

Chapter 3 presents the two kinds of memory management mechanisms—segmentation and paging—supported by the i386/i486. The memory management definition, memory address translation, and the method to use the memory are also discussed in this chapter.

Chapter 4 begins the sample programs and shows you how to incorporate the features of the i386/i486 processor in your program. This chapter explains how to set up the execution environment before entering and leaving the protected mode. The sample programs show you how to enter and leave the protected mode; it also shows how to keep a program from interfering with others in the protected mode.

Chapter 5 uses examples to show the memory paging management mechanism. The methods to set up the page tables (page directory table, second level page table) and to protect the page memory are included here.

Chapter 6 discusses how the i386/i486 keeps the operating system from interfering because of malfunctions in the application program. The discussion includes the definition of privilege level, control transfers between different processes, and control transfers between different privilege levels.

Chapter 7 shows multitasking support and how the i386/i486 does context switching during a task switch.

Chapter 8 introduces the four debugging aids supported by the i386/i486. This chapter concentrates on one of the aids—instruction-breakpoint fault and data-breakpoint trap.

Chapter 9 introduces the I/O port address, the I/O memory address, I/O privilege level protection, and I/O permission bit map protection in the i386/i486.

Chapter 10 discusses the differences between exceptions and interrupts, vectors, and the exception types defined in the i386/i486.

Chapter 11 explains how to enter the v86 mode, which is compatible with the 8086/88 processor but still contains the enhanced features in the i386/i486. The sample program also shows how to enable paging in the v86 mode.

For more information, can refer to the following books:

- *80386 Programmer's Reference Manual*, Intel Corporation.

- *80386 Assembly Language Reference Manual*, Intel Corporation.

- *i486 Microprocessor Programmer's Reference Manual*, Intel Corporation.

We hope this book can benefit you in your programming the i386/i486 and help you discover the true power of the i386/i486 processor.

Acknowledgements

We want to thank the following people who critiqued various aspects of the book during its preparation: Avatar Saini and Jay Sethuram of *Intel Corporation*, Hal Broome of *Sun Microsystem*, Steve Thomas of *Intergraph*, Deepak Verma of *VLSI Technology*, and Raghu Raghavan. We also want to thank Martha Cover and Ed Haas for correcting the language.

SECTION I

INTRODUCTION

CHAPTER 1

THE i386/i486 ARCHITECTURE

The revolution in desktop computing has made Intel's x86 architecture a *de facto* standard in the PC industry. The i386/i486 is not only an architectural upgrade of its predecessor, the 8086/88, it also incorporates multitasking, paging, hardware protection, debugging support, and a 32-bit address space. The i386/i486 microprocessor provides these new and powerful features that give microprocessor-based computers capabilities that used to be possible only with minicomputers.

To maintain compatibility with the 8086/88 generation, the i386/i486 processor preserves the features that permit 8086/88 programs to run on i386/i486 machines. In addition, ts multitasking feature supports multiple 8086/88 programs running simultaneously on the machine. This feature allows programmers to incorporate standard 8086/88 applications directly onto the i386/i486 system.

The i386/i486 system and its application architecture provides an extensive set of 32-bit resources in the assembly language programming environment.

1.1 Overview

The i386/i486's 32-bit architecture—32-bit programmer's register set, 32-bit data bus, and 32-bit address bus—directly provides large programming resources to application programs. The i386/i486's physical address space is 2^{32} bytes, and its logical address space is 2^{46} bytes. The i386/i486 instruction set supports 8-bit, 16-bit, and 32-bit data manipulation.

The operating system can directly provide virtual memory by using the memory management support in the i386/i486 processor. The i386/i486 processor supports two kinds of memory management—segmentation and paging. For systems whose segments are smaller than 64 kilobytes, segment-based virtual memory management can be used.

3

The i386/i486 demand paging is appropriate for large systems. The i386/i486 processor's present, dirty, and accessed bits for each page let you implement an efficient demand-paged virtual memory system.

Multitasking in the i386/i486 processor is also supported by hardware. By using a single assembly language instruction, the i386/i486 processor can switch the context from one task to another task in hardware, which gives better performance than the slow, software-controlled method of context switching in multitasking.

Any multitasking or time-sharing system must have a protection scheme that prevents each task from interfering with another task. The i386/i486 processor provides different levels and different types of protection which can be selectively used by the operating system or the programmer. These protection checks include privilege level checking (privilege level from 0 to 3), segment type checking (code, data segment), access right checking (read-only, write), segment limit checking, and privileged instruction checking.

The i386/i486 debug registers help you check the dynamic states of the processor. They significantly reduces program debugging time. By specifying the instruction breakpoint or the data breakpoint addresses in the debug registers, the i386/i486 processor generates breakpoint exception when it hits these addresses.

The i486 processor preserves all the features in the i386 processor and offers enhanced features to increase performance. An 8-kilobyte on-chip internal cache memory can reduce the memory access from an external bus. RISC design techniques reduce execution cycle time for frequently used instructions. The on-chip 387 math coprocessor supports the 32-, 64- and 80-bit data formats specified in the IEEE standard 754. The i486 processor supports multiprocessing on the system bus and instructions.

1.2 Operation Modes

The combination of the i386/i486 architecture and the compatibility with the 8086/88 is achieved by providing three distinct operation modes: protected mode, real-address mode, and virtual-8086 (v86) mode.

Protected mode

Protected mode is the native mode of the i386/i486 processor. In the protected mode, the operating system or programmer can use any feature supported by the i386/i486 processor.

Real-address mode

When the i386/i486 processor emulates the environment of the 8086/88 processor, it is in the real-address mode. This mode is independent of the protected mode and cannot use any feature supported in the protected mode. All the programs written for the 8086/88 environment can run under this mode. The i386/i486 processor goes into the real-address mode when the machine is powered on, since BIOS (Basic Input Output System) runs under the real-address mode.

Virtual-8086 mode

V86 mode is another emulation mode for the 8086/88 processor, but it is related to the protected mode. It can be thought of as running the 8086/88 processor emulation under the control of the protected mode. All the features supported in the protected mode are also available in this mode. For example, you can run multiple v86 tasks. The program written to run in v86 mode is the same as the program written for the 8086/88 processor. However, it requires a v86 monitor for initialization and exception handling. Since the protected mode controls the v86 mode, the i386/i486 processor must be in the protected mode before entering the v86 mode.

1.3 Registers

Most of the registers for the i386/i486 processor are 32 bits long, so the registers for the 8086, 80186, and 80286 processors are a subset of the i386/i486. Some of the registers have names you can use to access them.

Segment Registers

Six 16-bit segment registers hold the segment address in real-address mode and the segment selector in protected mode. The segment selector in the protected mode selects a segment descriptor defined in the descriptor table. Put the segment address or selector of the current code segment in the CS register, the segment address or selector of the current stack segment in SS register, and the segment address or selector of the data segment in the DS, ES, FS, and GS registers.

15	0	
CS		Code Segment
DS		Data Segment
ES		Extra Segment
SS		Stack Segment
FS		Data Segment
GS		Data Segment

Figure 1.1   i386/i486 Segment Registers

Instruction Pointer Register

The 32-bit instruction pointer register EIP holds the offset of the next instruction to execute. The lower 16 bits of the EIP can be accessed by the name IP, which can be used for 16-bit addressing. The related base address for the instruction pointer is always in the CS register. Figure 1.2 shows the EIP register format.

General Purpose Registers

There are eight 32-bit general purpose registers, named EAX, EBX, ECX, EDX, ESI, EDI, EBP, and ESP. Their lower 16-bit registers are named AX, BX, CX, DX, SI, DI, BP, and SP. You can access the lower 16-bit registers through these names. As in the 8086/88, the lower byte and the higher byte of the 16-bit registers, named AX, BX, CX, and DX, can be accessed as AL, BL, CL, DL, AH, BH, CH, and DH. These registers can hold data or address quantities.

Similar to the instruction pointer register, ESP holds the offset relative to the base address contained in the SS (stack segment) register. When other general purpose registers (except EBP and BP) are used as a memory address index (for example [BX]), the default relative base segment is DS. For the EBP and BP registers as a memory address index (for example [BP]), the default relative base segment is SS. Figure 1.2 shows the format for all the i386/i486 general purpose registers.

31	16	15	8	7	0	
		AH	A|X	AL		EAX
		BH	B|X	BL		EBX
		CH	C|X	CL		ECX
		DH	D|X	DL		EDX
		SI				ESI
		DI				EDI
		BP				EBP
		SP				ESP
		IP				EIP

Figure 1.2 General Purpose Registers and Instruction Pointer Register

EFLAGS Register

This 32-bit flags register defines bit and bit fields that control certain operations and it indicates the current status of the i386/i486 processor. The lower 12 bits field, which shows the current status, is the same as the flags used in the 8086/88 processor. Figures 1.3 and 1.4 show the format of EFLAGS.

31	17 16	15					7									0
Reserved	V	R	0	N	IO	O	D	I	T	S	Z	0	A	0	P	1	C
	M	F		T	PL	F	F	F	F	F	F		F		F		F

Figure 1.3 The i386 EFLAGS Register

31	18 17	16	15					7								0
Reserved	A	V	R	0	N	IO	O	D	I	T	S	Z	0	A	0	P	1	C
	C	M	F		T	PL	F	F	F	F	F	F		F		F		F

Figure 1.4 The i486 EFLAGS Register

You cannot access EFLAGS directly because the processor doesn't give it a name. Use *PUSHF* and *POPF* to access it indirectly.

IOPL (Input/Output Privilege Level, bits position 12-13)

The 2-bit IOPL field indicates the highest privilege level (from 0 to 3) permitted to execute I/O instructions. If the value of current privilege level (CPL) is greater than IOPL, the i386/i486 processor checks from the I/O bit map defined in TSS (task state segment). If the bit map shows "I/O not permitted" then the processor generates an exception.

NT (Nested Task Flag, bit position 14)

When you set this bit to 1, the current task is nested within another task. When you use a *CALL* instruction to switch tasks, the processor sets this bit to indicate a back link to the caller task. Execution of an *IRET* instruction in the called task with NT bit set switchs back to the caller task.

RF (Resume Flag, bit position 16)

Use this flag in conjunction with the instruction breakpoint exception. When you set this bit to 1, it suppresses multiple exceptions to the same instruction.

VM (Virtual-8086 Mode, bit position 17)

When you set this bit to 1, the processor enters v86 mode. This bit can only be set by the *IRET* instruction and by task switching in protected mode.

The i486 processor defines one more bit in the EFLAGS register than the i386 processor. This bit, the alignment check bit, is reserved in the i386 processor.

AC (Alignment Check, bit position 18)

When you set this bit to 1, it enables the i486 processor to check the alignment during any memory reference. Alignment check bit checks the address word boundary when accessing a word data, double word boundary when accessing a double word data, and 64 bits word boundary when accessing an 8 byte data. The i486 generates an alignment fault with error code 0 when it encounters a misaligned address. Only programs running on privilege level 3 can generate an alignment fault; the i486 processor ignores the alignment check bit when CPL (current privilege level) equals 0, 1, or 2. This bit is enabled by the alignment mask bit defined in the CR0 register (control register).

Control Register

The i386/i486 processor has three control registers: CR0, CR2, and CR3. CR1 register is reserved for future use. These registers either hold the global state or control the operation of the i386/i486 processor.

The formats of machine control register (CR0) defined in the i386 and i486 processor are shown in Figures 1.5 and 1.6.

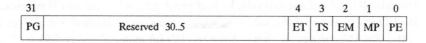

31			4	3	2	1	0
PG	Reserved 30..5		ET	TS	EM	MP	PE

Figure 1.5 The i386 CR0 Register

31	30	29		18	16		5	4	3	2	1	0
PG	CD	NW		AM	WP		NE	ET	TS	EM	MP	PE

Figure 1.6 The i486 CR0 Register

PG (Paging Enable, bit position 31)

Setting this bit to 1, enables memory paging.

ET (Processor Extension Type, bit position 4)

When you set this bit to 1, the 80387-compatible 32-bit protocol is used; otherwise, the 80287-compatible 16-bit protocol is used. This bit is always set to 1 for the i486 processor.

TS (Task Switched, bit position 3)

This bit is automatically set to 1 whenever a task switch happen. It gives the math-coprocessor trap handler an opportunity to save the 80287/80387 context during the task switch. Since this bit is not cleared by the i386/i486, the math-coprocessor trap handler needs to clear this bit before it can be reused.

EM (Emulate Coprocessor, bit position 2)

When you set this bit to 1, all coprocessor instructions generate the coprocessor-not-available exception. *WAIT* instruction ignores the setting of this bit.

MP (Math Present, bit position 1)

When you set both the TS bit and the MP bit to 1, executing *WAIT* or a coprocessor instruction in the program generates a coprocessor-not-available exception.

PE (Protection Enable, bit position 0)

The i386/i486 processor is executed in protected mode when you set this bit to 1 and in real-address mode when you set this bit to 0.

The i486 processor defines more bits in its CR0 register than the i386 processor. These bits are reserved in the i386.

CD (Cache Disable, bit position 30)

The internal cache fill mechanism is disabled when you set this bit to 1 and enabled when you set this bit to 0. When the addressed data cannot be found in the cache, the data is not written into the cache after the i486 processor fetches the data from main memory. The cache hit mechanism is never disabled. If the addressed data is found in the cache, the i486 can still read the data from the cache memory. The cache memory must be flushed to be completely disabled.

NW (Not Write-Through, bit position 29)

The i486 processor internal cache is a write-through and write-invalidate cache. It updates both the cache memory and the main memory during write operation when this bit is 0. This bit should coordinate with the cache disable bit. Table 1.1 summarizes the on-chip cache operating modes.

CD	NW	Description
1	1	Cache fill, write-through, and write-invalidate are disabled. In this mode, cache can be treated as a fast internal RAM. You must preload the data to cache memory.
1	0	Cache fill, write-through and write-invalidate are enabled. In this mode, cache can be used to store stale data.
0	1	This mode is invalid. The i486 generates general protection fault.
0	0	Cache fill, write-through and write-invalidate are enabled.

Table 1.1 On-Chip Cache Operating Mode

AM (Alignment Mask, bit position 18)

This bit controls alignment checking. When this bit is set to 1 and the current privilege level is 3, the i486 processor checks the alignment according to the AC bit defined in EFLAGS.

WP (Write Protect, bit position 16)

When paging is enabled in the i386 processor, all user level pages are readable and writable by the supervisor level process. The i486 processor provides a write protection mechanism to protect the page being written by the supervisor mode process. When this bit is set to 1, a read-only page that belongs to a user level cannot be written by any supervisor level process. The i486 processor paging behavior is the same as that of the i386 processor when this bit is cleared.

NE (Numeric Error, bit position 5)

Since the i486 processor contains the on-chip 80387 math coprocessor, it can perform floating-point operations. When this bit is set to 1, the i486 processor generates an unmasked floating-point fault through exception 16 to report floating-point numeric errors.

Page Fault Linear Address Register (CR2)

The CR2 register holds the 32-bit linear address that caused the page fault.

31   0

Page Fault Linear Address

Figure 1.7 CR2 Register

Page Directory Base Address Register (PDBR) (CR3)

The CR3 register must contain the physical base address of the page directory table when memory paging is enabled. The base address of the page directory table must in the page (4K) boundary, so the lower 12 bits of this address are always zero. In the i386 processor the lower 12 bits are reserved, if you attempt to write into these lower 12 bits, the contents become undefined. In the i486 processor, the bit 3 and bit 4 of the CR3 are defined as follows, whereas the other bits are reserved and have the same effect as in the i386 processor.

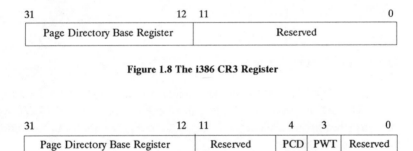

31   12 11   0

Page Directory Base Register	Reserved

Figure 1.8 The i386 CR3 Register

31   12 11   4   3   0

Page Directory Base Register	Reserved	PCD	PWT	Reserved

Figure 1.9 The i486 CR3 Register

PCD (Page Level Cache Disable, bit position 4)

The state of this bit coordinates with CD (Cache Disable) bit to drive the PCD pin during bus cycles when paging is disabled. It also drives the PCD pin where paging is not used to generate the address (for example, when updating the page directory entry) when paging is enabled.

PWT (Page Level Write-Through, bit position 3)

The state of this bit coordinates with the NW (Not Write-through) bit to drive the PWT pin during bus cycles when paging is disabled. It also drives the PWT pin where paging is not used to generate the address (for example, when updating the page directory entry) when paging is enabled.

Debug Registers (DR0 - DR7)

The debug registers can set the instruction and data breakpoints to help with program debugging. More explanation follows in Chapter 8.

Test Registers

Two TLB test registers, TR6 and TR7, control the testing of the translation look-aside buffer (TLB). The TLB is a cache buffer supported in the memory paging system. The i486 processor has three more cache test registers—TR3, TR4, and TR5—for internal on-chip cache testing.

System Address Register

The i386/i486 processor requires the creation of some system tables in the protected mode. These are the descriptor tables. There are three kinds of descriptor tables.

- Global Descriptor Table (GDT)

- Local Descriptor Table (LDT)

- Interrupt Descriptor Table (IDT)

Two registers, GDTR and IDTR, hold the linear base address and the limit for the GDT and IDT. The LDTR register holds the segment selector of the current LDT, where the invisible part (the shadow area in the figures) of the register holds the base address and the limit of current LDT.

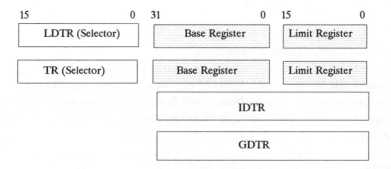

Figure 1.10 System Registers

The task register (TR) holds the segment selector of the current task state segment (TSS). TSS saves the context of the current task during a task switch. The invisible part of the TR register holds the base address and limit for current TSS.

Segment Descriptor Register

For each segment register, there is a corresponding segment descriptor register. These descriptor registers are invisible and cannot be accessed in any way. When you load a segment selector into any segment register, the selected descriptor defined in the descriptor table loads into its corresponding segment descriptor register. These registers allow quick segment references and segment protection checks for memory accesses.

32   0

CS	Descriptor Register (Invisible)
SS	Descriptor Register (Invisible)
DS	Descriptor Register (Invisible)
ES	Descriptor Register (Invisible)
FS	Descriptor Register (Invisible)
GS	Descriptor Register (Invisible)

Figure 1.11 Segment Descriptor Register

1.4 Protected Mode Data Structures

The execution environment in the protected mode is significantly different from the real-address mode. To execute a program in the protected mode, you must build required system data structures as follows.

Global Descriptor Table (GDT)

The GDT is an array of 8-byte descriptors and it is required for all programs that execute in the protected mode. This descriptor must define certain information about a segment. Generally, data, executable, and system segments are defined in the protected mode. Each segment descriptor has its own format and purpose to stand in the protected mode. The format and definition for each descriptor are shown at the end of this section. How to handle these descriptors is explained in the examples in Chapter 4 through Chapter 12. The linear base address of GDT must be loaded into the GDTR register before entering the protected mode.

Local Descriptor Table (LDT)

The LDT is optional. This table allows each task to define its private segment. You can use LDT to protect one task from interference by another. The difference between LDT and GDT is that GDT defines global segment descriptors which are shared by all tasks while LDT defines segment descriptors belong to one task. The LDT can only be accessed by the task who create it. If you don't want other tasks accidentally access data in your task then you can define your segment descriptors in your LDT.

Like GDT, the LDT is also an array of 8-byte descriptors. It also contains the same type of descriptors as the GDT does except for the type of LDT descriptor. Before a task can use the LDT, the task must define the LDT segment descriptor in the GDT and load this LDT segment selector into the LDTR register. At any time, the LDTR needs to contain the LDT segment selector for the current task. If no LDT is used, the LDTR should be initialized to 0 to avoid incidental usage. The contents of LDTR is exchanged during task switch.

Interrupt Descriptor Table (IDT)

The IDT has the same function as the interrupt table in the real-address mode. It can point out the address of up to 256 interrupt service routines. The IDT must have entries for every interrupt. The descriptor defined in the IDT can only have three types: task gate descriptor, trap gate descriptor, and interrupt gate descriptor. Put the linear base address of the IDT on the IDTR register.

Task State Segment (TSS)

Multitasking in the i386/i486 processor is supported in hardware. Switched contexts are stored in the TSS. During a task switch, the i386/i486 processor stores the machine state of the current task in the TSS for the current task and loads the new machine state from the new task's TSS. Then it transfers control to the new task. Before switching a task, the TR register must contain the segment selector of the current task's TSS.

ines different types of segment descriptors for different
ta segment descriptor, executable segment descriptor,
There are more types of descriptors defined for the
ures 1.13, 1.14 and 1.15 are the format of all types of
486 processor.

31	16	15		0	
I/O Map Base		Reserved		T	64
Reserved		LDT			60
Reserved		GS			5C
Reserved		FS			58
Reserved		DS			54
Reserved		SS			50
Reserved		CS			4C
Reserved		ES			48
EDI					44
ESI					40
EBP					3C
ESP					38
EBX					34
EDX					30
ECX					2C
EAX					28
EFLAGS					24
EIP					20
CR3					1C
Reserved		SS2			18
ESP2					14
Reserved		SS1			10
ESP1					0C
Reserved		SS0			8
ESP0					4
Reserved		Back Link to Previous TSS			0

Figure 1.12 Task State Segment Format

Base 31..24	G	B	0	V	Limit 19..16	P	DPL	1	0	E	W	A	Base 23..16	4
Segment Base 15..0						Segment Limit 15..0								0

G - Granularity
V - Available for programmer use
DPL - Descriptor Privilege Level
W - Writable

B - Big
P - Segment Present
E - Expand - Down
A- Accessed

Figure 1.13 Data Segment Descriptor Format

Base 31..24	G	D	0	V	Limit 19..16	P	DPL	1	1	C	R	A	Base 23..16	4
Segment Base 15..0						Segment Limit 15..0								0

D - Default operation size   C - Conforming
R - Readable

Figure 1.14 Executable Segment Descriptor Format

Reserved	P	DPL	0	0	1	0	1	Reserved	4
TSS Segment Selector		Reserved							0

Task Gate Descriptor

Offset in Segment 31..16	P	DPL	0	X	1	0	0	0	0	0	Count	4
Segment Selector		Offset in Segment 15..0										0

Call Gate Descriptor

X (= 0 - 286 CALL GATE, = 1 - 386 CALL GATE)

Offset in Segment 31..16	P	DPL	0	X	1	1	1	T	0	0	Reserved	4
Segment Selector		Offset in Segment 15..0										0

Interrupt/Trap Gate Descriptor

X (= 0 - 286, = 1 - 386)

T (= 0 - Interrupt Gate, = 1 - Trap Gate)

Base 31..24	G	0	0	V	Limit 19..16	P	DPL	0	0	0	1	0	Base 23..16	4
Segment Base 15..0						Segment Limit 15..0								0

LDT Descriptor

Figure 1.15 System Segment Descriptor Format (continued)

Base 31..24	G	0	0	V	Limit 19..16	P	DPL	0	X	0	B	1	Base 23..16	4
Segment Base 15..0						Segment Limit 15..0								0

TSS Descriptor

X (= 0 - 286 TSS, = 1 - 386 TSS)
B - Busy

Figure 1.15 System Segment Descriptor Format

1.5 Instructions

The i486 processor provides full support for the i386 processor instruction set and has six additional instructions. Three of these new instructions are application instructions and three are system instructions. The complete i386/i486 processor instruction set is given in Appendix B.

Application Instructions:

BSWAP (Byte Swap) This instruction reverses the byte order of a data stored in the 32-bit register.

XADD (Exchange and Add) This instruction loads the data from the destination operand to the source operand, retrieves the sum of the destination operand and the original source operand, then stores the sum to the destination operand.

CMPXCHG (Compare and Exchange) This instruction compares the data stored in accumulator with the destination operand. If they are equal, the source operand loads into the destination operand. Otherwise, the destination operand loads into the accumulator.

System Instructions:

INVD (Invalidate Cache) This instruction flushes the internal cache and signal the external cache to flush.

INVLPG (Invalidate TLB Entry) This instruction invalidates a single entry in the TLB.

WBINVD (Write-Back and Invalidate Cache) This instruction flushes the internal cache, signal the external cache to write-back, and then signal the external cache to flush.

1.6 Summary

This chapter has introduced the base architecture of the i386/i486 processor, the general registers, system registers, and system data structures. For compatibility with the 8086/88 processor, the i386/i486 processor can operate in three different modes—the real-address mode, the protected mode, and the v86 mode. The protected mode is the native mode of the i386/i486 processor; the real-address mode and v86 mode are two different emulation modes for compatibility with the 8086/88 processor. The i486 processor provides more functions and instructions set than the i386 processor.

SECTION II

REAL-ADDRESS MODE

CHAPTER 2

PROGRAMMING IN REAL-ADDRESS MODE

The i386/i486 system operates in the real-address mode when the processor emulates the execution of the 8086/88 processor. In this mode, the i386/i486 processor provides more instructions and extension registers (32-bit registers), which makes it the superset of the 8086/88 processor. The emulation consists of environment emulation and instruction execution emulation. This chapter explains how the i386/i486 processor performs this emulation.

2.1 Environment Emulation

For each segment register there is a corresponding invisible segment descriptor register. When the program wants to access data or instructions from any segment specified by a segment register, the i386/i486 system accesses the corresponding segment descriptor register instead of the segment register. From the information stored in this segment descriptor register, the i386/i486 system can get the linear base address of this segment and check the type, limit, and attribute (read, write) of this segment. If access to this segment violates the definition of this segment (for example, write to a read-only segment) the i386/i486 signals an exception to notify the system that the access is limited.

To make all the segments function as the segments in the 8086/88 processor, the information stored in the segment descriptor register must match the characteristics of the 8086/88 processor's segment.

The question arises how to define the value of these segment descriptor registers so programs have the same environment as in the 8086/88 processor. First define the descriptor register of the code segment (CS segment register) as an executable segment descriptor as in Figure 2.1.

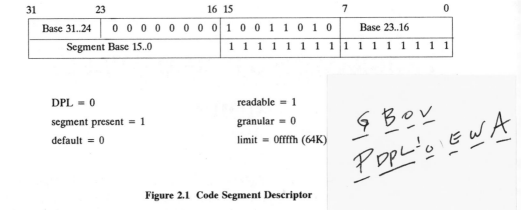

31	23	16	15	7	0
Base 31..24	0 0 0 0 0 0 0 0		1 0 0 1 1 0 1 0	Base 23..16	
Segment Base 15..0			1 1 1 1 1 1 1 1	1 1 1 1 1 1 1 1	

DPL = 0   readable = 1

segment present = 1   granular = 0

default = 0   limit = 0ffffh (64K)

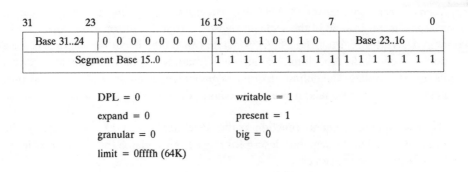

Figure 2.1 Code Segment Descriptor

Define the segment descriptor registers for other segment registers (SS, DS, ES, FS, GS) as in Figure 2.2.

31	23	16	15	7	0
Base 31..24	0 0 0 0 0 0 0 0		1 0 0 1 0 0 1 0	Base 23..16	
Segment Base 15..0			1 1 1 1 1 1 1 1	1 1 1 1 1 1 1 1	

DPL = 0   writable = 1

expand = 0   present = 1

granular = 0   big = 0

limit = 0ffffh (64K)

Figure 2.2 Data Segment Descriptor

The memory management mechanism supported in the 8086/88 processor (also in the real-address mode) is segmentation. It shifts the segment value left by four bits and adds the offset to form a 20-bit linear address. For example, if segment value is *0800h* and offset value is *765h*, the effective address (also the physical address) is *08765h*. There is no segment limit checking mechanism supported by the 8086/88 processor and the maximum size of a segment can be up to 0ffffh (64 kilobytes).

The i386/i486 processor loads the segment linear base address into the segment descriptor register when you load a segment address into the segment register. When the i386/i486 processor gets the segment address, it shifts the segment address value left by four bits to form the linear address and stores it into the segment base address field in the segment descriptor register.

2.2 Instruction Execution Emulation

The i386/i486 processor executes an instruction mainly depends on the current operation mode, the real-address mode, the protected mode, or the v86 mode. In different modes, the i386/i486 processor may execute the same instruction in different way. Thus, the i386/i486 processor can easily emulate the instruction operation of the 8086/88 processor.

After the system is powered on, the i386/i486 processor automatically initializes the segment descriptor registers to the state that matches the real-address mode and starts running in this mode. If you want to reenter the real-address mode from the protected mode, reinitialize the segment descriptor registers to the proper states (see Section 2.1) before reentering the real-address mode. Otherwise, the system might not execute properly in the real-address mode.

2.3 Real-Address Mode Operation

When the i386/i486 processor runs in the real-address mode, the execution environment is a superset of the 8086/88 processor. In fact, it gives you a high-speed 8086/88 processor with more instructions and extension registers (up to 32 bits). In addition, the i386/i486 processor provides an interrupt descriptor table register (IDTR) in the real-address mode that lets you set the interrupt table at any memory location.

When interrupts or exceptions occur, the i386/i486 processor gets the interrupt vector table base address from the IDTR register and according to the vector address defined in the interrupt table, dispatches control to the interrupt handler routine. After you reset the system, the IDTR register contains the address value *0* and the limit value *03ffh*, which is the interrupt vector table address defined in the 8086/88 processor. The instruction *LIDT* is used to load the base address and the limit value to the IDTR register and is available in both the real-address mode and the protected mode.

The sample program that follows explains the function of the IDTR register. You can set the interrupt vector table at any memory location in the IDTR register by using the *LIDT* instruction in real-address mode.

2.4 Interrupt Table Program

The following program runs in the real-address mode of the i386/i486 processor and the DOS environment. It first replaces the original interrupt vector table address in the IDTR register by its local interrupt vector table address. When this program executes a software interrupt instruction, the local interrupt service routine is called and this service routine displays a message that relate to this software interrupt on the screen. At the end of this program, it restores the original interrupt vector table address in the IDTR register and calls a DOS function to terminate itself.

File: REALIDT.ASM

```
.386p

;Define program Stack Segment

STACK           segment      STACK         use16
        db      100 DUP(0)
STACK           ends

;Define 16 (from 0 to 15) Local Interrupt Vector Table.
;Each vector contains the segment and offset address of its
;interrupt service procedure.


IDT     segment      para   public       'idt'         use16
        dd      Int0           ;interrupt 0 service routine vector
        dd      Int1           ;interrupt 1 service routine vector
        dd      Int2           ;interrupt 2 service routine vector
        dd      Int3           ;interrupt 3 service routine vector
        dd      Int4           ;interrupt 4 service routine vector
        dd      Int5           ;interrupt 5 service routine vector
        dd      Int6           ;interrupt 6 service routine vector
        dd      Int7           ;interrupt 7 service routine vector
        dd      Int8           ;interrupt 8 service routine vector
        dd      Int9           ;interrupt 9 service routine vector
        dd      Int10          ;interrupt 10 service routine vector
        dd      Int11          ;interrupt 11 service routine vector
        dd      Int12          ;interrupt 12 service routine vector
        dd      Int13          ;interrupt 13 service routine vector
        dd      Int14          ;interrupt 14 service routine vector
        dd      Int15          ;interrupt 15 service routine vector
idt_limit    equ   $
IDT     ends

;Define program Data Segment

DATA    segment    para  public '   data'        use16
IDT_addr     dw     idt_limit  ;new IDT segment limit
             dd     ?          ;new IDT base address,
                               ;initialized at run time
old_IDT_addr      dw    ?      ;DOS IDT segment limit
```

```
                dd      ?                 ;DOS IDT base address (0:0)
msg     db 'Program to Replace IDT address in real mode','$'
Int0M           db 'INTERRUPT 0', 0
Int1M           db 'INTERRUPT 1', 0
Int2M           db 'INTERRUPT 2', 0
Int3M           db 'INTERRUPT 3', 0
Int4M           db 'INTERRUPT 4', 0
Int5M           db 'INTERRUPT 5', 0
Int6M           db 'INTERRUPT 6', 0
Int7M           db 'INTERRUPT 7', 0
Int8M           db 'INTERRUPT 8', 0
Int9M           db 'INTERRUPT 9', 0
Int10M          db 'INTERRUPT 10', 0
Int11M          db 'INTERRUPT 11', 0
Int12M          db 'INTERRUPT 12', 0
Int13M          db 'INTERRUPT 13', 0
Int14M          db 'INTERRUPT 14', 0
Int15M          db 'INTERRUPT 15', 0
DATA    ends

;Program Code

code            segment         use16
        assume cs:code, ds:DATA, ss:STACK
start proc      far
        mov     ax,DATA           ;get data segment address
        mov     ds,ax             ;put in DS register
        mov     ah,9              ;display message on screen
        mov     dx,offset msg     ;by using DOS function call
        int     21h
;Get IDT base address and save it.
;The IDT address can be retrieved only during program run
;time.

        xor     eax,eax    ;clear eax register content
        mov     ax,IDT     ;get new IDT segment address
        shl     eax,4      ;convert to 32-bit linear address
        mov     dword ptr [IDT_addr+2],eax ;put it in data area

;Save old IDTR content

        sidt    fword ptr [old_IDT_addr]

;Load local IDT limit and base address into IDTR.

        lidt    fword ptr [IDT_addr]

;Execute a software interrupt instruction.

        int     5              ;Call interrupt 5 service routine.

;Restore old IDTR content.

        lidt    fword ptr [old_IDT_addr]

;Terminate the program
```

```
        mov    ax,4c00h              ;Terminate this program
        int    21h                   ;by calling DOS function call.
start endp
code    ends

;Local Interrupt service routine
;These routines will get the offset address of its message
;and display the message on the screen.

INTCODE       segment use16
       assume  cs:intcode,ds:data
Int0:         mov    si,offset Int0M
       jmp    dispmsg
Int1:         mov    si,offset Int1M
       jmp    dispmsg
Int2:         mov    si,offset Int2M
       jmp    dispmsg
Int3:         mov    si,offset Int3M
       jmp    dispmsg
Int4:         mov    si,offset Int4M
       jmp    dispmsg
Int5:         mov    si,offset Int5M
       jmp    dispmsg
Int6:         mov    si,offset Int6M
       jmp    dispmsg
Int7:         mov    si,offset Int7M
       jmp    dispmsg
Int8:         mov    si,offset Int8M
       jmp    dispmsg
Int9:         mov    si,offset Int9M
       jmp    dispmsg
Int10:        mov    si,offset Int10M
       jmp    dispmsg
Int11:        mov    si,offset Int11M
       jmp    dispmsg
Int12:        mov    si,offset Int12M
       jmp    dispmsg
Int13:        mov    si,offset Int13M
       jmp    dispmsg
Int14:        mov    si,offset Int14M
       jmp    dispmsg
Int15:        mov    si,offset Int15M

dispmsg:
       mov    di, 80 * 35
       call   dispit
       iret

;Message display routine
;Because DOS function call is not available at this time,
;we have to display it by ourself.

dispit        proc   near
       push   es              ;save ES register
       mov    ax,0b800h       ;video ram segment address
       mov    es,ax           ;put in ES register
       mov    ah,40h          ;display attribute
```

```
L1:     lodsb                   ;get display character
        cmp     al,0            ;end of display ?
        je      L2
        stosw                   ;store in video ram
        jmp     L1
L2:     pop     es              ;restore ES register
        ret
dispit          endp
INTCODE         ends
        end         start
```

2.5 Summary

The real-address mode of the i386/i486 processor uses two methods to emulate the 8086/88 processor—environment emulation and instruction execution emulation. Defining the proper value in the segment descriptor registers makes the environment act like the environment of the 8086/88 processor.

The i386/i486 processor is a superset of the 8086/88 processor, providing more instructions, extension registers (32-bit registers), and the IDTR register. The IDTR register lets you set the interrupt vector table at any system memory address. Because the i386/i486 processor depends on the IDTR register to get the base address of the interrupt vector table, you must program the IDTR register exactly as shown in the sample program to avoid incorrect execution.

SECTION III

PROTECTED MODE

CHAPTER 3

MEMORY MANAGEMENT

The i386/i486 processor supports two kinds of memory management: segmentation and paging. Each mechanism has its own merits and each can protect a program against interference from other programs. A typical example is when the operating system needs to be protected against the malfunctions in an application program.

Through the segmentation mechanism, the i386/i486 converts a logical address (segment:offset) to a linear address. Then through the paging mechanism, it converts a linear address to the physical address when paging is enabled. The linear address is actually the physical address if paging is not enabled. Figure 3.1 presents the i386/i486 memory address translation mechanisms.

3.1 Segmentation

Segmentation makes the memory completely simple but unstructured that a program can have several independent, protected address spaces. A segment is a block of address space whose size is variable. You can set the segment size as needed by the application but it must not exceed the memory limit. For each segment, you need to define the segment starting linear base address, the segment space range (limit), the segment type, and the segment attribute in its segment descriptor before the segment can be accessed.

When the i386/i486 processor access data or code from a segment, it checks the definition in its segment descriptor to ensure the access does not violate the segment rule. This checking procedure prevents interference between separate segments or multiple programs. However, it all depends on how the operating system allocates separate address blocks and defines proper segment descriptor for each segment. Different

31

segments can share the same segment block by defining their segment descriptors
with the same base address and limit.

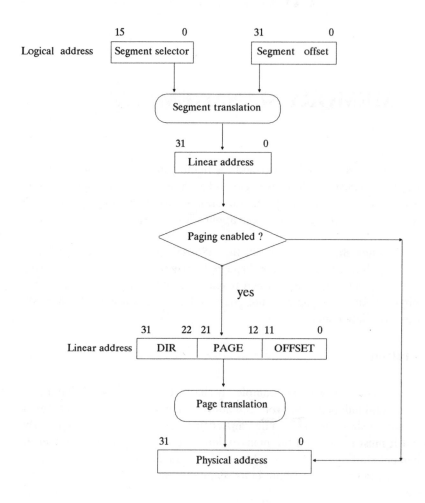

Figure 3.1 Address Translation Mechanism

3.2 Segmentation Address Translation

In the protected mode the segment selector points to the segment descriptor. The
segment selector should be an entry address in the descriptor table (GDT or LDT). Each
memory reference is associated with a segment selector. The segment descriptor must
include all information about a segment. The i386/i486 processor gets the segment linear
base address from the selected descriptor and adds the offset to form a 32-bit linear

address. At the same time it also checks the segment type, whether the segment is present or not, and the segment limit. An exception is generated if the memory reference violates the definition of the descriptor for example, the offset is beyond the segment limit. The maximum limit for each segment can be one megabytes (granularity bit = 0) or four gigabytes (granularity bit = 1).

Since the segment descriptor is eight bytes long, the least significant three bits of the segment selector are assumed to be zero while indexing into the descriptor table. The i386/i486 processor defines these three bits for other usage. One bit is a table indicator (TI) and the other two bits are requested privilege level (RPL). A clear table indicator bit (= 0) selects the descriptor from GDT. A set table indicator bit (= 1) selects the descriptor from the current LDT.

```
15                        3  2   1   0
  +-------------------------+----+-------+
  |         INDEX           | TI |  RPL  |
  +-------------------------+----+-------+
```

Figure 3.2 Segment Selector Format

3.3 Paging

Paging, unlike segmentation, divides the system memory into fixed memory blocks where each block is called a page. One page occupies four kilobytes of memory in the i386/i486 system. A linear address, which is translated from the logical address that given by user, is translated into its corresponding physical address by paging translation mechanism when paging is enabled.

Through the translation mechanism some disk storage space can also be treated as memory address space. The translation mechanism allows pages which reside in the disk to be read into memory and updating the mapping of linear addresses to physical addresses for that page. When the i386/i486 processor finds out that the desired page is not in memory, it generates an exception to enable the operating system to load the desired page into memory, and then restarts executing the program from the interrupted point. This provides the operating system an easy way to handle demand-paging virtual memory.

3.4 Page Address Translation

The i386/i486 processor uses two levels of page table mapping mechanism to translate a linear address to a physical address. The top-level page table is called the "page directory table," which maps to the second level "page table." The second level page table then maps to a page in physical memory. Both page tables have the same format. Figure 3.3 shows the page table entry format.

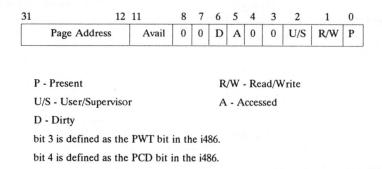

31	12 11		8	7	6	5	4	3	2	1	0
Page Address	Avail		0	0	D	A	0	0	U/S	R/W	P

P - Present   R/W - Read/Write

U/S - User/Supervisor   A - Accessed

D - Dirty

bit 3 is defined as the PWT bit in the i486.

bit 4 is defined as the PCD bit in the i486.

Figure 3.3 Page Table Entry Format

When paging is enabled, a task can only have one page directory table but several second level page tables at the same time. The CR3 register points to the physical base address of the page directory table. The CR3 register is also called the page directory base register (PDBR), because it holds the physical base address of the page directory table. Every page table is itself a page. It must be located on some page of the system and cannot cross the boundary of two pages. The 12 least significant bits in the CR3 register are treated as reserved because page tables are always aligned at a 4-kilobyte page boundary. The i386/i486 processor defines the 12 least significant bits in the page table entry for other usage, because these bits are never used during page address translation.

Figure 3.4 shows how the i386/i486 processor translates a linear address through the two-level page tables to a physical address. When paging is enabled, the linear address is interpreted as consisting of three fields—directory, page, and offset. The directory field chooses one entry from the page directory table, where the entry contains the physical base address of the second-level page table. The page field also chooses one entry from this second-level page table, where the entry contains the physical base address of the page frame. Since there are only 1024 entries in every page table, only 10 bits are needed for the directory and page field. The offset field contains the offset relative to the page that chosen by the directory and page field.

To make the translation from a linear address to a physical address take place quickly, the i386/i486 processor provides an on-chip cache called the translation look-aside buffer (TLB). When paging is enabled, the i386/i486 stores the most recently used page table entries in the TLB, and every address translation first goes through the TLB. This cache buffer can save the access time for a page table entry from the TLB instead of from the memory.

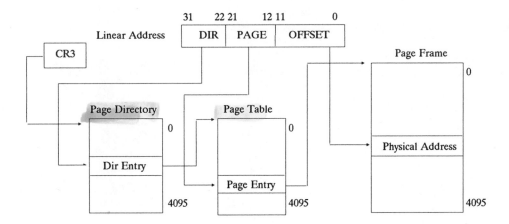

Figure 3.4 Page Translation

3.5 Summary

This chapter has discussed the i386/i486 segmentation and paging for memory management. Segmentation divides the system memory space into multiple variable-sized address spaces called the segment. The type, attribute, linear base address, and limit for each segment must be defined in its segment descriptor. The i386/i486 processor depends on the segment descriptor to get the segment information.

Paging divides the system memory space into multiple fixed-sized address spaces called the page. The i386/i486 processor uses two level page table mapping to convert a linear address to a physical address. A linear address is interpreted as an index into the page directory table (first level), then as an index into the page table (second level), and an offset to the actual page. Any operating system implemented in the i386/i486 system can support demand-paging virtual memory by using the paging mechanism.

CHAPTER 4

ENTER AND LEAVE PROTECTED MODE

The previous chapters mentioned that there are three different i386/i486 operation modes (real-address, protected, and v86 mode). This chapter describes how to enter and leave the protected mode. Before entering the protected mode, you have to set up the system data structures (GDT and IDT) and initialize system registers (GDTR and IDTR) in the program. When leaving the protected mode, you also have to reset the system registers (segment registers) to prepare the execution environment for the real-address mode.

4.1 Entering Protected Mode

When the i386/i486 system is powered on, the system startup program is running in the real-address mode. If you intend to run programs in the protected mode, certain setup procedures for entering the protected mode must be executed in the real-address mode. The setup procedures for entering the protected mode need to initialize all the system data structures and registers needed in the protected mode.

The global descriptor table (GDT) is the most important system data structure. It allows the i386/i486 access code and data in the protected mode. In the GDT, at least one segment descriptor should be defined for the code segment to let the i386/i486 processor continue to fetch and execute instructions. The segment descriptor for the data segment should be defined if the program needs to access data from the data segment. The linear base address and limit of the GDT must be loaded into the GDTR register before entering protected mode.

If you want the protected mode program to support the interrupt handler routines for exceptions or interrupts, the interrupt descriptor table (IDT) should be built to allow the execution of the interrupt handler routines when an interrupt or exception occurs.

37

Similar to the GDT, the IDT can be accessed only after the linear base address and limit of the IDT have been loaded into the IDTR register.

After the system data structures are set up, the program enters protected mode by enabling the PE bit in the CR0 register (see Figure 4.1). The program has to execute a *JMP* instruction immediately following the PE bit enable instruction. Since the i386/i486 processor overlaps the instruction fetch, decode, and execution, only the *JMP* instruction can flush the instruction queue and change the execution flow. The previous fetched and decoded instruction will be ignored.

At this point, when entering the protected mode with all the segment registers still holding the contents defined in the real-address mode, the program should reload the appropriate segment selector with these segment registers to fit the protected mode address translation. Now the program is executed in the protected mode with current privilege level (CPL) 0.

```
                .
                .
                .
        real-address mode program

        build GDT,IDT structure

        mov    eax,cr0              ;get cr0 register
        or     al,prot_enable       ;set protected mode enable
        mov    cr0,eax              ;restore cr0
        jmp    dword ptr cs:[enter_prot] ;far jump to flush
                                    ;instruction queue
enter_prot:
        dw     offset now_in_prot    ;EIP
        dw     code_sel             ;CS selector

now_in_prot:

        protected mode program
                .
                .
                .
```

Figure 4.1 Entering Protected Mode

4.2 Protected Mode Execution Environment

Figure 4.2 shows the relationship between the hardware structure and software structure while a program is executed in the protected mode. The GDTR and IDTR holds the linear base address (32 bits) and limits (16 bits) of the GDT and the IDT. The LDTR and the TR holds the segment selector which selects the segment descriptor of the LDT and TSS of the current task if it is needed by the program. Otherwise the LDTR and TR should be initialized to 0 to indicate a NULL selector.

The segment descriptor register is loaded with the segment descriptor whenever a segment register is loaded with the segment selector.

When any memory reference through any segment register or the LDTR and TR, the i386/i486 processor accesses the segment descriptor stored in the segment descriptor register instead of from the descriptor table. Accessing the segment descriptor from the segment descriptor register can save a lot of time and speed up program execution.

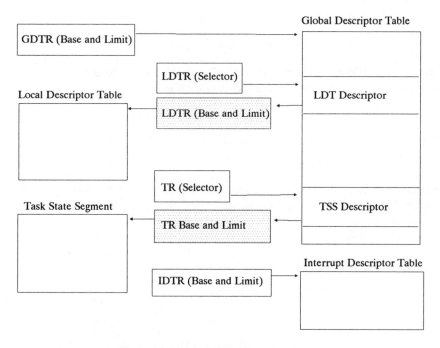

Figure 4.2 Protected Mode Execution Environment

4.3 Leaving Protected Mode

The i386/i486 processor can reenter the real-address mode when the PE bit of the CR0 register is cleared in the protected mode. To continue program execution in the real-address mode, certain system data structures need to be reset to allow the program to run in the real-address mode environment. Use the following steps before reentering the real-address mode:

- Change the privilege level for current task to 0, the privilege level for the real-address mode.

- Change the CS segment limit to *0ffffh* by transferring control to an executable segment that has a limit of *0ffffh*, the segment limit for CS in the real-address mode.

- Load all the segment registers except CS with a segment selector whose segment descriptor is defined as follows: data segment descriptor, DPL = *0*, writable = *1*, expand = *0*, present = *1*, granular = *0*, big = *0*, and limit = *0ffffh* (64 kilobytes). This sets the segment descriptor register to the states that are appropriate for the real-address mode.

- Disable the interrupt.

- To enter the real-address mode, clear the PE bit in the CR0 register .

- Execute a *JMP* instructionn to flush the instruction queue.

- Recover the IDTR register to the linear base address and to the limit of the interrupt vector table in the real-address mode if needed.

- Enable interrupt.

- The program now reenters the real-address mode. Reinitialize the segment registers in the real-address mode if needed.

Figure 4.3 shows the code and data segment descriptor format that is suitable for the segment in the real-address mode. Figure 4.4 shows an example of how to reenter real-address mode.

```
;level 0 code segment descriptor format:

code_sel     dw      0ffffh      ;limit (0 - 15)
             dw      ?           ;segment base (0 - 15)
             db      ?           ;segment base (16 - 23)
             db      9ah         ;present=1,readable = 1
             db      0           ;limit (16 - 19), G=0, D=0
             db      0           ;base (24 - 31)

;data segment descriptor format:

dmy_selec    dw      0ffffh      ;limit (0 - 15)
             dw      ?           ;segment base (0 - 15)
             db      ?           ;segment base (16 - 23)
             db      92h         ;present=1,writable = 1
             db      0           ;limit (16 - 19), G=0, D=0
             db      0           ;base (24 - 31)
```

Figure 4.3 Segment Definition for the Real-Address Mode

```
                    .
                    .
                    .
         protected mode program executed in level 0

         db     0eah                ;jump directly far
         dw     offset real_1       ;ip
         dw     code_sel            ;cs selector
real_1:
         mov    ax,dmy_selec        ;dummy selector
         mov    es,ax               ;reset segment registers
         mov    ds,ax
         mov    fs,ax
         mov    gs,ax
         mov    ss,ax
         cli                        ;disable interrupt
         mov    eax,cr0             ;load the content of CR0
         and    eax,not prot_enable      ;disable protected mode
         mov    cr0,eax             ;restore the content of CR0
         db     0eah                ;far jump to flush
                                    ;instruction queue
         dw     offset real_mode    ;new EIP
         dw     code                ;new CS segment
real_mode:                          ;executed in real-address mode
         mov    ax,data             ;get real mode data segment
                                    ;address
         mov    ds,ax               ;put in ds
         lidt   [oldidt]            ;load real address mode
                                    ;idt address
         cli
```

Figure 4.4 Reentering Real-Address Mode

4.4 Sample Program 1

The following program illustrates how to enter and leave between real-address and protected modes. This program only prepares the basic system data structures in order to enter the protected mode. It does not include all the structures and functions in the protected mode. There is no paging, multitasking, or protection in this sample program.

At the beginning of this program, two standard files *STRUCT* and *MACRO1* are included. The file *STRUCT* defines most of the data structures that is used in the protected mode. The other file, *MACRO1*, defines some routine code. To save coding time, these two files are separated from the main program and are defined as the "include" files.

File: STRUCT

```
;Structure for segment descriptor

dscp   struc
       D_lim1      dw      0
       D_base1     dw      0
       D_base2     db      0
       D_type      db      0
       D_lim2      db      0
       D_base3     db  .   0
dscp   ends

;Structure for stack after interrupt in v86 task

stkdef       struc
       oldeip      dw      0
                   dw      0
       oldcs       dw      0
                   dw      0
       oldflg      dw      0
                   dw      0
       oldsp       dw      0
                   dw      0
       oldss       dw      0
                   dw      0
       oldes       dw      0
                   dw      0
       olddds      dw      0
                   dw      0
       oldfs       dw      0
                   dw      0
       oldgs       dw      0
                   dw      0
stkdef       ends

;Structure for page table

page_tbl     struc
       pg_stat     db      ?
       pg_avail    db      ?
       pg_limit    db      ?
page_tbl     ends
```

File: MACRO1

```
;Macro for stack in TSS

TSS_stack          macro ss0,esp0,ss1,esp1,ss2,esp2
```

```
        dd      0
        dd      offset esp0
        dd      ss0
        dd      offset esp1
        dd      ss1
        dd      offset esp2
        dd      ss2
endm

;Macro for cr3 in TSS

TSS_cr3     macro
        dd      0
endm

;Macro for general register in TSS

TSS_regs
macro teip,tflg,teax,tebx,tecx,tedx,tesi,tedi,tebp,tesp
        dd      offset teip
        dd      tflg
        dd      teax
        dd      tecx
        dd      tedx
        dd      tebx
        dd      offset tesp
        dd      tebp
        dd      tesi
        dd      tedi
endm

;Macro for segment register in TSS

TSS_seg     macro tes,tcs,tss,tds,tfs,tgs
        dd      tes
        dd      tcs
        dd      tss
        dd      tds
        dd      tfs
        dd      tgs
endm

;Macro for far call

callf macro selector
        db      9ah
        dw      0
        dw      selector
endm

;Macro for far jump

jmpf    macro selector
        db      0eah
        dw      0
        dw      selector
endm
```

Program: EN.ASM

EN.ASM shows how to enter the protected mode from the real-address mode in DOS environment and leave the protected mode to reenter the DOS real-address mode. First, it sets up all the environment (GDT, IDT and TSS) for the protected mode while execution in the real-address mode, then enter the protected mode. Once in protected mode, this program displays a message on the screen then leaves protected mode reenters to the real-address mode. The program then terminates itself in the real-address mode and return to the DOS prompt.

Step 0: EQU definition.

Step 1: Define the global descriptor table (GDT)

The local descriptor table is not used in this program, so all the descriptors used in this program are defined in the global descriptor table. This table defines only the limit and the type of each descriptor and the linear base address is initialized at run time.

● The first descriptor must be a NULL descriptor.

● Video segment descriptor, not initiated at run time, has the linear base address *B8000H*.

Step 2: Define interrupt descriptor table (IDT)

This program defines 21 interrupt gate descriptors in the IDT, thereby providing 21 (0 - 20) interrupt service routines. The segment selector for these routines is *int_selec*. The offset of these routines is initialized at run time.

Step 3: Variable

● *pGDT* is a pointer to a six-byte data that has the linear base address and limit value for the GDT. These values are set at run time.

● *pIDT* is a pointer to a six-byte data that has the linear base address and limit value for the IDT. These values are set at run time.

● *pold* is a pointer to a six-byte data that has the linear base address and limit value for the interrupt vector table defined in real-address mode with DOS environment.

Step 4: Mapping table for each selector to segment

● This table defines those selectors whose linear base addresses need to be initialized in the descriptor. The corresponding segment is defined following the selector.

- *gdt_tab_size* has the entry number for this table.

Step 5: Define messages

Step 6: Define privilege level 0, 1, and 2 stack segment

Step 7: Set up task state segment

Step 8: Define a dummy segment that can give the proper value to the segment descriptor register when returning to the real-address mode

Step 9: Initialize the entry point of each interrupt descriptor defined in the IDT. Each interrupt service routine reserves 4 bytes and stays contiguous in the memory.

Step 10: The program gets the linear base address (32 bits) and the limit for the GDT and the IDT then saves it.

Step 11: Based on the segment address defined in the *gdt_phys_tab* table gets the linear base address (32 bits) and sets it in the descriptor corresponding to the segment selector.

Step 12: Switch to the protected mode

- Load the GDT linear address and limit into the GDTR.
- Load the IDT linear address and limit into the IDTR.
- Enable the protected mode bit in CR0.
- Use, a far *JMP* to flush the instruction queue.

Step 13: Set the LDTR, SS, SP, DS, ES, FS, and GS registers

Step 14: Now, the program displays a message on the screen.

Since there is no DOS system function in the protected mode, this program writes characters directly to the memory of the screen. First, it writes spaces into memory to clear the screen. Then it writes the messages to the screen.

Step 15: Load the current task state segment selector into the task register.

Step 16: Give a software interrupt that goes to the interrupt procedure through the interrupt descriptor defined in the IDT. The interrupt procedure displays the interrupt number and then return to the real-address mode with DOS environment.

Step 17: The interrupt service routines start from here. There are 21 interrupt routines in this program. Each routine has the same code and reserves 4 bytes in the memory.

Since these routines are defined contiguously, these routines appear as if they are defining a routine table.

Step 18: This entry point is called by every interrupt service routine. The actual interrupt number can be obtained as follows:

- *pop* the return address from the stack.

- get the offset of this return address from the starting address of the interrupt service routines.

- divide the offset by four, then get the interrupt number.

The program then displays the interrupt number on the screen.

Step 19: The program returns the system to the real-address mode with DOS environment.

- It resets the segment descriptors (except CS) by moving a dummy selector to the segment registers. The dummy selector has a limit of 64 kilobytes (limit equals *0ffffh*), byte granular (G bit equals to 0), expand up (E bit equals to 0), writable (W bit equals to 1), and present (P bit equals to 1), which are appropriate for real-address mode. Then it returns to real-address mode by clearing the PE bit in the CR0 register and flushes the instruction queue with a far *JMP* instruction.

Step 20: The code here is executed in the real-address mode. This program sets the DS, SS, and SP registers, which are used later.

Step 21: One more thing that needs to be done is to load the linear base address and limit of the DOS interrupt vector table in the real-address mode to the IDTR. Any interrupt that occurs after this point executes the interrupt routine defined by the DOS interrupt vector table.

Step 22: Finally, the program terminated by calling the DOS terminate process function.

File: EN.ASM

```
.386p
include struct
include macrol

;STEP 0: define equ

INTNO       equ   21        ;interrupt vector number
DSCPSIZE    equ   8         ;size of descriptor
INTSIZE     equ   4       ;size of interrupt service routine
TWO         equ   2
prot_enable equ   01h     ;protected mode enable bit in CR0
```

```
attribute    equ    07h              ;display character attribute
space        equ    20h              ;ASCII code for space

;STEP 1: Global Descriptor Table

GDT segment  para public use16 'GDT'
gdt_tab      label qword
null_selec   equ    $-gdt_tab            ;null selector
  dscp       <,,,,,>       ;first one must be a null descriptor

code_selec   equ    $-gdt_tab            ;code segment selector
  dscp       <0ffffh,,,09ah,,>           ;descriptor

task0_TSS_selec  equ  $-gdt_tab        ;TSS segment selector
  dscp       <task0_TSS_limit,,,,089h,,> ;descriptor

stk0_selec   equ    $-gdt_tab            ;level 0 stack segment
                                         ;selector
  dscp       <stk0_limit,,,92h,,>        ;descriptor with
                                         ;privilege level 0
stk1_selec   equ    $-gdt_tab or 1       ;level 1 stack
                                         ;segment selector
  dscp       <stk1_limit,,,0b2h,,>       ;descriptor with
                                         ;privilege level 1
stk2_selec   equ $-gdt_tab  or 2         ;level 2 stack
                                         ;segment selector
  dscp       <stk2_limit,,,0d2h,,>       ;descriptor with
                                         ;privilege level 2
dmy_selec    equ    $-gdt_tab            ;dummy segment selector
  dscp       <0ffffh,,,92h,,>            ;descriptor

video_selec  equ $-gdt_tab or 3          ;video segment selector
  dscp       <0ffffh,8000h,0bh,0f2h,,>       ;descriptor

gdata_selec  equ    $-gdt_tab            ;data segment selector
  dscp       <gdata_limit,,,0f2h,,>  ;descriptor

int_selec    equ    $-gdt_tab            ;interrupt segment
                                         ;selector
  dscp       <0ffffh,,,09ah,,>           ;descriptor
gdt_limit    equ    $-gdt_tab
GDT  ends

;STEP 2:    Interrupt Descriptor Table

IDT  segment para      public use16 'idt'
idt_tab equ $
     REPT   INTNO                        ;21 interrupt entries
     dscp   <,int_selec,0,0eeh,,>  ;DPL = 3
     ENDM
idt_limit    equ    $
IDT  ends

;DATA Segment

Gdata segment para public use16 'Gdata'
```

```
;STEP 3: variable to save GDT/IDT limit and linear address

pGDT   label fword
pGDT_limit   dw    ?              ;GDT limit
pGDT_addr    dd    ?              ;GDT base address

pIDT   label fword
pIDT_limit   dw    ?              ;IDT limit
pIDT_addr    dd    ?              ;IDT base address

pold   label fword
dIDT_limit   dw    03ffh          ;DOS IDT limit
dIDT_addr    dd    0              ;DOS IDT base address

;STEP 4: table to define the mapping of descriptor to
;        segment

gdt_phys_tab        label word
        dw    task0_TSS_selec     ;TSS segment selector
        dw    task0_TSS           ;TSS segment address
        dw    stk0_selec          ;stk0 segment selector
        dw    stk0                ;stk0 segment address
        dw    stk1_selec          ;stk1 segment selector
        dw    stk1                ;stk1 segment address
        dw    stk2_selec          ;stk2 segment selector
        dw    stk2                ;stk2 segment address
        dw    dmy_selec           ;dummy segment selector
        dw    dmy                 ;dummy segment address
        dw    code_selec          ;code segment selector
        dw    code                ;code segment address
        dw    gdata_selec         ;data segment selector
        dw    gdata               ;data segment address
        dw    int_selec           ;interrupt segment selector
        dw    code                ;code segment address
gdt_tab_size equ ($ - gdt_phys_tab) / 4    ;entry numbers in
                                           ;above table


;STEP 5: message definition area

in_protected        db    'in protected mode ',0
int_msg             db    'interrupt '
int_num             dw    ?
                    db    'H',0
Gdata_limit equ     $
Gdata ends

;STEP 6: Stack Segment for privilege level 0,1,2

stk0  segment       para public use16 'stk0'
        db    100h  dup(0)
stk0_limit  equ     $
stk0  ends

stk1  segment       para public use16 'stk1'
        db    100h  dup(0)
stk1_limit  equ     $
stk1  ends
```

```
stk2    segment        para public use16 'stk2'
        db     100h  dup(0)
stk2_limit  equ    $
stk2    ends


;STEP 7: Task State Segment

task0_TSS              segment        para public use16 'task0'
TSS_stack    stk0_selec,stk0_limit,stk1_selec,
             stk1_limit, stk2_selec,stk2_limit
TSS_cr3      0                    ;cr3
TSS_regs     0,0,0,0,0,0,0,0,0,stk0_limit
TSS_seg      gdata_selec,code_selec,stk0_selec,
             gdata_selec,gdata_selec,gdata_selec
             dd     0             ;LDT field
             dw     0             ;task trap flag
             dw     68h           ;I/O base
task0_TSS_limit    equ    $
task0_TSS    ends


;STEP 8: Dummy Segment

dmy    segment        para public use16 'dmy'
       db    128 dup(0)
dmy    ends



;CODE Segment

code   segment        para public use16 'code'
       assume         cs:code,ds:gdata
main   proc   far
       mov    ax,gdata        ;get gdata segment address
       mov    ds,ax           ;put in DS

;STEP 9: initialize IDT

       mov    ax,IDT                ;get IDT segment address
       mov    es,ax                 ;put in ES
       mov    di,offset idt_tab     ;get IDT offset address
       mov    ax,offset int_entry   ;get interrupt service
                                    ;routine address
       mov    cx,INTNO              ;get interrupt number
fillidt:
       mov    es:[di],ax            ;put entry address in IDT
       add    di,DSCPSIZE           ;adjust address in IDT
       add    ax,INTSIZE            ;adjust interrupt service
                         ;routine address, the size of each
                         ;routine is defined in INTSIZE
       loop   fillidt               ;keep filling

;STEP 10:    get GDT/IDT limit and linear address

       mov    ax,offset gdt_limit   ;get GDT segment limit
       mov    pGDT_limit,ax         ;put in pGDT_limit
       xor    eax,eax               ;clear eax
```

```
        mov    ax,GDT                      ;get GDT segment address
        shl    eax,4                       ;convert to 32 bit linear
                                           ;address
        mov    pGDT_addr,eax               ;put in pGDT_addr

        mov    ax,offset idt_limit         ;get IDT segment limit
        mov    pIDT_limit,ax               ;put in pGDT_limit
        xor    eax,eax                     ;clear eax
        mov    ax,idt                      ;get IDT segment address
        shl    eax,4                       ;convert to 32 bit
                                           ;linear address
        mov    pIDT_addr,eax               ;put in pIDT_addr

;STEP 11: based on gdt_phys_tab to set linear base address
;         for each corresponding descriptor

        mov    ax,GDT                      ;get gdt segment address
        mov    es,ax                       ;put in ES
        mov    si,offset gdt_phys_tab      ;get address of
                                           ;gdt_phys_tab
        mov    cx,gdt_tab_size             ;get gdt_phys_tab size
bdt1:
        lodsw                              ;get descriptor number
        mov    bx,ax                       ;put in BX
        and    bx,0fff8h                   ;mask off TI bit and RPL
        lodsw                              ;get corresponding
                                           ;segment address for
                                           ;the above descriptor
        push   ax                          ;save it
        shl    ax,4                        ;get lower 4 bytes offset
        mov    es:[bx][d_base1],ax         ;save it in descriptor
                                           ;base1 position
        pop    ax                          ;restore segment address
        shr    ax,12                       ;get the highest byte
        mov    es:[bx][d_base2],al         ;save it in descriptor
                                           ;base2 position
        loop   bdt1                        ;continue

;STEP 12: switch to protected mode

        cli                                ;clear interrupt
        lgdt   [pGDT]                      ;load GDT address and
                                           ;limit into GDTR
        lidt   [pIDT]                      ;load IDT address and
                                           ;limit into IDTR
        mov    eax,cr0                     ;get cr0 register
        or     al,prot_enable              ;set protected mode enable
        mov    cr0,eax                     ;restore cr0

        jmp    dword ptr cs:[enter_prot]      ;far jump to
                                           ;flush instruction queue
enter_prot:
        dw     offset now_in_prot          ;EIP
        dw     code_selec                  ;code segment selector

;STEP 13: execute in protected mode,set
;         LDTR,SS,SP,DS,ES,FS,GS
```

```
now_in_prot:
        xor     ax,ax                   ;clear ax
        lldt    ax                      ;load NULL selector
                                        ;to LDTR
        mov     ax,stk0_selec           ;get stack segment
                                        ;selector
        mov     ss,ax                   ;put in SS
        mov     sp,offset stk0_limit    ;set stack pointer
        mov     ax,gdata_selec    ;get data segment selector
        mov     ds,ax                   ;put in DS
        mov     es,ax                   ;put in ES
        mov     fs,ax                   ;put in FS
        mov     gs,ax                   ;put in GS

;STEP 14: display message in protected mode
                                        ;clear the screen first
        mov     ax,video_selec    ;get video segment selector
        mov     es,ax                   ;put in ES
        mov     cx,4000h                ;buffer size to clear
        xor     di,di                   ;screen starting address
        mov     ah,attribute            ;character attribute
        mov     al,space                ;space
        rep     stosw                   ;fill it
        mov     si,offset in_protected  ;get protected mode
                                        ;message address
        mov     di,320                  ;get display address
        call    disp_it                 ;call display procedure

;STEP 15:   load TSS to TR

        mov     ax,task0_TSS_selec      ;get TSS selector for
                                        ;current task
        ltr     ax                      ;load into task register

;STEP 16: switch back to real-address mode

        int     20                      ;interrupt 20

;STEP 17: Interrupt Service Routine

int_entry:                              ;entry point for
                                   ;interrupt service routine
        REPT    INTNO
        call    disp                    ;call the display message
        iret                            ;procedure
        ENDM

;STEP 18:   get interrupt number and display it

disp:
        pop     ax              ;get return address from stack
        mov     bx,gdata_selec          ;reload data segment
        mov     ds,bx
        sub     ax,offset int_entry     ;get offset from the
                                        ;interrupt entry
        shr     ax,TWO                  ;divide by 4 to get
```

```
                                        ;interrupt number
        mov     si,offset int_num       ;get ascii code address
        mov     cx,TWO                  ;convert to 2 ascii code
        call    htoa                    ;call convert procedure
        mov     si,offset int_msg       ;get interrupt message
                                        ;address
        mov     di,5*160                ;get display address
        call    disp_it                 ;call display procedure

;STEP 19:    return to real-address mode

        cli                             ;disable interrupt
        mov     ax,dmy_selec            ;dummy selector
        mov     es,ax                   ;reset segment registers
        mov     ds,ax
        mov     fs,ax
        mov     gs,ax
        mov     ss,ax
        mov     eax,cr0                 ;load the content of CR0
        and     eax,not prot_enable     ;disable protected mode
        mov     cr0,eax                 ;restore the content of
                                        ;CR0
        db      0eah                    ;far jump to flush
                                        ;instruction queue
        dw      offset next_instruction ;new EIP
        dw      code                    ;new CS

;STEP 20:    execute in real-address mode, set DS,SS and SP

next_instruction:
        mov     ax,Gdata                ;get data segment address
        mov     ds,ax                   ;put in DS
        mov     ax,stk0                 ;get stack segment address
        mov     ss,ax                   ;put in SS
        mov     sp,offset stk0_limit    ;set stack pointer

;STEP 21: set IDTR to DOS interrupt table

        lidt    [pold]                  ;load DOS interrupt vector
                                        ;table to IDTR register
        sti                             ;enable interrupt


;STEP 22: terminate this process

        mov     ax,4c00h                ;terminate process
        int     21h                     ;DOS function call
main    endp

;Procedure: disp_it
;Display string In protected mode
;Input: ds:si - string address, the end of the string must
;be 0

disp_it         proc  near
        mov     ax,video_selec          ;get video segment selector
        mov     es,ax                   ;put in ES
```

```
        mov     ah,attribute        ;display attribute
disp_it1:
        lodsb                       ;get display character
        stosw                       ;put it on screen
        cmp     al,0                ;end of display character ?
        jne     disp_it1            ;no, continue
        ret                         ;yes, return
disp_it         endp


;Procedure: htoa
;Convert hexadecimal code to ASCII code
;Input: si-- address to put ASCII code, cx-- hexadecimal
;code size,eax -- hexadecimal code

htoa_tab        db      '0123456789ABCDEF'
htoa    proc    near
        xor     ebx,ebx             ;clear EBX
        add     si,cx               ;adjust target address
        dec     si
htoa1:
        mov     bl,al               ;get hexadecimal code
        and     bl,0fh              ;distinguish it
        mov     bl,cs:[htoa_tab][ebx]   ;get indexed ascii
                                        ;character
        mov     byte ptr [esi],bl ;place in target address
        dec     esi                 ;adjust target address
        shr     eax,4               ;get rid of it
        loop    htoa1               ;continue
        ret                         ;return
htoa    endp
code    ends
        end     main
```

4.5 Protected Mode Exceptions

Exceptions are violations that might occur during the execution of instructions, such as accessing addresses beyond the segment limit. The reporting of these violations to the system software is known as exception handling. When the i386/i486 processor encounters this predefined violation, it generates a corresponding exception and transfers control to the exception handler.

The exception handler should try to recover the violation status if possible or stop execution. For example, if the system generates an exception because the desired page is not in memory, the exception handler can load the desired page from disk into memory, change the page mapping table, then restart the execution. If the program tries to access data that is beyond the segment limit, the exception handler can display a message or stop execution.

4.6 Sample Program 2

The following two programs, *sgnopres.asm* and *sgprotec.asm*, introduce exceptions that are related to segmentation memory management. Both of these programs show the i386/i486 segment protection mechanism.

To save coding time, some routines used to enter the protected mode are defined as macros and included in the file: *MACRO2*.

File: MACRO2

```
;Define macro to get GDT, IDT linear address and limit then
;save it

build_dtr    macro gdt,idt,pgdt,pidt,sizegdt,sizeidt
                                    ;define macro
       mov    ax,sizegdt              ;get GDT segment limit
       mov    word ptr [pgdt],ax      ;put in pGDT_limit
       xor    eax,eax                 ;clear eax
       mov    ax,gdt                  ;get GDT segment address
       shl    eax,4        ;convert to 32-bit linear address
       mov    dword ptr [pgdt+2],eax  ;put in pGDT_addr
;build idtr
       mov    ax,sizeidt              ;get IDT segment address
       mov    word ptr [pidt],ax      ;put in pIDT_limit
       xor    eax,eax                 ;clear eax
       mov    ax,idt              ;get IDT segment address
       shl    eax,4          ;convert to 32-bit linear address
       mov    dword ptr [pidt+2],eax  ;put in pIDT_addr
endm                                  ;end of macro

;Define macro to initialize the segment base address for
;each segment descriptor

build_dt    macro dtseg,dttable,dtcount    ;define macro
       local bdt1                  ;local label
       mov    ax,dtseg               ;get segment address
       mov    es,ax                  ;put in ES
       mov    si,offset dttable ;get address of gdt_phys_tab
       mov    cx,dtcount             ;get gdt_phys_tab size
bdt1:
       lodsw                          ;get descriptor number
       mov    bx,ax                   ;put in BX
       and    bx,0fff8h               ;mask off TI bit and RPL
       lodsw                          ;get corresponding segment
                                      ;address
                                      ;for the above descriptor
       push   ax                      ;save it
       shl    ax,4                    ;get lower 4 bytes offset
       mov    es:[bx][d_base1],ax     ;save it in descriptor
       pop    ax                      ;restore segment address
       shr    ax,12                   ;get the highest byte
       mov    es:[bx][d_base2],al     ;save it in descriptor
```

```
        loop   bdt1                 ;continue
endm                                ;end of macro

;Define macro to switch to protected mode and initialize
;data segment register

goto_prot    macro gdtptr,idtptr,cseg,stkseg,stkptr,dseg
        local enter_prot,now_in_prot        ;local label
        lgdt   [gdtptr]            ;load GDT address and limit
                                   ;into GDTR
        lidt   [idtptr]            ;load IDT address and limit
                                   ;into IDTR
        mov    eax,cr0             ;get cr0 register
        or     al,prot_enable      ;enable protected mode
        mov    cr0,eax             ;restore cr0
        jmp    dword ptr cs:[enter_prot]    ;far jump to
                                   ;flush instruction queue
enter_prot:
        dw     offset now_in_prot      ;EIP
        dw     cseg                ;code segment selector
now_in_prot:
        xor    ax,ax               ;clear ax
        lldt   ax                  ;load NULL selector to LDTR

        mov    ax,stkseg           ;get stack segment selector
        mov    ss,ax               ;put in SS
        mov    sp,stkptr           ;set stack pointer

        mov    ax,dseg             ;get data segment selector
        mov    ds,ax               ;put in DS
        mov    es,ax               ;put in ES
        mov    fs,ax               ;put in FS
        mov    gs,ax               ;put in GS
endm                                ;end of macro
```

Program: SGNOPRES.ASM

The program *sgnopres.asm* shows the segment protection when you try to load a "not present" segment to the data segment register. Figure 4.5 shows the segment descriptor format for a "not present" segment. When the i386/i486 processor executes this load segment register instruction and detects that the "present" bit of the desired segment descriptor is clear, it generates exception 11—segment not present fault. At this point, the exception handler can load the correct segment into memory and reset the "present" bit, then return to the breakpoint which generates the exception and reexecute the instruction. This program only displays the interrupt number on the screen and then goes back to DOS real-address mode. It does not handle the restarting of the instruction.

```
;not present data segment descriptor format:
notp_selec  dw    0ffffh     ;limit (0 - 15)
            dw    ?          ;segment base (0 - 15)
            db    ?          ;segment base (16 - 23)
            db    12h        ;present=0,writable = 1
            db    0          ;limit (16 - 19), G=0, D=0
            db    0          ;base (24 - 31)
```

Figure 4.5 Descriptor Format for "Not Present" Segment

Step 1.1: Define a segment selector and descriptor with segment not present.

Step 15.1: Move the segment selector which has the descriptor with "segment not present" to ES register. This instruction generates exception 11—"segment not present" fault.

In this program, if you load the "not present" segment selector into SS register instead of ES register, the i386/i486 processor generates exception 12—stack exception. This is a result of trying to load noncorrect status data to the SS register.

File: SGNOPRES.ASM

```
.386p
include struct
include macro1
include macro2

INTNO       equ   21         ;interrupt vector number
DSCPSIZE    equ   8          ;size of descriptor
INTSIZE     equ   4          ;size of interrupt service
                            ;routine
TWO         equ   2          ;
prot_enable equ   01h        ;protected mode enable bit
attribute   equ   07h        ;display character attribute
space       equ   20h        ;ASCII code for space

;Step 1: Global Descriptor Table

GDT    segment     para  public      use16 'GDT'
gdt_tab       label qword
null_selec equ    $-gdt_tab            ;null selector
   dscp        <,,,,,>        ;first one must be a null descriptor

code_selec equ    $-gdt_tab  ;code segment selector
   dscp        <0ffffh,,,09ah,,>        ;code segment descriptor

task0_TSS_selec   equ    $-gdt_tab  ;TSS segment selector
   dscp        <task0_TSS_limit,,,089h,,>    ;descriptor
```

```
stk0_selec  equ    $-gdt_tab        ;level 0 stack selector
   dscp        <stk0_limit,,,92h,,>  ;descriptor with
                                     ;privilege level 0
stk1_selec  equ    $-gdt_tab or 1   ;level 1 stack
                                     ;selector
   dscp        <stk1_limit,,,0b2h,,> ;descriptor with
                                     ;privilege level 1
stk2_selec  equ    $-gdt_tab  or 2  ;level 2 stack
                                     ;selector
   dscp        <stk2_limit,,,0d2h,,> ;descriptor with
                                     ;privilege level 2
dmy_selec   equ    $-gdt_tab        ;dummy segment selector
   dscp        <0ffffh,,,92h,,>      ;descriptor

video_selec equ    $-gdt_tab        ;video segment selector
   dscp        <0ffffh,8000h,0bh,0f2h,,>    ;descriptor

gdata_selec equ    $-gdt_tab        ;data segment selector
   dscp        <gdata_limit,,,0f2h,,> ;descriptor

int_selec   equ    $-gdt_tab        ;interrupt segment
                                     ;selector
   dscp        <0ffffh,,,09ah,,>     ;descriptor

;STEP 1.1: define segment not present descriptor in GDT

notp_selec  equ    $-gdt_tab        ;selector
   dscp        <0ffffh,,,072h,,>     ;descriptor with segment
                                     ;not present
GDT_limit   equ    $-gdt_tab
GDT    ends

;STEP 2:    Interrupt Descriptor Table

IDT    segment para      public use16      'idt'
idt_tab equ $
       REPT   INTNO                  ;21 interrupt entries
       dscp   <,int_selec,0,0eeh,,>  ;DPL = 3
       ENDM
idt_limit   equ    $
IDT    ends

;DATA        Segment

Gdata segment      para  public      use16 'Gdata'

;STEP 3: variable to save GDT/IDT limit and linear address.

pGDT   label fword
       dw     GDT_limit        ;GDT limit
       dd     0                ;GDT linear address
pIDT   label fword
       dw     IDT_limit        ;IDT limit
       dd     0                ;IDT linear address
pold   label fword
       dw     03ffh            ;DOS IDT limit
```

```
        dd      0                       ;DOS IDT linear address

;STEP 4: table to define the mapping of descriptor to
;        segment

gdt_phys_tab        label word
        dw      task0_TSS_selec     ;TSS segment selector
        dw      task0_TSS           ;TSS segment
        dw      stk0_selec          ;stk0 segment selector
        dw      stk0                ;stk0 segment
        dw      stk1_selec          ;stk1 segment selector
        dw      stk1                ;stk1 segment
        dw      stk2_selec          ;stk2 segment selector
        dw      stk2                ;stk2 segment
        dw      dmy_selec           ;dummy segment selector
        dw      dmy                 ;dummy segment
        dw      code_selec          ;code segment selector
        dw      code                ;code segment
        dw      gdata_selec         ;data segment selector
        dw      gdata               ;data segment
        dw      int_selec           ;interrupt segment selector
        dw      code                ;code segment
gdt_tab_size equ  ($ - gdt_phys_tab) / 4

;STEP 5: message definition area

in_protected        db      'in protected mode ',0
int_msg             db      'interrupt '
int_num             dw      ?
                    db      'H',0
Gdata_limit equ     $
Gdata ends

;STEP 6: Stack Segment for privilege level 0,1,2

stk0    segment     para  public use16 'stk0'
        db      100h  dup(0)
stk0_limit equ      $
stk0    ends

stk1    segment     para  public use16 'stk1'
        db      100h  dup(0)
stk1_limit equ      $
stk1    ends

stk2    segment     para  public use16 'stk2'
        db      100h  dup(0)
stk2_limit equ      $
stk2    ends

;STEP 7: Task State Segment

task0_TSS   segment     para  public use16 'task0'
TSS_stack   stk0_selec,stk0_limit,stk1_selec,
            stk1_limit,stk2_selec,stk2_limit
TSS_cr3     0                       ;cr3
TSS_regs    0,0,0,0,0,0,0,0,0,stk0_limit
```

```
TSS_seg        gdata_selec,code_selec,stk0_selec,
               gdata_selec,gdata_selec,gdata_selec
               dd    0            ;LDT field
               dw    0            ;task trap flag
               dw    68h          ;I/O base
task0_TSS_limit    equ    $
task0_TSS   ends

;STEP 8: Dummy Segment

dmy    segment     para  public use16 'dmy'
       db    128   dup(0)
dmy    ends

;CODE Segment

code   segment     para  public use16 'code'
       assume      cs:code,ds:gdata
main   proc  far
       mov   ax,gdata
       mov   ds,ax

;STEP 9:     initialize IDT

       mov   ax,IDT              ;get IDT segment address
       mov   es,ax               ;put in ES
       mov   di,offset idt_tab       ;get IDT offset address
       mov   ax,offset int_entry     ;get interrupt service
                                     ;routine address
       mov   cx,INTNO                ;get interrupt number
fillidt:
       mov   es:[di],ax          ;put entry address in IDT
       add   di,DSCPSIZE         ;adjust address in IDT
       add   ax,INTSIZE          ;adjust interrupt service
                                 ;routine address, the size
                                 ;of each routine is defined
                                 ;in INTSIZE
       loop  fillidt             ;keep filling


;STEP 10,11,12,13: set linear address for descriptor in GDT,
;     GDTR,IDTR and LDTR then switch to protected mode

       build_dtr   gdt,idt,pgdt,pidt,gdt_limit,idt_limit
       build_dt    gdt,gdt_phys_tab,gdt_tab_size
       cli
       goto_prot   pgdt,pidt,code_selec,stk0_selec,
                   stk0_limit,GDATA_selec

;STEP 14: display message in protected mode
                                 ;clear the screen first
       mov   ax,video_selec      ;get video segment selector
       mov   es,ax               ;put in ES
       mov   cx,4000h            ;screen size
       xor   di,di               ;screen starting address
       mov   ah,attribute
       mov   al,space            ;fill space and attribute
```

```
        rep    stosw                ;fill it
        mov    si,offset in_protected ;get protected mode
                                    ;message address
        mov    di,320               ;get display address
        call   disp_it              ;call display procedure

;STEP 15: load TSS to TR

        mov    ax,task0_TSS_selec   ;get TSS selector for
                                    ;current task
        ltr    ax                   ;load into task register

;STEP 15.1: try to load the selector with segment not
;present

        mov    ax,notp_selec        ;get the selector
        mov    es,ax                ;move into ES

;STEP 16:    switch back to real-address mode

        int    20                   ;interrupt 20

;STEP 17: Interrupt Service Routine

int_entry:                          ;entry point for interrupt
                                    ;service routine
        REPT   INTNO
        call   disp                 ;call the display message
                                    ;procedure
        iret
        ENDM

;STEP 18: get interrupt number and display it

disp:
        pop    ax                   ;get return address from stack
        sub    ax,offset int_entry  ;get offset from the
                                    ;interrupt entry
        shr    ax,TWO               ;divide by 4 to get
                                    ;interrupt number
        mov    si,offset int_num    ;get ascii code address
        mov    cx,TWO               ;convert to 2 ascii code
        call   htoa                 ;call convert procedure
        mov    si,offset int_msg    ;get interrupt message
                                    ;address
        mov    di,5*160             ;get display address
        call   disp_it              ;call display procedure

;STEP 19: Return to real-address mode

        cli                         ;disable interrupt

        mov    ax,dmy_selec         ;dummy selector
        mov    es,ax                ;reset segment register
        mov    ds,ax
        mov    fs,ax
        mov    gs,ax
```

```
        mov    ss,ax

        mov    eax,cr0                  ;load the content of CR0
        and    eax,not prot_enable      ;disable protected mode
        mov    cr0,eax                  ;restore the content of
                                        ;CR0 register
        db     0eah                     ;far jump to flush
                                        ;instruction queue
        dw     offset next_instruction
        dw     code

;STEP 20: execute in real-address mode, set DS,SS and SP

next_instruction:
        mov    ax,Gdata                 ;get data segment address
        mov    ds,ax                    ;set to DS register
        mov    ax,stk0             ;get stack segment address
        mov    ss,ax                    ;set to SS register
        mov    sp,offset stk0_limit     ;set stack pointer

;STEP 21: set IDTR to DOS interrupt table

        lidt   [pold]                   ;reset interrupt vector table
        sti                             ;enable interrupt

;STEP 22: terminate this process

        mov    ax,4c00h                 ;terminate process
        int    21h                      ;DOS system call
main    endp
code    ends
        end    main
```

Program: SGPROTEC.ASM

The program *sgprotec.asm* shows the segment level protection when the segment selector value goes beyond the GDT limit. When a memory address exceeding the corresponding segment limit, (for example, the segment limit is *60h* and you try to access an address in *70h*) the i386/i486 processor generates interrupt 13—general protection fault. Remember that the GDT limit is stored in the GDTR register. This program displays the interrupt number on the screen and then goes back to DOS real-address mode.

Step 1.1: Define a segment selector and descriptor which exceeds the GDT limit.

Step 15.1: Get the segment selector exceeding the GDT limit, and put it in ES. This instruction generates the exception 13—general protection fault.

File: SGPROTEC.ASM

```
.386p
include struct
```

```
        include macro1
        include macro2

INTNO       equ    21          ;interrupt vector number
DSCPSIZE    equ    8           ;size of descriptor
INTSIZE     equ    4      ;size of interrupt service routine
TWO         equ    2           ;
prot_enable equ    01h         ;protected mode enable bit
attribute   equ    07h         ;display character attribute
space       equ    20h         ;ASCII value for space

;STEP 1: Global Descriptor Table

GDT    segment     para  public use16 'GDT'
gdt_tab       label qword

null_selec  equ    $-gdt_tab            ;null selector
   dscp      <,,,,,>      ;first one must be a null descriptor

code_selec  equ    $-gdt_tab            ;code segment selector
   dscp      <0ffffh,,,09ah,,>          ;descriptor

task0_TSS_selec    equ    $-gdt_tab            ;TSS selector
   dscp      <task0_TSS_limit,,,089h,,>      ;descriptor

stk0_selec  equ    $-gdt_tab            ;level 0 stack selector
   dscp      <stk0_limit,,,92h,,>      ;descriptor with
                                       ;privilege level 0
stk1_selec  equ    $-gdt_tab or 1      ;selector for
                                       ;privilege level 1 stack
   dscp      <stk1_limit,,,0b2h,,>     ;descriptor with
                                       ;privilege level 1

stk2_selec  equ    $-gdt_tab or 2      ;selector for
                                       ;privilege level 2 stack
   dscp      <stk2_limit,,,0d2h,,>     ;descriptor with
                                       ;privilege level 2
dmy_selec   equ    $-gdt_tab            ;dummy segment selector
 dscp <0ffffh,,,92h,,>                  ;descriptor

video_selec equ    $-gdt_tab or 3      ;video segment selector
   dscp      <0ffffh,8000h,0bh,0f2h,,>      ;descriptor

gdata_selec equ    $-gdt_tab            ;data segment selector
   dscp      <gdata_limit,,,0f2h,,>    ;descriptor

int_selec   equ    $-gdt_tab            ;interrupt segment
                                        ;selector
   dscp      <0ffffh,,,09ah,,>          ;descriptor

;STEP 1.1: define selector beyond GDT limit

GDT_limit     equ    $-gdt_tab

beyond_selec equ    $-gdt_tab           ;selector value beyond
                                        ;GDT limit
   dscp      <0ffffh,,,0f2h,,>          ;descriptor
```

```
GDT     ends

;STEP 2: Interrupt Descriptor Table

IDT     segment para        public use16 'idt'
idt_tab equ $
        REPT   INTNO                    ;21 interrupt entries
        dscp   <,int_selec,0,0eeh,,>    ;DPL = 3
        ENDM
idt_limit    equ    $
IDT     ends

;DATA         Segment

Gdata segment       para   public       use16 'Gdata'

;STEP 3: variable to save GDT/IDT limit and linear address

pGDT   label fword
       dw     GDT_limit         ;GDT limit
       dd     0                 ;GDT linear address
pIDT   label fword
       dw     IDT_limit         ;IDT limit
       dd     0                 ;IDT linear address
pold   label fword
       dw     03ffh             ;DOS IDT limit
       dd     0                 ;DOS IDT linear address

;STEP 4: table to define the mapping of descriptor to
;        segment

gdt_phys_tab         label word
       dw     task0_TSS_selec   ;TSS segment selector
       dw     task0_TSS         ;TSS segment
       dw     stk0_selec        ;stk0 segment selector
       dw     stk0              ;stk0 segment
       dw     stk1_selec        ;stk1 segment selector
       dw     stk1              ;stk1 segment
       dw     stk2_selec        ;stk2 segment selector
       dw     stk2              ;stk2 segment
       dw     dmy_selec         ;dummy segment selector
       dw     dmy               ;dummy segment
       dw     code_selec        ;code segment selector
       dw     code              ;code segment
       dw     gdata_selec       ;data segment selector
       dw     gdata             ;data segment
       dw     int_selec         ;interrupt segment selector
       dw     code              ;code segment
gdt_tab_size         equ    ($ - gdt_phys_tab) / 4

;STEP 5: message definition area

in_protected         db     'in protected mode ',0
int_msg              db     'interrupt '
int_num              dw     ?
                     db     'H',0
Gdata_limit equ      $
```

```
Gdata ends

;STEP 6: Stack Segment for privilege level 0,1,2

stk0  segment      para  public use16 'stk0'
      db     100h  dup(0)
stk0_limit  equ    $
stk0  ends

stk1  segment      para  public use16 'stk1'
      db     100h  dup(0)
stk1_limit  equ    $
stk1  ends

stk2  segment      para  public use16 'stk2'
      db     100h  dup(0)
stk2_limit  equ    $
stk2  ends

;STEP 7: Task State Segment

task0_TSS    segment      para  public use16 'task0'
TSS_stack    stk0_selec,stk0_limit,stk1_selec,stk1_limit,
             stk2_selec,stk2_limit
TSS_cr3      0                   ;cr3
TSS_regs     0,0,0,0,0,0,0,0,0,stk0_limit
TSS_seg      gdata_selec,code_selec,stk0_selec,gdata_selec,
             gdata_selec,gdata_selec
             dd     0            ;LDT field
             dw     0            ;task trap flag
             dw     68h          ;I/O base
task0_TSS_limit    equ    $
task0_TSS    ends

;STEP 8: Dummy Segment

dmy   segment      para  public use16 'dmy'
      db     128   dup(0)
dmy   ends

;CODE Segment

code  segment      para  public use16 'code'
      assume       cs:code,ds:gdata
main  proc far
      mov    ax,gdata
      mov    ds,ax

;STEP 9:      initialize IDT

      mov    ax,IDT              ;get IDT segment address
      mov    es,ax               ;put in ES
      mov    di,offset idt_tab        ;get IDT offset address
      mov    ax,offset int_entry      ;get interrupt service
                                      ;routine address
      mov    cx,INTNO                 ;get interrupt number
fillidt:
```

```
        mov     es:[di],ax              ;put entry address in IDT
        add     di,DSCPSIZE             ;adjust address in IDT
        add     ax,INTSIZE              ;adjust interrupt service
                                        ;routine address, the size of
                              ;each routine is defined in INTSIZE
        loop    fillidt                 ;keep filling

;STEP 10,11,12,13: set base address for descriptor in GDT,
;       GDTR,IDTR and LDTR then switch to protected mode

        build_dtr   gdt,idt,pgdt,pidt,gdt_limit,idt_limit
        build_dt    gdt,gdt_phys_tab,gdt_tab_size
        cli
        goto_prot   pgdt,pidt,code_selec,stk0_selec,
                    stk0_limit,GDATA_selec

;STEP 14: display message in protected mode
                                        ;clear the screen first
        mov     ax,video_selec          ;get video segment selector
        mov     es,ax                   ;put in ES
        mov     cx,4000h                ;screen size
        xor     di,di                   ;screen starting address
        mov     ah,attribute
        mov     al,space                ;fill space and attribute
        rep     stosw                   ;fill it

        mov     si,offset in_protected  ;get protected mode
                                        ;message address
        mov     di,320                  ;get display address
        call    disp_it                 ;call display procedure


;STEP 15: load TSS to TR

        mov     ax,task0_TSS_selec      ;get TSS selector for
                                        ;current task
        ltr     ax                      ;load into task register

;STEP 15.1: load the selector beyond GDT limit

        mov     ax,beyond_selec         ;get the selector
        mov     es,ax                   ;put in ES


;STEP 16: switch back to real-address mode

        int     20                      ;interrupt 20

;STEP 17: Interrupt Service Routine
                                        ;entry point for interrupt
int_entry:                              ;service routine
        REPT    INTNO
        call    disp                    ;call the display procedure
        iret
        ENDM
```

```
;STEP 18: get interrupt number and display it

disp:
        pop     ax                      ;get return address from stack
        sub     ax,offset int_entry     ;get offset from the
                                        ;interrupt entry
        shr     ax,TWO                  ;divide by 4 to get
                                        ;interrupt number
        mov     si,offset int_num       ;get ascii code address
        mov     cx,TWO                  ;convert to 2 ascii code
        call    htoa                    ;call convert procedure
        mov     si,offset int_msg ;get interrupt message address
        mov     di,5*160                ;get display address
        call    disp_it                 ;call display procedure

;STEP 19: Return to real-address mode

        cli                             ;disable interrupt
        mov     ax,dmy_selec            ;dummy selector
        mov     es,ax                   ;reset segment register
        mov     ds,ax
        mov     fs,ax
        mov     gs,ax
        mov     ss,ax

        mov     eax,cr0                 ;load the content of CR0
        and     eax,not prot_enable     ;disable protected mode
        mov     cr0,eax                 ;restore the content of
                                        ;CR0
        db      0eah                    ;far jump to flush
                                        ;instruction queue
        dw      offset next_instruction ;ip
        dw      code                    ;cs

;STEP 20: execute in real-address mode, set DS,SS and SP

next_instruction:
        mov     ax,Gdata                ;get data segment address
        mov     ds,ax                   ;set to DS register
        mov     ax,stk0                 ;get stack segment address
        mov     ss,ax                   ;set to SS register
        mov     sp,offset stk0_limit    ;set stack pointer

;STEP 21: set IDTR to DOS interrupt table

        lidt    [pold]                  ;reset interrupt vector table
        sti                             ;enable interrupt

;STEP 22: terminate this process

        mov     ax,4c00h                ;terminate process
        int     21h                     ;DOS system call
main    endp
code    ends
        end     main
```

4.7 Summary

Before entering the protected mode, you need to create the system data structures: GDT and IDT. GDT includes all the segment descriptors for all the segments that you use during program execution in the protected mode. You also need to define the segment type, segment attribute, segment linear base address, and segment limit in the segment descriptor. IDT contains the interrupt segment descriptors for the interrupt or exception handler routines. When the system data structure is ready, enabling the PE bit in the CR0 register, the program starts executing in the protected mode. After entering the protected mode, the program has to execute a jump instruction immediately to flush the instruction queue and change the execution flow.

To make the program execute properly after reentering the real-address mode from the protected mode, you must reset the segment definitions in the segment descriptor registers to match the real-address mode requirement. After entering the real-address mode by clearing the PE bit in the CR0 register, a jump instruction is also necessary to flush the instruction queue and change the execution flow.

CHAPTER 5

PAGE PROGRAMMING

The operating system running on the i386/i486 system can easily support demand-paging virtual memory by enabling memory paging. Paging uses two-level page table mapping to translate a linear address to a physical address. A linear address specifies an index in the first level page table (page directory table), an index in the second level page table, and an offset within that page.

The paging structure and paging mechanism are introduced in Chapter 3. This chapter uses sample programs to explain how to prepare the page directory table and the second level page table for memory paging. It also presents the i386/i486 paging memory protection. Before enabling paging support, you must create the page directory table and the second level page table, then put the physical base address of the page directory table in the CR3 (page directory base address) register.

5.1 Sample Program 1

This program shows page memory management and page level protection with "page not present." The page mapping in this program is very simple. Only one page directory table and one second level page table are needed. Both page tables must be located at the 4K-byte boundary and are themselves pages.

The page directory table in this program defines one (the first) entry, which contains the physical base address of the second level page table. The second level page table defines 256 entries. Each entry contains the physical base address of the page, from page 0 to page 255. Figure 5.1 shows the second level page table example. Entry 0 contains the physical base address of page 0, entry 1 contains the physical base address of page 1 and so on. After setting the PG bit in the CR0 register which enabling paging, this program tries to access data from a page defined as "not present" and it generates exception 14—page fault. Figure 5.2 shows the definition of a page table format for a "not present" page.

```
;page table starts from here. Define each page entry
;according to its sequence.
;entry 0 maps to page 0, entry 1 map to page 1. Each page
;is in supervisor mode, writable and present.

page_table_start label dword

page_table_entry  dd ($-page_table_start)/4 * 1000h + 07h
                  dd ($-page_table_start)/4 * 1000h + 07h
                                .
                                .
                                .
```

Figure 5.1 Sample Second-Level Page Table Entry

```
;the following page entry defines a not present page.

page_table_entry1 dd  (&- page_table_start)/4 * 1000h + 03h
```

Figure 5.2 Page Table Entry Format for a "Not Present" Page

Program: MP.ASM

Step 0.1: EQU definition.

Step 1.1: Define segment selector and descriptor for a segment. The linear base address of this segment is *00090000h*, which means page directory entry 0, page table entry 90h, and offset 0.

Step 5.1: Define a variable to save the physical base address of the page directory table.

Step 8.1: Reserve space for the page table and the page directory table.

Step 8.2: Reserve 4 K bytes to align the page table and page directory table to the 4 K bytes boundary.

Step 8.3: Predefine the page table entry. Only 256 entries in the page table are defined. Each entry has user level, writable and "present" specification.

Step 8.4: Define the page table size.

Step 8.5: Define the page directory table. In this program, one entry in the page directory table is enough.

Step 8.6: Define variable to save aligned page directory table address.

Step 9.1: Call procedure to align the page table and page directory table. Also, clear the present bit in entry 90h of the page table.

Step 9.2: Set the physical base address of the page directory table in the CR3 register.

Step 15.1: Enable memory paging by turning on the paging bit in the CR0 register.

Step 15.2: Get the segment selector for page 90h and access data from this page. A page fault is generated.

Step 19.1: Disable memory paging before returning to the real-address mode.

File: MP.ASM

```
.386p
include struct
include macro1
include macro2

INTNO        equ   21        ;interrupt vector number
DSCPSIZE     equ   8         ;size of descriptor
INTSIZE      equ   4         ;size of interrupt service routine
TWO          equ   2         ;
attribute    equ   07h
space        equ   20h       ;ASCII code for character space
prot_enable  equ   01h       ;CR0 protected mode enable bit

;STEP 0.1: define more equ

pg_enable    equ   80000000h ;CR0 page enable bit
pg_present   equ   01h       ;page present bit
pte_mask     equ   07h       ;user level,read write, and
                             ;page present
pdbr_offset  equ   1000h     ;4k

;STEP 1: Global Descriptor Table

GDT    segment      para public use16 'GDT'
```

```
gdt_tab              label qword
null_selec   equ    $-gdt_tab            ;null selector
   dscp      <,,,,,>        ;first one must be a null descriptor

CODE_selec   equ    $-gdt_tab            ;code segment selector
   dscp      <0ffffh,,,09ah,,>           ;descriptor

task0_TSS_selec   equ    $-gdt_tab       ;TSS selector
   dscp      <task0_TSS_limit,,,089h,,>      ;TSS descriptor

stk0_selec   equ    $-gdt_tab            ;level 0 stack segment
                                         ;selector
   dscp      <stk0_limit,,,92h,,>        ;descriptor with
                                         ;privilege level 0

stk1_selec   equ    $-gdt_tab or 1       ;level 1 stack
                                         ;segment selector
   dscp      <stk1_limit,,,0b2h,,>       ;descriptor with
                                         ;privilege level 1

stk2_selec   equ    $-gdt_tab or 2       ;level 2 stack
                                         ;segment selector
   dscp      <stk2_limit,,,0d2h,,>       ;descriptor with
                                         ;privilege level 2

dmy_selec    equ    $-gdt_tab            ;dummy segment selector
   dscp      <0ffffh,,,92h,,>            ;descriptor

video_selec  equ    $-gdt_tab or 3       ;video segment selector
   dscp      <0ffffh,8000h,0bh,0f2h,,>         ;descriptor
gdata_selec  equ    $-gdt_tab            ;data segment selector
   dscp      <gdata_limit,,,0f2h,,>      ;descriptor

int_selec    equ    $-gdt_tab            ;interrupt segment
                                         ;selector
   dscp      <0ffffh,,,09ah,,>           ;descriptor

;STEP 1.1: define descriptor for page 90h

page_selec   equ    $-gdt_tab     ;selector for specific page
      dscp   <0ffffh,0h,09h,0f2h,,>  ;page 90h, offset 0
GDT_limit    equ    $-gdt_tab
GDT    ends

;STEP 2: Interrupt Descriptor Table

IDT    segment para        public use16 'idt'
idt_tab equ $
       REPT   INTNO                     ;21 interrupt entries
       dscp   <,int_selec,0,0eeh,,>     ;DPL = 3
       ENDM
idt_limit    equ    $
IDT    ends

;DATA         Segment

Gdata segment        para   public use16 'Gdata'
```

```
;STEP 3: define variable to save GDT/IDT limit and linear
;address.

pGDT    label   fword
        dw      GDT_limit           ;GDT limit
        dd      0                   ;GDT linear address
pIDT    label   fword
        dw      IDT_limit           ;IDT limit
        dd      0                   ;IDT linear address
pold    label   fword
        dw      03ffh               ;DOS IDT limit
        dd      0                   ;DOS IDT linear address

;STEP 4: table to define the mapping of descriptor to
;        segment

gdt_phys_tab        label word
        dw      task0_TSS_selec     ;TSS segment selector
        dw      task0_TSS           ;TSS segment
        dw      stk0_selec          ;stk0 segment selector
        dw      stk0                ;stk0 segment
        dw      stk1_selec          ;stk1 segment selector
        dw      stk1                ;stk1 segment
        dw      stk2_selec          ;stk2 segment selector
        dw      stk2                ;stk2 segment
        dw      dmy_selec           ;dummy segment selector
        dw      dmy                 ;dummy segment
        dw      CODE_selec          ;code segment selector
        dw      code                ;code segment
        dw      gdata_selec         ;data segment selector
        dw      gdata               ;data segment
        dw      int_selec           ;interrupt segment selector
        dw      code                ;code segment
gdt_tab_size        equ    ($ - gdt_phys_tab) / 4

;STEP 5: working area and message definition area

in_protected    db      'in protected mode ',0
int_msg         db      'interrupt '
int_num         dw      ?
                db      'H',0

;STEP 5.1: define variable

pdbr        dd      ?       ;page directory linear address
Gdata_limit equ     $
Gdata ends

;STEP 6: Stack Segment for privilege level 0,1,2

stk0    segment     para  public use16 'stk0'
        db      100h  dup(0)
stk0_limit  equ     $
stk0  ends

stk1    segment     para  public use16 'stk1'
```

```
        db      100h  dup(0)
stk1_limit   equ    $
stk1  ends

stk2  segment       para  public use16 'stk2'
        db      100h  dup(0)
stk2_limit   equ    $
stk2  ends

;STEP 7: Task State Segment

task0_TSS    segment       para  public use16 'task0'
TSS_stack    stk0_selec,stk0_limit,stk1_selec,
             stk1_limit, stk2_selec,stk2_limit
TSS_cr3      0                      ;cr3
TSS_regs     0,0,0,0,0,0,0,0,0,stk0_limit
TSS_seg      gdata_selec,code_selec,stk0_selec,
             gdata_selec,gdata_selec,gdata_selec
             dd    0                ;LDT field
             dw    0                ;task trap flag
             dw    68h              ;I/O base
task0_TSS_limit     equ    $
task0_TSS    ends

;STEP 8: Dummy Segment

dmy   segment       para  public use16 'dmy'
        db      128  dup(0)
dmy   ends

;STEP 8.1: page segment

pagetbl      segment para public 'pagetbl' use16

;STEP 8.2: reserve 4K area to adjust page table address

        db      4096  dup(0)

;STEP 8.3: define page table entry

tmp_ptbl     label byte
        rept  256
        dd    (($-tmp_ptbl)/4*1000h + pte_mask)
        endm

;STEP 8.4: page table size

page_tbl_size      equ    ($-tmp_ptbl)/4

;STEP 8.5: page directory

        org   tmp_ptbl+pdbr_offset    ;2000h
        dd    ?                 ;first entry for page directory

;STEP 8.6: working area to save page table address

ptbl_addr          dw     ?
```

```
pagetbl_limit      equ     $
pagetbl     ends

;CODE Segment

code    segment     para  public use16 'code'
        assume      cs:code,ds:gdata
main    proc  far
        mov   ax,gdata          ;get data segment
        mov   ds,ax             ;put in DS

;STEP 9: initialize IDT

        mov   ax,IDT            ;get IDT segment address
        mov   es,ax             ;put in ES
        mov   di,offset idt_tab ;get IDT offset address
        mov   ax,offset int_entry       ;get interrupt service
                                ;routine address
        mov   cx,INTNO          ;get interrupt number
fillidt:
        mov   es:[di],ax        ;put entry address in IDT
        add   di,DSCPSIZE       ;adjust address in IDT
        add   ax,INTSIZE        ;adjust interrupt service
                                ;routine address, the size of
                                ;each routine is defined in
                                ;INTSIZE
        loop  fillidt           ;keep filling


;STEP 9.1: set page table and pdbr

        call  setup_pgtbl       ;call procedure to set up
                                ;page table
        mov   eax,pdbr          ;get page directory table
                                ;linear address
        mov   cr3,eax           ;store in CR3

;STEP 10,11,12,13: set GDTR,IDTR,LDTR and switch to
;protected mode

        build_dtr   gdt,idt,pgdt,pidt,gdt_limit,idt_limit
        build_dt    gdt,gdt_phys_tab,gdt_tab_size
        cli
        goto_prot   pgdt,pidt,CODE_selec,stk0_selec,
                    stk0_limit,GDATA_selec

;STEP 14: display message in protected mode

                                ;clear the screen first
        mov   ax,video_selec    ;get video segment selector
        mov   es,ax             ;put in ES
        mov   cx,4000h          ;screen size
        xor   di,di             ;screen starting address
        mov   ah,attribute      ;fill attribute
        mov   al,space          ;and space
        rep   stosw             ;fill it
```

```
        mov     si,offset in_protected  ;get protected mode
                                        ;message address
        mov     di,320                  ;get display address
        call    disp_it                 ;call display procedure

;STEP 15: load TSS to TR

        mov     ax,task0_TSS_selec      ;get TSS selector for
                                        ;current task
        ltr     ax                      ;load into task register

;STEP 15.1: enable memory paging

        mov     eax,cr0                 ;load the content of CR0
        or      eax,pg_enable           ;enable memory paging
        mov     cr0,eax                 ;restore the content of CR0

;STEP 15.2: access data from page 90h

        mov     ax,page_selec           ;get the specific page selector
        mov     es,ax                   ;put it in ES register
        mov     ax,word ptr es:[0100h]  ;access one word from
                                        ;this page

;STEP 16: switch back to real-address mode

        int     20                      ;interrupt 20


;STEP 17: Interrupt Service Routine

int_entry:                              ;entry point for interrupt
        REPT    INTNO                   ;service routine
        call    disp            ;call the display message procedure
        iret
        ENDM

;STEP 18: get interrupt number and display it

disp:
        pop     ax                      ;get return address from stack
        sub     ax,offset int_entry     ;get offset from the
                                        ;interrupt entry
        shr     ax,TWO                  ;divide by 4 to get
                                        ;interrupt number
        mov     si,offset int_num       ;get ascii code address
        mov     cx,TWO                  ;convert to 2 ascii code
        call    htoa                    ;call convert procedure
        mov     si,offset int_msg       ;get interrupt message
                                        ;address
        mov     di,5*160                ;get display address
        call    disp_it                 ;call display procedure

;STEP 18.1: disable memory paging

        mov     eax,cr0                         ;load the content of CR0
```

```
        and    eax,not pg_enable      ;disable memory paging
        mov    cr0,eax                ;restore the content of
                                      ;CR0
;STEP 19: Return to real-address mode

goto_real:
        cli                    ;disable interrupt
        mov    ax,dmy_selec    ;dummy selector
        mov    es,ax           ;put in ES
        mov    ds,ax           ;put in DS
        mov    fs,ax           ;put in FS
        mov    gs,ax           ;put in GS
        mov    ss,ax           ;put in SS

        mov    eax,cr0         ;load the content of CR0
        and    eax,not prot_enable    ;disable protected mode
        mov    cr0,eax         ;restore the content of CR0

        db     0eah        ;far jump to flush instruction queue
        dw     offset next_instruction     ;new EIP
        dw     code            ;new CS

;STEP 20: execute in real-address mode, set DS,SS, and SP.

next_instruction:
        mov    ax,Gdata        ;get data segment address
        mov    ds,ax           ;set to DS register
        mov    ax,stk0         ;get stack segment address
        mov    ss,ax           ;set to SS register
        mov    sp,offset stk0_limit    ;set stack pointer
;STEP 21: set IDTR to DOS interrupt table

        lidt   [pold]          ;reset interrupt vector table
        sti                    ;enable interrupt

;STEP 22: terminate this process

        mov    ax,4c00h        ;terminate process
        int    21h             ;DOS system call
main    endp

;Procedure:setup_pgtbl
;Align the predefined page table to page boundary. Set the
;first entry of page directory table to this aligned page
;table. The page directory table will be set below the page
;table.

setup_pgtbl proc   near
        push   ds              ;save DS
        push   es              ;save ES
        assume         ds:pagetbl
        mov    ax,pagetbl      ;get page table segment address
        mov    ds,ax           ;put in DS
        mov    es,ax           ;put in ES
        mov    cx,page_tbl_size ;get page table size
        mov    bx,ax           ;bx has page table segment
                               ;address
```

```
        and     bx,00ffh              ;bx is in 4K range (segment)
        xor     edi,edi
        mov     di,100h               ;di has 4K size (segment)
        sub     di,bx                 ;address for 4K boundary,also
                                      ;page table address
        shl     di,4                  ;convert to offset
        mov     ptbl_addr,di          ;save page table address
        push    di                    ;save it
        mov     si,offset tmp_ptbl    ;get predefined page
                                      ;table address
        rep     movsd                 ;move it to the page boundary
                                      ;address
        pop     di                    ;restore di
;set pdbr & pdir
        xor     ebx,ebx               ;clear ebx
        mov     bx,ax                 ;get page table segment address
        shl     ebx,4                 ;convert to 20-bit address
        add     ebx,edi               ;page table linear base address
        or      bl,pte_mask           ;user level,read-write,present
        mov     dword ptr [di].pdbr_offset,ebx  ;put in first
                                      ;entry in page directory table
        add     ebx,offset pdbr_offset  ;page directory base
                                      ;address
        push    ds
        assume ds:gdata
        mov     ax,gdata              ;get gdata segment
        mov     ds,ax                 ;put in DS
        and     ebx,0fffff000h        ;PDBR
        mov     pdbr,ebx              ;save page directory address
        pop     ds
        assume ds:pagetbl
        mov     bx,ptbl_addr          ;get page table address
        add     bx,90h shl 2          ;get entry 90h (1 entry has 4
                                      ;bytes)
        and     [bx][pg_stat],not pg_present  ;set page 90h
                                      ;not present
        pop     es                    ;restore ES
        pop     ds                    ;restore DS
        ret
setup_pgtbl endp
code    ends
        end     main
```

5.2 Sample Program 2

This program shows the page level protection when a user level task tries to write data to a user level, read-only page. When paging is enabled, it groups the CPL (current privilege level) into two levels. A task is running in the supervisor level if the CPL of this task equals 0, 1, or 2. Otherwise, it is running in the user level. To be a user level task in the paging system, the task itself has to change its CPL to 3. How to change a task's CPL is described in Chapter 6.

Program: PP.ASM

Step 0.2: EQU definition.

Step 1.1: Define the segment selector and descriptor for page 90h, privilege level 3 code segment, and level 3 stack segment.

Step 4.1: Add mapping for level 3 code segment.

Step 5.1: Define data for paging variable and paging message.

Step 6.1: Define stack segment for privilege level 3 task.

Step 9.1: Call procedure to align the page table and page directory table. Also, clear the read/write (means read-only) bit in entry 90h of the page table.

Step 15.2: Change the CPL from 0 (supervisor level) to 3 (user level) for current task.

Step 15.3: Display message after the level changes.

Step 15.4: Write data to page 90h. This generates the page fault.

File: PP.ASM

```
.386p
include struct
include macro1
include macro2

INTNO        equ   21              ;interrupt vector number
DSCPSIZE     equ   8               ;size of descriptor
INTSIZE      equ   4        ;size of interrupt service routine
TWO          equ   2               ;
attribute    equ   07h             ;character attribute
space        equ   20h             ;space
prot_enable equ    01h             ;protected mode enable bit

;STEP 0.1: define more equ

pg_enable    equ   80000000h   ;page enable bit
pg_present   equ   01h         ;page present bit
pdbr_offset equ    1000h       ;4k
pte_mask     equ   07h         ;user level, read-write,
                               ;and present
read_only    equ   0fffffffdh  ;read only

;STEP 1: Global Descriptor Table

GDT    segment       para  public use16 'GDT'
gdt_tab              label qword
null_selec equ       $-gdt_tab   ;null selector
```

```
    dscp        <,,,,,>         ;first one must be a null descriptor

code_selec  equ    $-gdt_tab            ;code segment selector
    dscp        <0ffffh,,,09ah,,>        ;descriptor

task0_TSS_selec    equ    $-gdt_tab    ;TSS selector
    dscp       <task0_TSS_limit,,,089h,,>    ;TSS descriptor

stk0_selec  equ    $-gdt_tab    ;level 0 stack segment
                                         ;selector
    dscp        <stk0_limit,,,92h,,>     ;descriptor with
                                         ;privilege level 0
stk1_selec  equ    $-gdt_tab or 1        ;level 1 stack
                                         ;segment selector
    dscp        <stk1_limit,,,0b2h,,>    ;descriptor with
                                         ;privilege level 1
stk2_selec  equ    $-gdt_tab or 2        ;level 2 stack
                                         ;segment selector
    dscp        <stk2_limit,,,0d2h,,>    ;descriptor with
                                         ;privilege level 2
dmy_selec   equ    $-gdt_tab    ;dummy segment selector
    dscp        <0ffffh,,,92h,,>             ;dummy segment descriptor

video_selec equ    $-gdt_tab or 3    ;video segment selector
    dscp        <0ffffh,8000h,0bh,0f2h,,>    ;descriptor

gdata_selec equ    $-gdt_tab            ;data segment selector
    dscp        <gdata_limit,,,0f2h,,>   ;descriptor

int_selec   equ    $-gdt_tab    ;interrupt segment selector
    dscp        <0ffffh,,,09ah,,>        ;descriptor

;STEP 1.1: selector and descriptor for paging

page_selec  equ    $-gdt_tab            ;selector for specific
                                         ;page
    dscp        <0ffffh,0h,09h,0f2h,,>   ;page 90h, offset 0

code3_selec equ    $-gdt_tab or 3        ;level 3 code segment
                                         ;selector, (RPL = 3)
    dscp        <0ffffh,,,0fah,,>        ;code segment descriptor
                                         ;(DPL = 3)
stk3_selec         equ    $-gdt_tab or 3    ;level 3 stack
                                         ;segment selector
    dscp        <stk3_limit,,,0f2h,,>    ;descriptor with
                                         ;privilege level 3
GDT_limit   equ    $-gdt_tab
GDT    ends

;STEP 2: Interrupt Descriptor Table

IDT    segment para      public use16 'idt'
idt_tab equ $
       REPT   INTNO                      ;21 interrupt entries
       dscp   <,int_selec,0,0eeh,,>   ;DPL = 3
       ENDM
idt_limit    equ    $
```

```
IDT    ends

;DATA        Segment

Gdata segment      para  public use16 'Gdata'

;STEP 3: define variable to save GDT/IDT limit and linear
;address.

pGDT  label fword
      dw    GDT_limit          ;GDT limit
      dd    0                  ;GDT linear address
pIDT  label fword
      dw    IDT_limit          ;IDT limit
      dd    0                  ;IDT linear address
pold  label fword
      dw    03ffh              ;DOS IDT limit
      dd    0                  ;DOS IDT linear address

;STEP 4: table to define the mapping of descriptor to
;segment

gdt_phys_tab        label word
      dw    task0_TSS_selec    ;TSS segment selector
      dw    task0_TSS          ;TSS segment
      dw    stk0_selec         ;stk0 segment selector
      dw    stk0               ;stk0 segment
      dw    stk1_selec         ;stk1 segment selector
      dw    stk1               ;stk1 segment
      dw    stk2_selec         ;stk2 segment selector
      dw    stk2               ;stk2 segment
      dw    dmy_selec          ;dummy segment selector
      dw    dmy                ;dummy segment
      dw    code_selec         ;code segment selector
      dw    code               ;code segment
      dw    gdata_selec        ;data segment selector
      dw    gdata              ;data segment
      dw    int_selec          ;interrupt segment selector
      dw    code               ;code segment

;STEP 4.1: selector for level 3 code and stack segment

      dw    code3_selec        ;code segment selector
      dw    code               ;code segment
      dw    stk3_selec         ;stk3 segment selector
      dw    stk3               ;stk3 segment

gdt_tab_size        equ  ($ - gdt_phys_tab) / 4

;STEP 5: message definition area

in_protected        db   'in protected mode ',0
int_msg             db   'interrupt '
int_num             dw   ?
                    db   'H',0
level_msg           db   'change to user level ',0
```

```
;STEP 5.1: paging working area

pdbr        dd    ?         ;address of page directory table
Gdata_limit equ   $
Gdata ends

;STEP 6: Stack Segment for privilege level 0,1,2

stk0   segment      para  public use16 'stk0'
       db    100h  dup(0)
stk0_limit equ     $
stk0 ends

stk1   segment      para  public use16 'stk1'
       db    100h  dup(0)
stk1_limit equ     $
stk1 ends

stk2   segment      para  public use16 'stk2'
       db    100h  dup(0)
stk2_limit equ     $
stk2 ends

;STEP 6.1: Stack Segment for privilege level 3

stk3   segment      para  public use16 'stk3'
       db    100h  dup(0)
stk3_limit equ     $
stk3 ends

;STEP 7: Task State Segment for task 0

task0_TSS    segment      para  public use16 'task0'
TSS_stack    stk0_selec,stk0_limit,stk1_selec,
             stk1_limit,stk2_selec,stk2_limit
TSS_cr3      0                    ;cr3
TSS_regs     0,0,0,0,0,0,0,0,0,stk0_limit
TSS_seg      gdata_selec,code_selec,stk0_selec,
             gdata_selec,gdata_selec,gdata_selec
             dd    0              ;LDT field
             dw    0              ;task trap flag
             dw    68h            ;I/O base
task0_TSS_limit   equ    $
task0_TSS   ends

;STEP 8: Dummy Segment

dmy    segment      para  public use16 'dmy'
       db    128   dup(0)
dmy    ends

;STEP 8.1: page segment

pagetbl      segment para public 'pagetbl' use16

;STEP 8.2: reserve 4K area to adjust page table address
```

```
        db      4096   dup(0)

;STEP 8.3: define page table entry

tmp_ptbl    label byte
        rept  256
        dd    (($-tmp_ptbl)/4*1000h + pte_mask)
        endm

;STEP 8.4: page table size

page_tbl_size      equ    ($-tmp_ptbl)/4

;STEP 8.5: page directory

        org   tmp_ptbl+pdbr_offset          ;2000h
        dd    ?                  ;first entry for page directory

;STEP 8.6: working area to save page table address

ptbl_addr           dw    ?
pagetbl_limit       equ   $
pagetbl    ends
;CODE Segment

code    segment      para  public use16      'code'
        assume       cs:code,ds:gdata
main    proc  far
        mov   ax,gdata
        mov   ds,ax

;STEP 9: initialize IDT

        mov   ax,IDT             ;get IDT segment address
        mov   es,ax              ;put in ES
        mov   di,offset idt_tab  ;get IDT offset address
        mov   ax,offset int_entry    ;get interrupt service
                                     ;routine address
        mov   cx,INTNO           ;get interrupt number
fillidt:
        mov   es:[di],ax         ;put entry address in IDT
        add   di,DSCPSIZE        ;adjust address in IDT
        add   ax,INTSIZE         ;adjust interrupt service
                                 ;routine address, the size of
                                 ;each routine is defined in
                                 ;INTSIZE
        loop  fillidt            ;keep filling

;STEP 9.1: call procedure to set up page table

        call  setup_pgtbl        ;set up page table

;STEP 9.2: set PDBR

        mov   eax,pdbr           ;get page directory linear
                                 ;address
        mov   cr3,eax            ;store in CR3
```

```
;STEP 10,11,12,13: set GDTR,IDTR,LDTR and switch to
protected mode

        build_dtr    gdt,idt,pgdt,pidt,gdt_limit,idt_limit
        build_dt     gdt,gdt_phys_tab,gdt_tab_size
        cli
        goto_prot    pgdt,pidt,CODE_selec,stk0_selec,
                     stk0_limit,GDATA_selec

;STEP 14: display message in protected mode

                                  ;clear the screen first
        mov   ax,video_selec      ;get video segment selector
        mov   es,ax               ;put in ES
        mov   cx,4000h            ;screen size
        xor   di,di               ;screen starting address
        mov   ah,attribute        ;fill attribute
        mov   al,space            ;and space
        rep   stosw               ;fill it

        mov   si,offset in_protected  ;get protected mode
                                     ;message address
        mov   di,320              ;get display address
        call  disp_it             ;call display procedure

;STEP 15: set load TSS to TR

        mov   ax,task0_TSS_selec      ;get TSS selector for
                                     ;current task
        ltr   ax                      ;load into task register

;STEP 15.1: enable memory paging

        mov   eax,cr0             ;load the content of CR0
        or    eax,pg_enable       ;enable paging bit
        mov   cr0,eax             ;restore the content of CR0

;STEP 15.2: change current task to level 3 (user level)

        mov   ax,stk3_selec       ;get ss with level 3
        push  ax                  ;push ss
        mov   ax,offset stk3_limit    ;get sp with level 3
        push  ax                  ;push sp
        mov   ax,code3_selec      ;get cs with level 3
        push  ax                  ;push cs
        mov   ax,offset level     ;get eip
        push  ax                  ;push eip
        retf                      ;return far

;STEP 15.3: display change level message

level:
        mov   si,offset level_msg     ;get display message
        mov   di,3*160            ;get display position
        call  disp_it             ;display it
```

```
;STEP 15.4: write data to page with read only

        mov    ax,page_selec      ;get the page selector for
                                   ;page 90h
        mov    es,ax              ;put it in ES register
        mov    word ptr es:[0100h],ax  ;write data to this page

;STEP 16: switch back to real-address mode

        int    20                 ;interrupt 20

;STEP 17: Interrupt Service Routine

int_entry:             ;entry point for interrupt service routine
        REPT   INTNO
        call   disp               ;call the display message procedure
        iret
        ENDM

;STEP 18: get interrupt number and display it

disp:
        pop    ax                 ;get return address from stack
        sub    ax,offset int_entry   ;get offset from the
                                      ;interrupt entry
        shr    ax,TWO             ;divide by 4 to get interrupt
                                  ;number
        mov    si,offset int_num     ;get ascii code address
        mov    cx,TWO             ;convert to 2 ASCII code
        call   htoa               ;call convert procedure
        mov    si,offset int_msg  ;get interrupt message address
        mov    di,5*160           ;get display address
        call   disp_it            ;call display procedure

;STEP 18.1: disable memory paging

        mov    eax,cr0            ;load the content of CR0
        and    eax,not pg_enable  ;disable memory paging
        mov    cr0,eax            ;store to CR0

;STEP 19: Return to real-address mode

goto_real:
        cli                       ;disable interrupt

        mov    ax,dmy_selec       ;get dummy segment selector
        mov    es,ax              ;put in ES
        mov    ds,ax              ;put in DS
        mov    fs,ax              ;put in FS
        mov    gs,ax              ;put in GS
        mov    ss,ax              ;put in SS

        mov    eax,cr0            ;load the content of CR0
        and    eax,not prot_enable   ;disable protected mode
        mov    cr0,eax            ;restore the content of CR0

        db     0eah               ;far jump to flush instruction queue
```

```
          dw      offset next_instruction ;ip
          dw      code                    ;cs

;STEP 20: execute in real-address mode, and set DS,SS and SP

next_instruction:
          mov     ax,Gdata              ;get data segment address
          mov     ds,ax                 ;set to DS register
          mov     ax,stk0               ;get stack segment address
          mov     ss,ax                 ;set to SS register
          mov     sp,offset stk0_limit     ;set stack pointer

;STEP 21: set IDTR to DOS interrupt table

          lidt    [pold]                ;reset interrupt vector table
          sti                           ;enable interrupt

;STEP 22: terminate this process

          mov     ax,4c00h              ;terminate process
          int     21h                   ;DOS system call
main      endp

;Procedure: setup_pgtbl
;Align the predefined page table to page boundary. Set the
;first entry of page directory table to this aligned page
;table. The page directory table will be set below the page
;table.

setup_pgtbl proc   near
          push    ds                    ;save DS
          push    es                    ;save ES
          assume        ds:pagetbl
          mov     ax,pagetbl            ;get page table segment address
          mov     ds,ax
          mov     es,ax
          mov     bx,ax
          mov     cx,page_tbl_size      ;get page table size
          and     bx,00ffh              ;bx is in 4K range (segment)
          xor     edi,edi
          mov     di,100h               ;di has 4K size (segment)
          sub     di,bx                 ;address for 4K boundary,
                                        ;also page table address
          shl     di,4                  ;convert to offset
          mov     ptbl_addr,di          ;save page table address
          push    di                    ;save it
          mov     si,offset tmp_ptbl       ;get predefined page
                                           ;table address
          rep     movsd                 ;move it to the page boundary
                                        ;address
          pop     di                    ;restore di
;set pdbr & pdir
          xor     ebx,ebx
          mov     bx,ax                 ;get page table segment address
          shl     ebx,4                 ;convert to 20-bit address
          add     ebx,edi               ;page table linear base address
          or      bl,pte_mask           ;user level,read-write,present
```

```
        mov    dword ptr [di].pdbr_offset,ebx       ;put in page
                                      ;directory table
        add    ebx,offset pdbr_offset  ;page directory base
                                       ;address
        push   ds
        assume      ds:gdata
        mov    ax,gdata          ;get gdata segment
        mov    ds,ax             ;put in DS
        and    ebx,0fffff000h    ;PDBR
        mov    pdbr,ebx          ;save page directory address
        pop    ds
        assume      ds:pagetbl
        mov    bx,ptbl_addr      ;get page table address
        add    bx,90h shl 2      ;get entry 90h (1 entry has
                                 ;4 bytes)
        and    [bx][pg_stat],read_only ;set page 90h to read only
        pop    es                ;restore ES
        pop    ds                ;restore DS
        ret
setup_pgtbl endp
code   ends
        end    main
```

5.3 Summary

This chapter has presented sample programs for page programming, showing how to build the page directory table and the second level page table. Before enabling the paging, the CR3 register must hold the physical base address of the page directory table. This chapter also has presented two memory paging protection mechanisms supported by the i386/i486 processor, page "not present" protection and page level protection.

CHAPTER 6

CONTROL TRANSFERS

In the multitasking environment, enough protection is necessary to ensure that multitasking is reliable. In end-user systems, the operating system should be protected against damage from user programs or should recover automatically. The i386/i486 processor uses privilege levels to implement such protection. Each task has four privilege levels, numbered from 0 to 3. Lesser numbers mean higher privilege levels. This chapter discusses the definition of privilege level and its effect during control transfers between different processes and different privilege levels.

6.1 Privilege Level

The i386/i486 processor defines four privilege levels, numbered 0 to 3, for each task. The lesser the number, the higher the privileges. A general protection exception is generated if a lower privilege level task tries to access data from a higher privilege level segment. The operating system can be protected against a program by giving the operating system the highest privilege level and the program a lower privilege level.

The privilege level can also apply to control transfers. The i386/i486 processor provides very flexible control transfer checking, which gives the operating system a easy way to control the execution flow and protect the system.

There are three kinds of privilege levels available in the i386/i486 system: current, descriptor, and requested privilege level.

Current Privilege Level (CPL)

CPL indicates the privilege level of the task currently being executed in the system. The CPL value is defined in the lowest two bits of the CS segment register. When execution control transfers to a different level of procedure or task, the CPL value is changed according to the privilege level of the target procedure or task. The lowest two bits of the SS segment register must have the same value as the CPL.

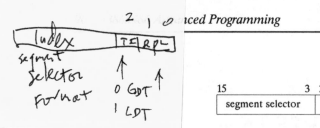

```
15              3 2 1  0
 ┌─────────────────┬──┬────┐
 │ segment selector│  │ CPL│
 └─────────────────┴──┴────┘
```

Figure 6.1 CS Segment Register

Descriptor Privilege Level (DPL)

DPL is a field defined in the segment descriptor. It defines the privilege level value for this segment. When execution control is transferred to a new code segment, the i386/i486 processor gets the DPL value of this new code segment and copies it to the CPL.

Figure 6.2 Control Transfer to a New Code Segment

Requested Privilege Level (RPL)

RPL is defined in the lowest two bits of any segment selector. (see Figure 3.2 for the segment selector format.) The value of RPL is given by any procedure uses this segment selector to access a segment. During the privilege level checking to this accessed segment, RPL checks instead of CPL if the RPL value is greater than CPL. The purpose of RPL is to create a lower privilege level checking than the current privilege level for the use of a segment.

The privilege level checking is performed when a segment selector is loaded into a segment register. There are two kinds of checking, one for data access and the other for control transfers.

6.2 Data Access Privilege Checking

When an instruction loads a segment selector into a data segment register (DS,ES,FS,GS), if the selected segment descriptor is a data segment or readable, executable segment, the privilege level checking is passed only when the DPL of the loaded segment is greater than (lower privilege) or equal to both the CPL and the segment selector's RPL. Otherwise, the i386/i486 processor generates a general protection exception.

There is one exception in the privilege level checking when loading a conforming, readable, and executable segment. The i386/i486 processor does not perform any checking when loading a conforming, executable segment into a data segment register. It treats the privilege level of this conforming, executable segment the same as the CPL, regardless of its DPL and RPL.

The privilege level checking is more restricted when loading a segment selector into the SS segment register. The DPL of the selected segment and the selector's RPL must equal the CPL. A general protection exception is generated for any of these violations.

6.3 Control Transfers Privilege Checking

The i386/i486 processor provides two kinds of control transfers. One is the control transfers between different privilege levels in one task. The other is the control transfers to a different task (task switch). Figure 6.3 shows the differences between these two kinds of control transfers.

A task has four privilege levels where every level in the task is independent of each other. To keep the independence and protection, each level must define its own stack and code segment. The individual stack can avoid the stack sharing problem, and it can save the current level states during different levels of control transfers (if necessary). Any control transfers in the i386/i486 processor that change CPL must cause a change of stack at the same time. Both CPL and SS segment's RPL must hold the same value.

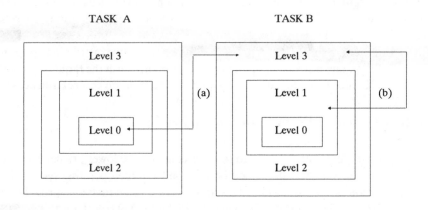

(a) control transfers between two tasks (task A and task B, task switch)

(b) control transfers inside one task (level 3 and level 1 of task B)

Figure 6.3 Control Transfers

In Figure 6.3, task B shows the control transfers between different privilege levels within a task. This kind of control transfers can be put into three categories; from higher privilege level to lower privilege level, from lower privilege level to higher privilege level, and transfer between the same privilege level.

With the i386/i486 processor, control transfers can be done through the *JMP*, *CALL*, *RET*, and *IRET* instructions. The i386/i486 depends on the instruction's operand data type to decide which categories of the control transfers an instruction requires, then it performs different privilege level checking. The exceptions and interrupts are other mechanisms to do control transfers and are discussed in Chapter 10.

Task switch between task A and task B (as shown in Figure 6.3) does not require any privilege level checking. It is much more complicated than control transfer within a task and is discussed in Chapter 7.

6.4 Control Transfers From Higher to Lower Level

Generally, it is common for a task to transfer control from a higher privilege level to a lower privilege level (switch to outer-level). For example, an application program in the lower privilege level can be executed when the operating system in the higher privilege level transfers control to it. In the i386/i486 system, this kind of control transfer does not require any privilege level checking. If the DPL of the target executable segment has a lower privilege level than the CPL, after control transfers to the target segment, the CPL is replaced by the DPL of the target segment.

It has already been noted that each privilege level in one task must have its own stack segment. The SS segment register must be reloaded when control transfers to a different privilege level. Since the i386/i486 generates an exception if reloading the CS and SS segment register separately, the only way to reload the CS and SS segment in one instruction is by using far *RET* and *IRET* instructions. These two instructions pop the SS, SP, CS, and IP in one instruction operation. You can first push the target segment's SS, SP, CS, and IP into stack, then use these two instructions to do control transfers.

6.5 Control Transfers From Lower to Higher Level

Sometimes, it is necessary for tasks to transfer control from lower privilege level to higher privilege level. Such transfers need permission from the operating system. For example, application programs may be allowed to execute some functions provided by the operating system. The i386/i486 mechanism to do this kind of transfer is through the *CALL* and *JMP* instruction to a call gate descriptor.

Call gate descriptor is used for control transfers from a lower privilege level to a higher privilege level. So the CPL must be the same or less privileged than the DPL of the target code segment selected by the call gate descriptor. The other check for call gate is both the CPL and the call gate selector's RPL must have equal or greater privilege than the DPL of the call gate descriptor. This check gives call gate a chance to specify the privilege level required to enter the task level defined by the call gate descriptor.

When there is no violation during privilege checking, control can be transferred to the task level whose segment and entry points are defined in the call gate descriptor. When control transfers through a call gate, the i386/i486 processor automatically reloads the SS and SP relative to the target segment's privilege level from current TSS. The value of SS and SP must be predefined in the current TSS, and the TR register must hold the base address of the TSS.

The privilege level checking during control transfers from lower privilege to higher privilege also has one exception for the executable conforming segment. Control can be transferred through *JMP* far and *CALL* far instructions directly to an executable conforming segment only if the DPL of the conforming code segment is more privileged than the CPL.

You can also transfer control from lower privilege to higher privilege through interrupt and exception. When interrupt or exception occurs, the i386/i486 gets the handler address from IDT. Only interrupt, trap, and task gate descriptor can be defined in the IDT. The Interrupt and trap gate have the same function and privilege level checking rule as the call gate. The difference is that the trap and interrupt gate cannot be called directly; they can only be invoked by interrupt instruction, exception, or external interrupt.

6.6 Control Transfers in the Same Privilege Level

For control transfers between the same privilege level, there are no restrictions. You can use *CALL* far, *JUMP* far, *RET* far, and *IRET* instructions directly transfer control to the code segment with the same privilege level.

6.7 Sample Program

The following two sample programs, *trans.asm* and *clgt.asm*, show control transfers between different privilege levels in one task. The first example uses far *RET* instruction to transfer control from a higher privilege level to a lower privilege level. The second example uses call gate to transfer control from a lower privilege level to a higher privilege level.

Program: TRANS.ASM

This program transfers control to a lower privilege level segment by using the far *RET* instruction. Before executing the far *RET* instruction, we must push the value of CS, IP, SS, and SP relative to the target segment's privilege level into the stack (Figure 6.4).

```
            execute in privilege level 0
                       .
                       .
                       .
      mov    ax,stk2_selec           ;get ss with level 2
      push   ax                      ;push ss
      mov    ax,offset stk2_limit    ;get sp with level 2
      push   ax                      ;push sp
      mov    ax,task0_code2_selec    ;get cs with level 2
      push   ax                      ;push cs
      mov    ax,offset level2        ;get ip
      push   ax                      ;push ip
      retf                           ;return far
```

Figure 6.4 Control Transfer from Higher Level to Lower Level

Step 1.1: Define the segment selector and descriptor with privilege level 2.

Step 4.1: Define mapping for segment base address and segment descriptor.

Step 5.1: Define display message.

Step 15.1: Push SS, SP, CS, IP for privilege level 2 segment into stack, then use far *RET* instruction to return to level 2 segment.

Step 15.2: Display message after changed level.

File: TRANS.ASM

```
.386p
include struct
include macro1
include macro2

INTNO       equ    21      ;interrupt vector number
DSCPSIZE    equ    8       ;size of descriptor
INTSIZE     equ    4       ;size of interrupt service routine
TWO         equ    2       ;
prot_enable equ    01h     ;protected mode enable bit in CR0
attribute   equ    07h     ;display character attribute
space       equ    20h     ;ASCII code for space

;STEP 1: Global Descriptor Table

GDT    segment    para   public use16 'GDT'
gdt_tab           label  qword
null_selec        equ    $-gdt_tab              ;null selector
  dscp      <,,,,,>        ;first one must be a null descriptor
```

```
code_selec  equ   $-gdt_tab    ;task 0 code segment selector
   dscp       <0ffffh,,,09ah,,>       ;descriptor for task 0

task0_TSS_selec   equ   $-gdt_tab   ;task 0 TSS selector
   dscp       <task0_TSS_limit,,,089h,,>    ;descriptor

stk0_selec  equ   $-gdt_tab            ;level 0 stack segment
                                       ;selector
   dscp       <stk0_limit,,,92h,,>     ;descriptor with
                                       ;privilege level 0
stk1_selec  equ   $-gdt_tab or 1       ;level 1 stack
                                       ;segment selector
   dscp       <stk1_limit,,,0b2h,,>    ;descriptor with
                                       ;privilege level 1
stk2_selec  equ   $-gdt_tab or 2       ;level 2 stack
                                       ;segment selector
   dscp       <stk2_limit,,,0d2h,,>    ;descriptor with
                                       ;privilege level 2
dmy_selec   equ   $-gdt_tab            ;dummy segment selector
   dscp       <0ffffh,,,92h,,>         ;dummy segment descriptor

video_selec equ   $-gdt_tab or 3    ;video segment selector
   dscp       <0ffffh,8000h,0bh,0f2h,,>    ;descriptor

gdata_selec equ   $-gdt_tab or 3    ;data segment selector
   dscp       <gdata_limit,,,0f2h,,>   ;descriptor

int_selec   equ   $-gdt_tab    ;interrupt segment selector
   dscp       <0ffffh,,,09ah,,>        ;descriptor

;STEP 1.1: privilege level 2 code segment

task0_code2_selec equ   $-gdt_tab or 2    ;level 2 code
                                          ;segment selector
   dscp       <0ffffh,,,0dah,,>          ;descriptor with
GDT_limit   equ   $-gdt_tab              ;DPL = 2
GDT   ends

;STEP 2: Interrupt Descriptor Table

IDT   segment para       public use16 'idt'
idt_tab equ $
      REPT   INTNO                      ;21 interrupt entries
      dscp   <,int_selec,0,0eeh,,>  ;DPL = 3
      ENDM
idt_limit   equ   $
IDT   ends

;DATA       Segment

Gdata segment       para   public use16 'Gdata'

;STEP 3: define variable to save GDT/IDT limit and linear
;address.

pGDT   label fword
```

```
        dw      GDT_limit               ;GDT limit
        dd      0                       ;GDT linear address
pIDT  label fword
        dw      IDT_limit               ;IDT limit
        dd      0                       ;IDT linear address
pold  label fword
        dw      03ffh                   ;DOS IDT limit
        dd      0                       ;DOS IDT linear address

;STEP 4: table to define the mapping of descriptor to
;        segment

gdt_phys_tab            label word
        dw      task0_TSS_selec         ;task 0 TSS segment selector
        dw      task0_TSS               ;task 0 TSS segment
        dw      stk0_selec              ;stk0 segment selector
        dw      stk0                    ;stk0 segment
        dw      stk1_selec              ;stk1 segment selector
        dw      stk1                    ;stk1 segment
        dw      stk2_selec              ;stk2 segment selector
        dw      stk2                    ;stk2 segment
        dw      dmy_selec               ;dummy segment selector
        dw      dmy                     ;dummy segment
        dw      code_selec              ;code segment selector
        dw      code                    ;code segment
        dw      gdata_selec             ;data segment selector for
        dw      gdata                   ;data segment
        dw      int_selec               ;interrupt segment selector
        dw      code                    ;code segment

;STEP 4.1: selector and segment for level 2 segment

        dw      task0_code2_selec
        dw      code
gdt_tab_size            equ     ($ - gdt_phys_tab) / 4

;STEP 5: message definition area

in_protected    db      'in protected mode ',0
int_msg         db      'interrupt '
int_num         dw      ?
                db      'H',0

;STEP 5.1: message definition area for task switch

level_msg   db      'change task to privilege level 2',0
Gdata_limit equ     $
Gdata ends

;STEP 6:     Stack Segment for privilege level 0,1,2

stk0   segment      para  public use16 'stk0'
        db      100h  dup(0)
stk0_limit  equ     $
stk0   ends

stk1   segment      para  public use16 'stk1'
```

```
         db      100h  dup(0)
stk1_limit   equ     $
stk1  ends

stk2  segment      para  public use16 'stk2'
         db      100h  dup(0)
stk2_limit   equ     $
stk2  ends
```

;STEP 7: Task State Segment for task 0

```
task0_TSS    segment      para  public use16 'task0'
TSS_stack    stk0_selec,stk0_limit,stk1_selec,stk1_limit,
             stk2_selec,stk2_limit
TSS_cr3      0                      ;cr3
TSS_regs     0,0,0,0,0,0,0,0,0,stk0_limit
TSS_seg      gdata_selec,code_selec,stk0_selec,
             gdata_selec,gdata_selec,gdata_selec
             dd      0              ;LDT field
             dw      0              ;task trap flag
             dw      68h            ;I/O base
task0_TSS_limit   equ     $
task0_TSS    ends
```

;STEP 8: Dummy Segment

```
dmy   segment      para  public use16 'dmy'
      db      128   dup(0)
dmy   ends
```

;CODE Segment

```
code  segment      para  public use16 'code'
      assume       cs:code,ds:gdata
main  proc  far
      mov   ax,gdata
      mov   ds,ax
```

;STEP 9: initialize IDT

```
      mov   ax,IDT               ;get IDT segment address
      mov   es,ax                ;put in ES
      mov   di,offset idt_tab    ;get IDT offset address
      mov   ax,offset int_entry  ;get interrupt service
                                 ;routine address
      mov   cx,INTNO             ;get interrupt number
fillidt:
      mov   es:[di],ax           ;put entry address in IDT
      add   di,DSCPSIZE          ;adjust address in IDT
      add   ax,INTSIZE           ;adjust interrupt service
                                 ;routine address, the size of
                                 ;each routine is defined in
                                 ;INTSIZE
      loop  fillidt             ;keep filling
```

```
;STEP 10,11,12,13: set GDTR,IDTR,LDTR and switch to
;                  protected mode

        build_dtr   gdt,idt,pgdt,pidt,gdt_limit,idt_limit
        build_dt    gdt,gdt_phys_tab,gdt_tab_size
        cli
        goto_prot   pgdt,pidt,CODE_selec,stk0_selec,
                    stk0_limit,GDATA_selec

;STEP 14: display message in protected mode

                                    ;clear the screen first
        mov     ax,video_selec      ;get video segment selector
        mov     es,ax               ;put in ES
        mov     cx,4000h            ;screen size
        xor     di,di               ;screen starting address
        mov     ah,attribute
        mov     al,space            ;fill space and attribute
        rep     stosw               ;fill it

        mov     si,offset in_protected  ;get protected mode
                                        ;message address
        mov     di,320              ;get display address
        call    disp_it             ;call display procedure

;STEP 15: set load TSS to TR

        mov     ax,task0_TSS_selec      ;get TSS selector for
                                        ;current task
        ltr     ax                      ;load into task register

;STEP 15.1: change privilege level from 0 to 2

        xor     eax,eax                 ;clear eax
        mov     ax,stk2_selec           ;get ss with level 2
        push    eax                     ;push ss
        xor     eax,eax                 ;clear eax
        mov     ax,offset stk2_limit    ;get sp with level 2
        push    eax                     ;push sp
        xor     eax,eax                 ;clear eax
        mov     ax,task0_code2_selec    ;get cs with level 2
        push    eax                     ;push cs
        mov     eax,offset level        ;get ip
        push    eax                     ;push ip
        db      66h                     ;32 bit operand size
        retf                            ;return far

;STEP 15.2: display message after the level changes

level:
        mov     si,offset level_msg ;get message address
        mov     di,4*160            ;get display address
        call    disp_it             ;call display

;STEP 16: switch back to real-address mode
```

```
        int    20                      ;interrupt 20
;STEP 17: Interrupt Service Routine

int_entry:             ;entry point for interrupt service routine
        REPT   INTNO
        call   disp          ;call the display message procedure
        iret
        ENDM

;STEP 18: get interrupt number and display it

disp:
        pop    ax                     ;get return address from stack
        sub    ax,offset int_entry    ;get offset from the
                                      ;interrupt entry
        shr    ax,TWO                 ;divide by 4 to get interrupt
                                      ;number
        mov    si,offset int_num      ;get ascii code address
        mov    cx,TWO                 ;convert to 2 ascii code
        call   htoa                   ;call convert procedure
        mov    si,offset int_msg ;get interrupt message address
        mov    di,6*160               ;get display address
        call   disp_it                ;call display procedure

;STEP 19: Return to real-address mode

        cli                           ;disable interrupt

        mov    ax,dmy_selec           ;get dummy selector
        mov    es,ax                  ;put in ES
        mov    ds,ax                  ;put in DS
        mov    fs,ax                  ;put in FS
        mov    gs,ax                  ;put in GS
        mov    ss,ax                  ;put in SS

        mov    eax,cr0                ;load the content of CR0
        and    eax,not prot_enable    ;disable protected mode
        mov    cr0,eax                ;restore the content of CR0

        db     0eah          ;far jump to flush instruction queue
        dw     offset next_instruction ;ip
        dw     code                    ;cs

;STEP 20: execute in real-address mode, and set DS,SS and SP

next_instruction:
        mov    ax,Gdata               ;get data segment address
        mov    ds,ax                  ;set to DS register
        mov    ax,stk0                ;get stack segment address
        mov    ss,ax                  ;set to SS register
        mov    sp,offset stk0_limit   ;set stack pointer

;STEP 21: set IDTR to DOS interrupt table

        lidt   [pold]                 ;reset interrupt vector table
        sti                           ;enable interrupt
```

```
;STEP 22: terminate this process

        mov    ax,4c00h             ;terminate process
        int    21h                  ;DOS system call
main    endp
code    ends
        end    main
```

Program: CLGT.ASM

This program calls a call gate descriptor to transfer control from a lower privilege
level to a higher privilege level. Call gate can only be used in control transfers from lower
level to higher level. This program first changes its privilege level to 2 as *trans.asm* does
and then transfer control to a privilege level 1 procedure through call gate. Figure 6.5
shows the definition format for a call gate descriptor, where *gate_enter* specifies the target
procedure offset, and *code1_selec* specifies the target segment selector. Figure 6.6 shows
the instruction to call the call gate.

```
gate_selec   dw     gate_enter1        ;offset (0..15)
             dw     code1_selec        ;code segment selector
             db     0                  ;dword count = 0
             db     8ch                ;present, 386 call gate
             db     gate_enter2        ;offset (16..31)
```

Figure 6.5 Call Gate Descriptor Format

```
        callf gate_selec              ;call gate selector
```

Figure 6.6 Call a Procedure Through Call Gate

Step 1.1: Define call gate, code segment with level 1, and level 2 selector and descriptor.

Step 4.1: Define segment base address for code segment with level 1 and level 2.

Step 5.1: Define message.

Step 15.1: Change current task level from 0 to 2.

Step 15.2: Display change level message.

Step 15.3: Call procedure through call gate (note *callf* is macro).

Step 15.4: Display message in the called procedure.

File: CLGT.ASM

```
.386p
include struct
include macro1
include macro2

INTNO       equ   21      ;interrupt vector number
DSCPSIZE    equ   8       ;size of descriptor
INTSIZE     equ   4       ;size of interrupt service routine
TWO         equ   2       ;
prot_enable equ   01h     ;
attribute   equ   07h     ;
space       equ   20h     ;

;STEP 1: Global Descriptor Table

GDT    segment      para  public      use16 'GDT'
gdt_tab             label qword
null_selec          equ   $-gdt_tab   ;null selector
  dscp      <,,,,,>         ;first one must be a null descriptor

code_selec equ   $-gdt_tab          ;code segment selector
  dscp      <0ffffh,,,09ah,,>        ;descriptor

task0_TSS_selec  equ   $-gdt_tab     ;TSS segment selector
  dscp      <task0_TSS_limit,,,089h,,>    ;TSS descriptor

stk0_selec equ   $-gdt_tab          ;level 0 stack segment
                                    ;selector
  dscp<stk0_limit,,,92h,,>           ;descriptor with
                                    ;privilege level 0
stk1_selec equ   $-gdt_tab or 1     ;level 1 stack
                                    ;segment selector
  dscp<stk1_limit,,,0b2h,,>          ;descriptor with
                                    ;privilege level 1
stk2_selec equ   $-gdt_tab or 2     ;level 2 stack
                                    ;segment selector
  dscp      <stk2_limit,,,0d2h,,>    ;descriptor with
                                    ;privilege level 2
dmy_selec  equ   $-gdt_tab          ;dummy segment selector
  dscp      <0ffffh,,,92h,,>         ;dummy segment descriptor

video_selec equ   $-gdt_tab or 3    ;video segment selector
  dscp      <0ffffh,8000h,0bh,0f2h,,>      ;descriptor

gdata_selec equ   $-gdt_tab         ;data segment selector
  dscp      <gdata_limit,,,0f2h,,>  ;descriptor

int_selec  equ   $-gdt_tab          ;interrupt segment
                                    ;selector
  dscp      <0ffffh,,,09ah,,>        ;descriptor
```

```
;STEP 1.1: Define descriptor

code1_selec equ    $-gdt_tab or 1    ;level 1 code segment
                                     ;selector (RPL = 1)
   dscp         <0ffffh,,,0bah,,>    ;descriptor (DPL = 1)

code2_selec equ    $-gdt_tab or 2    ;level 2 code segment
                                     ;selector (RPL = 2)
   dscp         <0ffffh,,,0dah,,>    ;descriptor (RPL = 2)

gate_selec  equ    $-gdt_tab         ;call gate selector
   dscp         <gate_enter,code1_selec,,0ech,,>    ;call gate
                                     ;descriptor (DPL = 3)
GDT_limit   equ    $-gdt_tab
GDT   ends

;STEP 2: Interrupt Descriptor Table

IDT    segment para      public use16 'idt'
idt_tab equ $
      REPT   INTNO                   ;20 interrupt
      dscp   <,int_selec,0,0eeh,,>   ;DPL = 3
      ENDM
idt_limit   equ    $
IDT   ends

;DATA       Segment

Gdata segment      para   public use16 'Gdata'

;STEP 3: define variable to save GDT/IDT limit and linear
;address.

pGDT  label fword
      dw    GDT_limit         ;GDT limit
      dd    0                 ;GDT linear address
pIDT  label fword
      dw    IDT_limit         ;IDT limit
      dd    0                 ;IDT linear address
pold  label fword
      dw    03ffh             ;DOS IDT limit
      dd    0                 ;DOS IDT linear address

;STEP 4: table to define the mapping of descriptor to
;        segment

gdt_phys_tab          label word
      dw    task0_TSS_selec   ;TSS segment selector
      dw    task0_TSS         ;TSS segment
      dw    stk0_selec        ;stk0 segment selector
      dw    stk0              ;stk0 segment
      dw    stk1_selec        ;stk1 segment selector
      dw    stk1              ;stk1 segment
      dw    stk2_selec        ;stk2 segment selector
      dw    stk2              ;stk2 segment
      dw    dmy_selec         ;dummy segment selector
```

```
        dw      dmy                     ;dummy segment
        dw      code_selec              ;code segment selector
        dw      code_                   ;code segment
        dw      gdata_selec             ;data segment selector
        dw      gdata_                  ;data segment
        dw      int_selec               ;interrupt segment selector
        dw      code_                   ;code segment

;STEP 4.1: Define level 1 and 2 code segment

        dw      code1_selec             ;level 1 code segment selector
        dw      code_                   ;code segment
        dw      code2_selec             ;level 2 code segment selector
        dw      code_                   ;code segment
gdt_tab_size        equ     ($ - gdt_phys_tab) / 4

;STEP 5: message definition area

in_protected    db      'in protected mode ',0
int_msg         db      'interrupt '
int_num         dw      ?
                db      'H',0

;STEP 5.1: more message definition area

level_msg           db      'changed to level 2',0
gate_msg            db      'call gate procedure',0
Gdata_limit         equ     $
Gdata_ends

;STEP 6: Stack Segment for privilege level 0,1,2

stk0  segment       para  public use16 'stk0'
      db      100h  dup(0)
stk0_limit  equ     $
stk0_ ends

stk1  segment       para  public use16 'stk1'
      db      100h  dup(0)
stk1_limit  equ     $
stk1_ ends

stk2  segment       para  public use16 'stk2'
      db      100h  dup(0)
stk2_limit  equ     $
stk2_ ends

;STEP 7: Task State Segment for task 0

task0_TSS           segment      para  public use16 'task0'
TSS_stack   stk0_selec,stk0_limit,stk1_selec,
            stk1_limit,stk2_selec,stk2_limit
TSS_cr3     0                       ;cr3
TSS_regs    0,0,0,0,0,0,0,0,0,stk0_limit
TSS_seg     gdata_selec,code_selec,stk0_selec,
            gdata_selec,gdata_selec,gdata_selec
            dd      0               ;LDT field
```

```
                dw      0               ;task trap flag
                dw      68h             ;I/O base
task0_TSS_limit equ     $
task0_TSS       ends

;STEP 8: Dummy Segment

dmy     segment         para  public use16 'dmy'
        db      128     dup(0)
dmy     ends

;CODE Segment

code    segment         para  public use16 'code'
        assume          cs:code,ds:gdata
main    proc    far
        mov     ax,gdata
        mov     ds,ax

;STEP 9:      initialize IDT

        mov     ax,IDT          ;get IDT segment address
        mov     es,ax           ;put in ES
        mov     di,offset idt_tab ;get IDT offset address
        mov     ax,offset int_entry     ;get interrupt service
                                ;routine address
        mov     cx,INTNO        ;get interrupt number
fillidt:
        mov     es:[di],ax      ;put entry address in IDT
        add     di,DSCPSIZE     ;adjust address in IDT
        add     ax,INTSIZE      ;adjust interrupt service
                                ;routine address, the size of
                                ;each routine is defined in
                                ;INTSIZE
        loop    fillidt         ;keep filling

;STEP 10,11,12,13: set GDTR,IDTR,LDTR and switch to
;                  protected mode

        build_dtr   gdt,idt,pgdt,pidt,gdt_limit,idt_limit
        build_dt    gdt,gdt_phys_tab,gdt_tab_size
        cli
        goto_prot   pgdt,pidt,CODE_selec,stk0_selec,
                    stk0_limit,GDATA_selec

;STEP 14: display message in protected mode

                                ;clear the screen first
        mov     ax,video_selec  ;get video segment selector
        mov     es,ax           ;put in ES
        mov     cx,4000h        ;screen size
        xor     di,di           ;screen starting address
        mov     ah,attribute
        mov     al,space        ;fill space and attribute
        rep     stosw           ;fill it

        mov     si,offset in_protected  ;get protected mode
```

```
                                        ;message address
        mov    di,320                   ;get display address
        call   disp_it                  ;call display procedure

;STEP 15: Load TSS to TR

        mov    ax,task0_TSS_selec       ;get TSS selector for
                                        ;current task
        ltr    ax                       ;load into task register

;STEP 15.1: change current task to level 2

        mov    ax,stk2_selec            ;get ss2
        push   ax                       ;push it
        mov    ax,offset stk2_limit     ;get sp2
        push   ax                       ;push it
        mov    ax,code2_selec     ;get cs selector with level 2
        push   ax                       ;push it
        mov    ax,offset level          ;get eip
        push   ax                       ;push it
        retf                            ;far return

;STEP 15.2: display change level message

level:
        mov    si,offset level_msg      ;get message
        mov    di,4*160                 ;get display position
        call   disp_it                  ;display it

;STEP 15.3: call procedure through call gate

        callf gate_selec                ;call gate selector

;STEP 15.4: called procedure entry point

gate_enter:
        mov    si,offset gate_msg       ;get message
        mov    di,6*160                 ;get display position
        call   disp_it                  ;display it

;STEP 16: switch back to real-address mode

        int    20                       ;interrupt 20

;STEP 17: Interrupt Service Routine

int_entry:          ;entry point for interrupt service routine
        REPT   INTNO
        call   disp        ;call the display message procedure
        iret
        ENDM

;STEP 18: get interrupt number and display it

disp:                       ;get interrupt number and display it
        pop    ax                   ;get return address from stack
        sub    ax,offset int_entry  ;get offset from the
```

```
                                    ;interrupt entry
          shr    ax,TWO       ;divide by 4 to get interrupt number
          mov    si,offset int_num      ;get ascii code address
          mov    cx,TWO                ;convert to 2 ascii code
          call   htoa                  ;call convert procedure
          mov    si,offset int_msg ;get interrupt message address
          mov    di,8*160              ;get display address
          call   disp_it              ;call display procedure

;STEP 19: Return to real-address mode

goto_real:
          cli                          ;disable interrupt

          mov    ax,dmy_selec      ;get dummy selector
          mov    es,ax             ;put in ES
          mov    ds,ax             ;put in DS
          mov    fs,ax             ;put in FS
          mov    gs,ax             ;put in GS
          mov    ss,ax             ;put in SS

          mov    eax,cr0           ;load the content of CR0
          and    eax,not prot_enable      ;disable protected mode
          mov    cr0,eax           ;restore the content of CR0

          db     0eah              ;far jump to flush
                                   ;instruction queue
          dw     offset next_instruction ;ip
          dw     code                 ;cs

;STEP 20: execute in real-address mode, and set DS,SS and SP

next_instruction:
          mov    ax,Gdata          ;get data segment address
          mov    ds,ax             ;set to DS register
          mov    ax,stk0           ;get stack segment address
          mov    ss,ax             ;set to SS register
          mov    sp,offset stk0_limit    ;set stack pointer

;STEP 21: set IDTR to DOS interrupt table

          lidt   [pold]            ;reset interrupt vector table
          sti                      ;enable interrupt

;STEP 22: terminate this process

          mov    ax,4c00h          ;terminate process
          int    21h               ;DOS system call
main      endp
code      ends
          end    main
```

6.8 Summary

This chapter has discussed how the i386/i486 processor supports the protection mechanisms within one task. The i386/i486 processor defines four privilege levels for each task, numbered from 0 to 3. Lower numbers mean higher privilege levels. A task with a lower privilege level cannot access any data from a higher privilege level segment. There are no restrictions to transfer control from a higher privilege level to a lower privilege level or the same privilege level. Control transfers from a lower privilege level to a higher privilege level must go through call gate, trap gate, or interrupt gate.

CHAPTER 7

MULTITASKING

In multitasking systems, during a task switch it is necessary to save the machine state of the current task to continue execution after control returns. The i386/i486 processor directly supports this operation in hardware, which can rapidly switch between tasks. When a task switch is invoked, the i386/i486 processor saves the state of the current task in its TSS, loads the context from the new task's TSS, performs protection checks, and then starts executing the new task. In the following sections, we discuss how to do a task switch in the i386/i486 system.

7.1 Task State Segment

Task state segment (TSS) is a segment that i386/i486 processor saves and loads the machine state of the current task and the new task during a task switch. The format of TSS is shown in Chapter 1. The TSS is a part of the system data structures and is protected from access by application programs. The i386/i486 system requires that the limit of a TSS must be greater than 103 bytes, in order to put certain values, and can be as large as 4 gigabytes. The operating system can store additional information following the required state value in the TSS during task switch if the information is needed.

Each task must have a TSS associated with it during a task switch. The i386/i486 processor stores the old task state to the old task's TSS and loads the new task state from the TSS of the new task. The segment selector of the current task's TSS must be stored in the task register (TR). The new task's TSS should be specified by the TSS segment selector or task gate segment selector given by the task switch instruction. During a task switch, the i386/i486 processor reloads the new task's TSS segment selector to the task register (TR).

7.2 Task Switch

A task switch can be invoked by using the *CALL* or *JMP* instruction to a TSS segment descriptor or a task gate descriptor. It can also be invoked through interrupts or exceptions by putting a task gate descriptor in the IDT. The TSS segment descriptor can only reside in the GDT. If a task switch instruction attempts to access a TSS segment descriptor from the LDT, the i386/i486 generates an exception.

When a task switch is through a *CALL* or *INT* instruction, it must go through the *IRET* (not *RET*) instruction to return to the switched task. When a program uses these two instructions to do a task switch, the i386/i486 processor puts the TSS segment selector of the interrupted task in the back link field of the new task's TSS and sets the NT bit in the EFLAGS register. Only the *IRET* instruction checks the NT bit and decides to perform a regular return or task return.

There is no privilege level checking between two switched tasks. Because each task is isolated by its address space and the TSS, one task can switch to any level of the other task from any level.

7.3 Sample Program

The following program does a task switch from task0 to task1 by using a *JMP* instruction to the TSS descriptor of task1. After switching to task1, it then switches back to task0 by using a software interrupt instruction. This specific software interrupt descriptor, residing in the IDT, is a task gate descriptor which points to the TSS descriptor of task0.

Program: mult.asm

Before task switching, we have to prepare the TSS for each switched task. Figures 7.1 and 7.2 show the TSS definition for these two tasks (task0 and task1). Since the TSS of task0 stores the state of task0, we don't need to initialize its contents. But we do have to initialize the contents of task1's TSS because the i386/i486 processor loads the machine state from task1's TSS.

```
TSS0        dd      0                           ;back link
            dd      0,0                         ;esp0,ss0
            dd      0,0                         ;esp1,ss1
            dd      0,0                         ;esp2,ss2
            dd      0                           ;cr3
            dd      0                           ;eip
            dd      0                           ;eflags
            dd      0,0,0,0,0,0,0,0             ;eax,ecx,ebx,edx,
                                                ;esp,ebp,esi,edi
            dd      0,0,0,0,0,0                 ;es,cs,ss,ds,fs,gs
            dd      0                           ;LDT field
TSS0_limit  equ     $
```

Figure 7.1 TSS Definition for Task0

```
TSS1    dd      0                               ;back link
        dd      task1_esp0,task1_ss0            ;esp0,ss0
        dd      task1_esp1,task1_ss1            ;esp1,ss1
        dd      task1_esp2,task1_ss2            ;esp2,ss2
        dd      0                               ;cr3
        dd      task1_eip                       ;eip
        dd      task1_eflags                    ;eflags
        dd      task1_eax,task1_ecx,task1_ebx,task1_edx
                                                ;eax,ecx,ebx,edx
        dd      task1_esp,task1_ebp,task1_esi,task1_edi
                                                ;esp,ebp,esi,edi
        dd      task1_es,task1_cs,task1_ss,task1_ds
        dd      task1_fs,task1_gs               ;es,cs,ss,ds,fs,gs
        dd      task1_ldt                       ;LDT field
        dw      0                               ;task trap flag
TSS1_limit  equ   $
```

Figure 7.2 TSS Definition for task1

Figure 7.3 shows the TSS descriptor definition for both tasks. We also have to load the current task's (task0) TSS segment selector into the TR register, shown in Figure 7.4. Figure 7.5 shows a task switch from task0 to task1 by jumping to task1's TSS descriptor. When the i386/i486 processor executes this instruction, it gets task0's TSS from the TR register, saves the machine state in this TSS, then loads the new state from the TSS pointed to by the new TSS descriptor.

```
task0_TSS_selec label word      ;TSS descriptor for task 0
      dw      TSS0_limit        ;TSS 0 limit (0..15)
      dw      TSS0_base1        ;TSS 0 base address (0..15)
      db      TSS0_base2        ;TSS 0 base address (16..23)
      db      89h               ;present,and available 386 TSS
      db      0
      db      0

task1_TSS_selec label word      ;TSS descriptor for task 1
      dw      TSS1_limit        ;TSS 1 limit (0..15)
      dw      TSS1_base1        ;TSS 1 base address (0..15)
      db      TSS1_base2        ;TSS 1 base address (16..23)
      db      89h               ;present,and available 386 TSS
      db      0
      db      0
```

Figure 7.3 TSS Descriptor Definition

```
      mov     ax,task0_tss_selec    ;get task 0 TSS selector
      ltr     ax                    ;load into TR register
```

Figure 7.4 Load Current Task TSS Into TR Register

```
        jmpf    task1_TSS_selec    ;jump to task 1 TSS selector
```

Figure 7.5 Task Switch by Using Jump Instruction

Step 1.1: Define task1 TSS and code segment selector and descriptor.

Step 2.1: Define a task gate descriptor in IDT, which points to the TSS of task0.

Step 4.1: Define mapping descriptor and segment for task1. The descriptor base address for these selectors is initialized at run time.

Step 5.1: Message definition area for task switch.

Step 7.1: Define task state segment for task1. The content of CS and EIP are initialized to the code segment of task1 and its entry point.

Step 15.1: Switch to task1 by jumping to task1's TSS segment selector (*jmpf* is a macro).

Step 15.2: Display message after returning from task1.

Step 23: Task1 code segment.

Step 25: By using a software interrupt instruction, switch back to task0 through a task gate located in IDT.

File: MULT.ASM

```
.386p
include struct
include macro1
include macro2

INTNO         equ    21           ;interrupt vector number
DSCPSIZE      equ    8            ;size of descriptor
INTSIZE       equ    4           ;size of interrupt service routine
TWO           equ    2            ;
prot_enable   equ    01h          ;protected mode enable bit in CR0
attribute     equ    07h          ;display character attribute
space         equ    20h          ;ASCII code for space

;STEP 1: Global Descriptor Table

GDT    segment      para  public use16 'GDT'
gdt_tab              label qword
null_selec           equ   $-gdt_tab           ;null selector
  dscp       <,,,,,>       ;first one must be a null descriptor
```

```
code_selec   equ    $-gdt_tab    ;task 0 code segment selector
   dscp        <0ffffh,,,09ah,,>         ;descriptor for task 0

task0_TSS_selec   equ   $-gdt_tab    ;task 0 TSS selector
   dscp        <task0_TSS_limit,,,089h,,>    ;descriptor

stk0_selec   equ    $-gdt_tab    ;level 0 stack segment selector
   dscp        <stk0_limit,,,92h,,>     ;descriptor with
                                        ;privilege level 0

stk1_selec   equ    $-gdt_tab or 1    ;level 1 stack
                                      ;segment selector
   dscp        <stk1_limit,,,0b2h,,>    ;descriptor with
                                        ;privilege level 1
stk2_selec   equ    $-gdt_tab or 2    ;level 2 stack
                                      ;segment selector
   dscp        <stk2_limit,,,0d2h,,>    ;descriptor with
                                        ;privilege level 2
dmy_selec    equ    $-gdt_tab         ;dummy segment selector
   dscp        <0ffffh,,,92h,,>        ;descriptor

video_selec equ    $-gdt_tab or 3    ;video segment selector
   dscp        <0ffffh,8000h,0bh,0f2h,,>    ;descriptor

gdata_selec equ    $-gdt_tab or 3    ;data segment selector
   dscp        <gdata_limit,,,0f2h,,>   ;descriptor

int_selec    equ    $-gdt_tab    ;interrupt segment selector
   dscp        <0ffffh,,,09ah,,>        ;descriptor

;STEP 1.1: task1 selector and descriptor

task1_TSS_selec    equ    $-gdt_tab or 1    ;level 1 TSS
                                           ;selector for task1
   dscp        <task1_TSS_limit,,,0a9h,,>    ;descriptor DPL = 1

task1_code_selec   equ    $-gdt_tab or 1    ;level 1 code
                                           ;segment selector for task1
   dscp        <task1_seg_limit,,,0bah,,>    ;descriptor DPL = 1

GDT_limit    equ    $-gdt_tab
GDT    ends

;STEP 2: Interrupt Descriptor Table

IDT    segment para       public use16 'idt'
idt_tab equ $
       REPT   INTNO                 ;21 interrupt entries
       dscp   <,int_selec,0,0eeh,,>   ;DPL = 3
       ENDM

;STEP 2.1: define task gate in IDT

   dscp        <,task0_TSS_selec,0,0e5h,,>    ;interrupt 21,
                                             ;task gate descriptor
idt_limit    equ    $
IDT    ends
```

```
        ;DATA           Segment

        Gdata segment      para   public use16 'Gdata'

        ;STEP 3: define variable to save GDT/IDT limit and linear
        ;address.

        pGDT  label fword
              dw    GDT_limit           ;GDT limit
              dd    0                   ;GDT linear address
        pIDT  label fword
              dw    IDT_limit           ;IDT limit
              dd    0                   ;IDT linear address
        pold  label fword
              dw    03ffh               ;DOS IDT limit
              dd    0                   ;DOS IDT linear address

        ;STEP 4: table to define the mapping of descriptor to
        ;        segment

        gdt_phys_tab        label word
              dw    task0_TSS_selec     ;task0 TSS segment selector
              dw    task0_TSS           ;task0 TSS segment
              dw    stk0_selec          ;stk0 segment selector
              dw    stk0                ;stk0 segment
              dw    stk1_selec          ;stk1 segment selector
              dw    stk1                ;stk1 segment
              dw    stk2_selec          ;stk2 segment selector
              dw    stk2                ;stk2 segment
              dw    dmy_selec           ;dummy segment selector
              dw    dmy                 ;dummy segment
              dw    code_selec          ;code segment selector
              dw    code                ;code segment
              dw    gdata_selec         ;data segment selector
              dw    gdata               ;data segment
              dw    int_selec           ;interrupt segment selector
              dw    code                ;code segment

        ;STEP 4.1: selector and segment for task1

              dw    task1_TSS_selec     ;task1 TSS segment selector
              dw    task1_TSS           ;task1 TSS segment
              dw    task1_code_selec    ;task1 code segment selector
              dw    task1_seg           ;task1 code segment
        gdt_tab_size        equ    ($ - gdt_phys_tab) / 4

        ;STEP 5: message definition area

        in_protected     db    'in protected mode ',0
        int_msg          db    'interrupt '
        int_num          dw    ?
                         db    'H',0

        ;STEP 5.1: message definition area for task switch

        task1_msg        db    'switch to task 1',0
        retmsg           db    'return to task 0',0
```

```
Gdata_limit equ    $
Gdata ends

;STEP 6: Stack Segment for privilege level 0,1,2

stk0   segment     para  public use16 'stk0'
       db    100h  dup(0)
stk0_limit  equ    $
stk0  ends

stk1   segment     para  public use16 'stk1'
       db    100h  dup(0)
stk1_limit  equ    $
stk1  ends

stk2   segment     para  public use16 'stk2'
       db    100h  dup(0)
stk2_limit  equ    $
stk2  ends

;STEP 7: Task State Segment for task0

task0_TSS    segment     para  public use16 'task0'
TSS_stack    stk0_selec,stk0_limit,stk1_selec,
             stk1_limit,stk2_selec,stk2_limit
TSS_cr3      0                ;cr3
TSS_regs     0,0,0,0,0,0,0,0,0,stk0_limit
TSS_seg      gdata_selec,code_selec,stk0_selec,
             gdata_selec,gdata_selec,gdata_selec
             dd    0          ;LDT field
             dw    0          ;task trap flag
             dw    68h        ;I/O base
task0_TSS_limit    equ    $
task0_TSS    ends

;STEP 7.1: Task State Segment for task1

task1_TSS    segment     para  public use16 'task1'
TSS_stack    stk0_selec,stk0_limit,stk1_selec,
             stk1_limit, stk2_selec,stk2_limit
TSS_cr3      0                ;cr3
TSS_regs     task1_entry,2,0,0,0,0,0,0,0,stk1_limit
TSS_seg      gdata_selec,task1_code_selec,stk1_selec,
             gdata_selec,gdata_selec,gdata_selec
             dd    0          ;LDT field
             dw    0          ;task trap flag
             dw    68h        ;I/O base
task1_TSS_limit    equ    $
task1_TSS    ends

;STEP 8: Dummy Segment

dmy    segment     para  public use16 'dmy'
       db    128   dup(0)
dmy    ends

;CODE Segment
```

```
code    segment       para  public use16 'code'
        assume        cs:code,ds:gdata
main    proc far
        mov   ax,gdata
        mov   ds,ax

;STEP 9: initialize IDT

        mov   ax,IDT                     ;get IDT segment address
        mov   es,ax                      ;put in ES
        mov   di,offset idt_tab          ;get IDT offset address
        mov   ax,offset int_entry        ;get interrupt service
                                         ;routine address
        mov   cx,INTNO                   ;get interrupt number
fillidt:
        mov   es:[di],ax       ;put entry address in IDT
        add   di,DSCPSIZE      ;adjust address in IDT
        add   ax,INTSIZE       ;adjust interrupt service
                              ;routine address, the size of
                              ;each routine is defined in
                              ;INTSIZE
        loop  fillidt         ;keep filling

;STEP 10,11,12,13: set GDTR,IDTR,LDTR and switch to
;protected mode

        build_dtr  gdt,idt,pgdt,pidt,gdt_limit,idt_limit
        build_dt   gdt,gdt_phys_tab,gdt_tab_size
        cli
        goto_prot  pgdt,pidt,CODE_selec,stk0_selec,
                   stk0_limit,GDATA_selec

;STEP 14: display message in protected mode

                              ;clear the screen first
        mov   ax,video_selec  ;get video segment selector
        mov   es,ax           ;put in ES
        mov   cx,4000h        ;screen size
        xor   di,di           ;screen starting address
        mov   ah,attribute
        mov   al,space        ;fill space and attribute
        rep   stosw           ;fill it

        mov   si,offset in_protected  ;get protected mode
                                      ;message address
        mov   di,320                  ;get display address
        call  disp_it                 ;call display procedure

;STEP 15: set load TSS to TR

        mov   ax,task0_TSS_selec      ;get TSS selector
                                      ;for current task
        ltr   ax                      ;load into task register

;STEP 15.1: jump to task1 through task1 selector
```

```
        jmpf    task1_TSS_selec    ;jump to task1 TSS selector

;STEP 15.2: display message after returning from task1

        mov     si,offset retmsg        ;get message address
        mov     di,5*160                ;get display address
        call    disp_it                 ;display it

;STEP 16: switch back to real-address mode

        int     20                      ;interrupt 20

;STEP 17: Interrupt Service Routine

int_entry:              ;entry point for interrupt service routine
        REPT    INTNO
        call    disp            ;call the display message procedure
        iret
        ENDM

;STEP 18: get interrupt number and display it

disp:
        pop     ax                      ;get return address from stack
        sub     ax,offset int_entry     ;get offset from the
                                        ;interrupt entry
        shr     ax,TWO                  ;divide by 4 to get
                                        ;interrupt number
        mov     si,offset int_num       ;get ascii code address
        mov     cx,TWO                  ;convert to 2 ascii code
        call    htoa                    ;call convert procedure
        mov     si,offset int_msg       ;get interrupt message
                                        ;address
        mov     di,6*160                ;get display address
        call    disp_it                 ;call display procedure

;STEP 19: Return to real-address mode

        cli                             ;disable interrupt

        mov     ax,dmy_selec            ;get dummy selector
        mov     es,ax                   ;put in ES
        mov     ds,ax                   ;put in DS
        mov     fs,ax                   ;put in FS
        mov     gs,ax                   ;put in GS
        mov     ss,ax                   ;put in SS

        mov     eax,cr0                 ;load the content of CR0
        and     eax,not prot_enable     ;disable protected mode
        mov     cr0,eax                 ;restore the content of CR0

        db      0eah            ;far jump to flush instruction queue
        dw      offset next_instruction ;ip
        dw      code                    ;cs
;STEP 20: execute in real-address mode, and set DS,SS and SP
next_instruction:
        mov     ax,Gdata                ;get data segment address
```

```
        mov    ds,ax                ;set to DS register
        mov    ax,stk0              ;get stack segment address
        mov    ss,ax                ;set to SS register
        mov    sp,offset stk0_limit    ;set stack pointer

;STEP 21: set IDTR to DOS interrupt table

        lidt   [pold]               ;reset interrupt vector table
        sti                         ;enable interrupt

;STEP 22: terminate this process

        mov    ax,4c00h             ;terminate process
        int    21h                  ;DOS system call
main    endp
code    ends

;STEP 23: Task1 Code Segment

task1_seg    segment      para  public use16 'task1_seg'
        assume       cs:task1_seg, ds:gdata
task1_entry proc   near

;STEP 24: display message when entering task1

        mov    si,offset task1_msg     ;get display message
        mov    di,160*3             ;get display position
        call   disp2                ;call display procedure

;STEP 25: switch back to task0 using interrupt instruction
;          through task gate

        int    21                   ;task gate reside in IDT (INT 21)
task1_entry endp

;procedure: disp2
;display string in protected mode
;input: ds:si - string address, the end of the string must
;              be 0

disp2 proc   near
        mov    ax,video_selec       ;get video segment selector
        mov    es,ax                ;put in ES
        mov    ah,attribute         ;display attribute
disp21:
        lodsb                       ;get display character
        stosw                       ;put it on screen
        cmp    al,0                 ;end of display character ?
        jne    disp21               ;no, continue
        ret                         ;yes, return
disp2 endp
task1_seg_limit    equ    $
task1_seg    ends
        end    main
```

We can also use the *CALL* TSS descriptor instruction to switch to task1. Then in task1 use the *IRET* instruction to return to task0. There is an exception related to task switching—exception 10, invalid TSS. If we set the task1 code segment as a "not present" segment (see Figure 7.6), the program generates an invalid TSS exception.

```
task1_cs    dw    task1_limit1    ;segment limit (0..15)
            dw    task1_base1     ;segment base (0..15)
            db    task1_base2     ;segment base (16..23)
            db    29h             ;segment not present
            db    task1_limit2    ;segment limit (16..19)
            db    task1_base3     ;segment base (24..31)
```

Figure 7.6 Task1 CS Descriptor Definition

7.4 Summary

Multitasking in the i386/i486 processor is through hardware, which can speed up the task context switching time. During a task switch, the i386/i486 processor stores the current machine state in the TSS of the current task, loads the new state from the new task's TSS, then starts executing the new task. The TR register must hold the TSS segment selector of the current task before doing a task switch.

CHAPTER 8

DEBUGGING

The i386/i486 processor provides advanced debugging features that give you a convenient way to examine program execution states. There are four debugging methods supported by the i386/i486 processor.

- instruction breakpoint
- single step trap
- instruction-breakpoint fault and data-breakpoint trap
- task-switch trap

This chapter briefly introduces these four methods but concentrates on describing the instruction-breakpoint fault and data-breakpoint trap. The i386/i486 processor provides four debug address registers (DR0 - DR3), one debug control register (DR7), and one debug status register (DR6) to let you set and examine the instruction-breakpoint fault and data-breakpoint trap.

8.1 Breakpoint and Trap

Generally, the debugging aids can be classified into four categories:

Instruction Breakpoint

You can set instruction breakpoint with the *INT 3* (opcode *0cch*) instruction. When the i386/i486 processor executes this instruction, it generates a breakpoint trap exception (exception 3). The exception handler can dump and examine the machine states. The value of the returned CS:EIP (or CS:IP), which was pushed into the stack, is the address that follows the *INT 3* instruction.

121

Single Step Trap

Everytime before the i386/i486 processor executes an instruction, it checks the TF bit defined in the EFLAGS register. If the TF bit is set(= 1), the i386/i486 processor generates a single step trap exception (exception 1). You can also dump and examine the machine states in the exception handler.

Instruction-Breakpoint Fault and Data-Breakpoint Trap

The i386/i486 processor provides a set of debug registers that can generate the instruction-breakpoint fault and data-breakpoint trap (exception 1) by setting these debug registers. You need to set the 32-bit linear address of the instruction or data breakpoint in the debug address registers and enable the debug control register when using this method.

Task-Switch Trap

After the i386/i486 processor does a task switch, it checks the task trap bit defined in the new task's TSS (see TSS format in Chapter 1). If this bit is set(= 1), a task-switch trap exception (exception 1) is generated. This allows you to check the new task's state after task switching but before executing the first instruction of the new task.

8.2 Debug Register

Figures 8.1, 8.2 and 8.3 show the format of each debug register. There are four debug address registers (DR0 - DR3), which can hold four 32-bit breakpoint linear addresses. The linear address is translated to a physical address by the paging mechanism when paging is enabled.

31	0	
Breakpoint 0 Linear Address		DR0
Breakpoint 1 Linear Address		DR1
Breakpoint 2 Linear Address		DR2
Breakpoint 3 Linear Address		DR3
Reserved		DR4
Reserved		DR5

Figure 8.1 Debug Address Registers

The debug status register (DR6) reports the breakpoint that triggered the debug exception. B0-B3 are set to 1, if the exception matches the conditions presented in the control register (DR7) and the relative debug address registers (DR0-DR3). The task-switch trap sets the BT bit, and the single step trap sets the BS bit. The BD bit is used by in-circuit emulation. The i386/i486 processor sets the DR6 register, but never clears it. The debug exception handler must clear the DR6 register before it is used to avoid any confusion.

31	16	15	14	13		3	2	1	0	
Reserved		BT	BS	BD	Reserved	B3	B2	B1	B0	DR6

Figure 8.2 Debug Status Register (DR6)

The fields defined in the debug control register (DR7) are related to each debug address register (DR0-DR3). The LENn (n relative to DR0-DR3) field specifies the memory size of the breakpoint location. The R/Wn field specifies the type of the breakpoint. Tables 8.1 and 8.2 explain how the i386/i486 processor defines these fields. The Ln (local enable) and Gn (global enable) bits are used to enable the breakpoint operations. The local enable bit enables breakpoint function for a local task. The global enable bit enables breakpoint function for all tasks. Local enable bits are cleared during task switching. The LE or GE bit should be set when "exact data breakpoint match" condition is desired. If one of these two bits is set, the i386/i486 processor slows instruction execution and reports the data breakpoint exactly at the instruction execution which triggered the data breakpoint, rather than the execution of the next instruction.

31	30	29	28 27	26 25	24 23	22 21	20 19	18 17	16
LEN3		R/W3	LEN2	R/W2	LEN1	R/W1	LEN0	R/W0	

15		10 9	8	7	6	5	4	3	2	1	0
Reserved		GE	LE	G3	L3	G2	L2	G1	L1	G0	L0

Figure 8.3 Debug Control Register (DR7)

R/W	Description
00	Breakpoint at instruction execution only
01	Breakpoint at data writes only
10	Undefined
11	Breakpoint at data reads or writes but not instruction execution

Table 8.1 Meaning for R/W Field

LEN	Description
00	Breakpoint is one byte long
01	Breakpoint is two byte long
10	Undefined
11	Breakpoint is four byte long

Table 8.2 Meaning for LEN Field

8.3 Examples

The following sample programs, *dbrd.asm*, *dbri.asm*, and *dbrt.asm*, show how to set the data-breakpoint trap, instruction-breakpoint fault, and task-switch trap in a program by using the debug address register, debug control register, and TSS. You must calculate the 32-bit linear address of the breakpoint before setting it in the debug address register. The first sample sets the data breakpoint, the second sets the instruction breakpoint, and the third sets the trap bit in TSS. All these programs generate exception 1.

Program: DBRD.ASM

This program sets the breakpoint address in one of the debug address registers and sets the type field relative to the debug address register in debug control register (DR7) as a data breakpoint. (Figure 8.4.) When this breakpoint address is hit during data access, the processor generates exception 1—data address breakpoint trap.

```
mov    eax,brk_address     ;get breakpoint linear address
mov    dr1,eax             ;put in debug address register
       ;set debug control register field relative to DR1
mov    dr7,00000000111100000000001100001100b     ;four byte
                           ;long, break on data read and write
```

Figure 8.4 Set Debug Address and Control Register as Data Breakpoint

Step 5.1: Reserve some data space.

Step 9.1: Set the breakpoint address at the address of variable *pos1*. First gets the linear address of *pos1* and then puts it in the DR1 register.

Step 9.2: Set the debug control register DR7 relative to the DR1 register as data reads or writes breakpoint, and the breakpoint length is four bytes. Also enable the breakpoint function for DR1 register.

Step 9.3: The DR6 register reports the breakpoint status at the time the debug exception is generated. Clear it to get the correct information after debug exception.

Step 15.1: Read data from variable *pos1*. This generates the debug exception.

Step 18.1: If a debug exception is generated, dump the contents of the DR6 register then clear the DR6, DR7 and DR1 registers before returning to the real-address mode.

File: DBRD.ASM

```
.386p
include struct
include macro1
include macro2

INTNO         equ    21      ;interrupt vector number
DSCPSIZE      equ    8       ;size of descriptor
INTSIZE       equ    4       ;size of interrupt service routine
TWO           equ    2       ;
prot_enable   equ    01h     ;protected mode enable bit in cr0
attribute     equ    07h     ;display character attribute
space         equ    20h     ;ASCII code for space

;STEP 1: Global Descriptor Table

GDT    segment        para  public use16 'GDT'
gdt_tab               label qword
null_selec    equ    $-gdt_tab           ;null selector
   dscp       <,,,,,>              ;first one must be a null descriptor

CODE_selec    equ    $-gdt_tab    ;code segment selector
   dscp       <0ffffh,,,09ah,,>         ;descriptor

task0_TSS_selec    equ    $-gdt_tab    ;TSS segment selector
   dscp       <task0_TSS_limit,,,089h,,>    ;descriptor

stk0_selec    equ    $-gdt_tab               ;level 0 stack segment
                                             ;selector
   dscp       <stk0_limit,,,92h,,>    ;descriptor with
                                      ;privilege level 0

stk1_selec    equ    $-gdt_tab or 1    ;level 1 stack
                                       ;segment selector
   dscp       <stk1_limit,,,0b2h,,>   ;descriptor with
                                      ;privilege level 1
stk2_selec    equ    $-gdt_tab  or 2    ;level 2 stack
                                        ;segment selector
   dscp       <stk2_limit,,,0d2h,,>   ;descriptor with
                                      ;privilege level 2
dmy_selec     equ    $-gdt_tab         ;dummy segment selector
   dscp       <0ffffh,,,92h,,>         ;descriptor
video_selec   equ    $-gdt_tab or 3    ;video segment selector
   dscp       <0ffffh,8000h,0bh,0f2h,,>     ;descriptor
```

```
gdata_selec equ    $-gdt_tab               ;data segment selector
  dscp       <gdata_limit,,,0f2h,,>            ;descriptor

int_selec   equ    $-gdt_tab     ;interrupt segment selector
  dscp       <0ffffh,,,09ah,,>           ;descriptor

GDT_limit   equ    $-gdt_tab
GDT   ends

;STEP 2: Interrupt Descriptor Table

IDT    segment para      public use16 'idt'
idt_tab equ $
       REPT   INTNO                     ;21 interrupt entries
       dscp   <,int_selec,0,0eeh,,>   ;DPL = 3
       ENDM
idt_limit   equ    $
IDT   ends

;DATA          Segment

Gdata segment      para  public      use16 'Gdata'

;STEP 3: variable to save GDT/IDT limit and linear address

pGDT   label fword
       dw     GDT_limit             ;GDT limit
       dd     0                     ;GDT linear address
pIDT   label fword
       dw     IDT_limit             ;IDT limit
       dd     0                     ;IDT linear address
pold   label fword
       dw     03ffh                 ;DOS IDT limit
       dd     0                     ;DOS IDT linear address

;STEP 4: table to define the mapping of descriptor to
;        segment

gdt_phys_tab        label word
       dw     task0_TSS_selec     ;TSS segment selector
       dw     task0_TSS           ;TSS segment
       dw     stk0_selec          ;stk0 segment selector
       dw     stk0                ;stk0 segment
       dw     stk1_selec          ;stk1 segment selector
       dw     stk1                ;stk1 segment
       dw     stk2_selec          ;stk2 segment selector
       dw     stk2                ;stk2 segment
       dw     dmy_selec           ;dummy segment selector
       dw     dmy                 ;dummy segment
       dw     CODE_selec          ;code segment selector
       dw     code                ;code segment
       dw     gdata_selec         ;data segment selector
       dw     gdata               ;data segment
       dw     int_selec           ;interrupt segment selector
       dw     code                ;code segment
gdt_tab_size        equ    ($ - gdt_phys_tab) / 4
```

```
;STEP 5: message definition area

in_protected        db      'in protected mode ',0
int_msg             db      'interrupt '
int_num             dw      ?
                    db      'H',0

;STEP 5.1: working data area

dr6_msg     db      'DR6:'
dr6_off     db      9       dup(0)
pos1        dd      0       ;data breakpoint is set here
Gdata_limit equ     $
Gdata ends

;STEP 6: Stack Segment for privilege level 0,1,2

stk0    segment     para  public use16 'stk0'
        db      100h  dup(0)
stk0_limit  equ     $
stk0    ends

stk1    segment     para  public use16 'stk1'
        db      100h  dup(0)
stk1_limit  equ     $
stk1    ends

stk2    segment     para  public use16 'stk2'
        db      100h  dup(0)
stk2_limit  equ     $
stk2    ends

;STEP 7: Task State Segment

task0_TSS   segment     para  public use16 'task0'
TSS_stack   stk0_selec,stk0_limit,stk1_selec,
            stk1_limit,stk2_selec,stk2_limit
TSS_cr3     0                       ;cr3
TSS_regs    0,0,0,0,0,0,0,0,0,stk0_limit
TSS_seg     gdata_selec,code_selec,stk0_selec,
            gdata_selec,gdata_selec,gdata_selec
            dd      0               ;LDT field
            dw      0               ;task trap flag
            dw      68h             ;I/O base
task0_TSS_limit     equ     $
task0_TSS   ends

;STEP 8: Dummy Segment

dmy     segment     para  public use16 'dmy'
        db      128   dup(0)
dmy     ends

;CODE Segment
code    segment     para  public use16 'code'
        assume      cs:code,ds:gdata
main    proc    far
```

```
          mov    ax,gdata
          mov    ds,ax

;STEP 9:       initialize IDT

          mov    ax,IDT              ;get IDT segment address
          mov    es,ax               ;put in ES
          mov    di,offset idt_tab      ;get IDT offset address
          mov    ax,offset int_entry    ;get interrupt service
                                        ;routine address
          mov    cx,INTNO               ;get interrupt number
fillidt:
          mov    es:[di],ax          ;put entry address in IDT
          add    di,DSCPSIZE         ;adjust address in IDT
          add    ax,INTSIZE          ;adjust interrupt service
                                     ;routine address. The size of
                                     ;each routine is defined in
                                     ;INTSIZE
          loop   fillidt             ;keep filling

;STEP 9.1: set DR1 at linear address pos1 in gdata segment

          xor    eax,eax             ;clear EAX
          mov    ax,gdata            ;get gdata segment address
          shl    eax,4               ;shift 4 bits left
          lea    esi,pos1            ;get offset address of pos1
          add    eax,esi             ;get linear address of pos1
          mov    dr1,eax             ;set debug register #1

;STEP 9.2: set DR7

          mov    eax,0f0030ch        ;breakpoint on data reads or
                                     ;write. breakpoint length is
                                     ;four bytes
          mov    dr7,eax             ;set debug control register

;STEP 9.3: clear DR6

          xor    eax,eax             ;clear eax
          mov    dr6,eax             ;put in dr6

;STEP 10,11,12,13: set GDTR,IDTR,LDTR and switch to
;                   protected mode

          build_dtr   gdt,idt,pgdt,pidt,gdt_limit,idt_limit
          build_dt    gdt,gdt_phys_tab,gdt_tab_size
          cli
          goto_prot   pgdt,pidt,CODE_selec,stk0_selec,
                      stk0_limit,GDATA_selec

;STEP 14: display message in protected mode
                                     ;clear the screen first
          mov    ax,video_selec      ;get video segment selector
          mov    es,ax               ;put in ES
          mov    cx,4000h            ;screen size
          xor    di,di               ;screen starting address
          mov    ah,attribute
```

```
        mov   al,space            ;fill space and attribute
        rep   stosw               ;fill it

        mov   si,offset in_protected  ;get protected mode
                                      ;message address
        mov   di,320              ;get display address
        call  disp_it             ;call display procedure

;STEP 15: set load TSS to TR

        mov   ax,task0_TSS_selec      ;get TSS selector for
                                      ;current task
        ltr   ax                  ;load into task register

;STEP 15.1: access data from pos1

        mov   eax,pos1            ;access data in pos1

;STEP 16: switch back to real-address mode

        int   20                  ;interrupt 20

;STEP 17: Interrupt Service Routine

int_entry:            ;entry point for interrupt service routine
        REPT  INTNO
        call  disp            ;call the display message procedure
        iret
        ENDM

;STEP 18: get interrupt number and display it

disp:
        pop   ax                  ;get return address from stack
        sub   ax,offset int_entry     ;get offset from the
                                      ;interrupt entry
        shr   ax,TWO              ;divide by 4 to get interrupt
                                 ;number
        push  ax
        mov   si,offset int_num  ;get ASCII code address
        mov   cx,TWO             ;convert to 2 ASCII code
        call  htoa              ;call convert procedure
        mov   si,offset int_msg ;get interrupt message address
        mov   di,5*160          ;get display address
        call  disp_it           ;call display procedure
        pop   ax

;STEP 18.1: check if debug exception then display dr6

        cmp   ax,1                ;debug exceptions ?
        jne   goto_real
        call  dump                ;call dump dr6 procedure
        xor   eax,eax             ;clear eax
        mov   dr6,eax             ;put in dr6
        mov   dr7,eax             ;put in dr7
        mov   dr1,eax             ;put in dr1
```

```
;STEP 19: Return to real-address mode

goto_real:
        cli                             ;disable interrupt

        mov     ax,dmy_selec            ;dummy selector
        mov     es,ax
        mov     ds,ax
        mov     fs,ax
        mov     gs,ax
        mov     ss,ax

        mov     eax,cr0                 ;load the content of CR0
        and     eax,not prot_enable     ;disable protected mode
        mov     cr0,eax                 ;restore the content of CR0

        db      0eah            ;far jump to flush instruction queue
        dw      offset next_instruction ;ip
        dw      code                    ;cs

;STEP 20: execute in real-address mode, and set DS,SS and SP

next_instruction:
        mov     ax,Gdata                ;get data segment address
        mov     ds,ax                   ;set to DS register
        mov     ax,stk0                 ;get stack segment address
        mov     ss,ax                   ;set to SS register
        mov     sp,offset stk0_limit    ;set stack pointer

;STEP 21: set IDTR to DOS interrupt table

        lidt    [pold]                  ;reset interrupt vector table
        sti                             ;enable interrupt

;STEP 22: terminate this process

        mov     ax,4c00h                ;terminate process
        int     21h                     ;DOS system call
main    endp

;procedure: dump
;This procedure dumps the content of DR6 on the screen

dump    proc    near
        mov     esi,offset dr6_off
        mov     eax,dr6
        mov     cx,8
        call    htoa
        mov     esi,offset dr6_msg
        mov     edi,9*80
        call    disp_it
        ret
dump    endp
code    ends
        end     main
```

Program: DBRI.ASM

This program sets the breakpoint address in one of the debug address registers and sets the type field relative to the debug address register in debug control register (DR7) as instruction breakpoint. (Figure 8.5) When the instruction execution hits this breakpoint, it generates exception 1—instruction address breakpoint fault.

```
mov     eax,brk_address            ;get breakpoint linear address
mov     dr1,eax                    ;put in debug address register
        ;set debug control register field relative to DR1
mov     dr7,1100b           ;break on instruction execution
```

Figure 8.5 Set Debug Address and Control Register as Instruction Breakpoint

Step 5.1: Reserve space to display the contents of the DR6 register.

Step 9.1: Get the linear address of label *pos1* and put it in the DR1 register.

Step 9.2: Set debug control register (DR7) relative to DR1 register as the instruction-breakpoint and enable the breakpoint function for the DR1 register. If it is set as the instruction-breakpoint, the length field must be 0.

Step 9.3: Clear the content of the DR6 debug status register.

Step 15.1: Execute instruction in the address of label *pos1*. This generates the debug exception.

Step 18.1: If this is debug exception, dump the contents of the DR6 register and clear the DR6, DR7 and DR1 registers before returning to the real-address mode.

File: DBRI.ASM

```
.386p
include struct
include macro1
include macro2

INTNO         equ    21      ;interrupt vector number
DSCPSIZE      equ    8       ;size of descriptor
INTSIZE       equ    4       ;size of interrupt service routine
TWO           equ    2       ;
prot_enable   equ    01h     ;protected mode enable bit in CR0
attribute     equ    07h     ;display character attribute
space         equ    20h     ;ASCII code for space
```

```
;STEP 1: Global Descriptor Table

GDT     segment      para  public use16 'GDT'
gdt_tab              label qword
null_selec   equ     $-gdt_tab             ;null selector
   dscp        <,,,,,>        ;first one must be a null descriptor

code_selec   equ     $-gdt_tab    ;code segment selector
   dscp        <0ffffh,,,09ah,,>        ;descriptor

task0_TSS_selec   equ     $-gdt_tab          ;TSS selector
   dscp        <task0_TSS_limit,,,,089h,,>    ;descriptor

stk0_selec   equ     $-gdt_tab          ;level 0 stack segment
                                        ;selector
   dscp        <stk0_limit,,,92h,,>     ;descriptor with
                                        ;privilege level 0
stk1_selec   equ     $-gdt_tab or 1     ;level 1 stack
                                        ;segment selector
   dscp        <stk1_limit,,,0b2h,,>    ;descriptor with
                                        ;privilege level 1
stk2_selec   equ     $-gdt_tab or 2     ;level 2 stack
                                        ;segment selector
   dscp<stk2_limit,,,0d2h,,>            ;descriptor with
                                        ;privilege level 2
dmy_selec    equ     $-gdt_tab          ;dummy segment selector
   dscp        <0ffffh,,,92h,,>         ;descriptor

video_selec  equ     $-gdt_tab or 3     ;video segment selector
   dscp        <0ffffh,8000h,0bh,0f2h,,>        ;descriptor

gdata_selec  equ     $-gdt_tab          ;data segment selector
   dscp        <gdata_limit,,,0f2h,,>          ;descriptor

int_selec    equ     $-gdt_tab    ;interrupt segment selector
   dscp        <0ffffh,,,09ah,,>        ;descriptor
GDT_limit    equ     $-gdt_tab
GDT     ends

;STEP 2: Interrupt Descriptor Table

IDT     segment para      public use16 'idt'
idt_tab equ $
        REPT    INTNO                    ;21 interrupt entries
        dscp    <,int_selec,0,0eeh,,>    ;DPL = 3
        ENDM
idt_limit    equ     $
IDT     ends

;DATA         Segment

Gdata segment      para  public use16 'Gdata'

;STEP 3: variable to save GDT/IDT limit and linear address

pGDT    label fword
        dw      GDT_limit    ;GDT limit
```

```
        dd      0                       ;GDT linear address
pIDT    label   fword
        dw      IDT_limit               ;IDT limit
        dd      0                       ;IDT linear address
pold    label   fword
        dw      03ffh                   ;DOS IDT limit
        dd      0                       ;DOS IDT linear address

;STEP 4: table to define the mapping of descriptor to
;        segment

gdt_phys_tab            label word
        dw      task0_TSS_selec  ;TSS segment selector
        dw      task0_TSS        ;TSS segment
        dw      stk0_selec       ;stk0 segment selector
        dw      stk0             ;stk0 segment
        dw      stk1_selec       ;stk1 segment selector
        dw      stk1             ;stk1 segment
        dw      stk2_selec       ;stk2 segment selector
        dw      stk2             ;stk2 segment
        dw      dmy_selec        ;dummy segment selector
        dw      dmy              ;dummy segment
        dw      code_selec       ;code segment selector
        dw      code             ;code segment
        dw      gdata_selec      ;data segment selector
        dw      gdata            ;data segment
        dw      int_selec        ;interrupt segment selector
        dw      code             ;code segment
gdt_tab_size    equ     ($ - gdt_phys_tab) / 4

;STEP 5: message definition area

in_protected    db      'in protected mode ',0
int_msg         db      'interrupt '
int_num         dw      ?
                db      'H',0

;STEP 5.1: working data area

dr6_msg         db      'DR6:'
dr6_off         db      9       dup(0)
Gdata_limit equ     $
Gdata ends

;STEP 6: Stack Segment for privilege level 0,1,2

stk0    segment         para  public use16 'stk0'
        db      100h    dup(0)
stk0_limit      equ     $
stk0    ends

stk1    segment         para  public use16 'stk1'
        db      100h    dup(0)
stk1_limit      equ     $
stk1    ends
```

```
stk2    segment     para  public use16 'stk2'
        db    100h  dup(0)
stk2_limit  equ    $
stk2_   ends


;STEP 7: Task State Segment

task0_TSS   segment     para  public use16  'task0'
TSS_stack   stk0_selec,stk0_limit,stk1_selec,stk1_limit,
            stk2_selec,stk2_limit
TSS_cr3     0                   ;cr3
TSS_regs    0,0,0,0,0,0,0,0,0,stk0_limit
TSS_seg     gdata_selec,code_selec,stk0_selec,
            gdata_selec,gdata_selec,gdata_selec
            dd    0             ;LDT field
            dw    0             ;task trap flag
            dw    68h           ;I/O base
            db    100h  dup(0ffh)  ;I/O bit maps
task0_TSS_limit  equ    $
task0_TSS_  ends


;STEP 8: Dummy Segment

dmy     segment     para  public use16 'dmy'
        db    128   dup(0)
dmy     ends


;CODE Segment

code    segment     para  public use16 'code'
        assume      cs:code,ds:gdata
main    proc  far
        mov   ax,gdata
        mov   ds,ax


;STEP 9: initialize IDT

        mov   ax,IDT            ;get IDT segment address
        mov   es,ax             ;put in ES
        mov   di,offset idt_tab     ;get IDT offset address
        mov   ax,offset int_entry   ;get interrupt service
                                    ;routine address
        mov   cx,INTNO         ;get interrupt number
fillidt:
        mov   es:[di],ax       ;put entry address in IDT
        add   di,DSCPSIZE      ;adjust address in IDT
        add   ax,INTSIZE       ;adjust interrupt service
                              ;routine address. The size of
                              ;each routine is defined in
                              ;INTSIZE
        loop  fillidt          ;keep filling

;STEP 9.1: set DR1 at linear address pos1 in code segment

        xor   eax,eax          ;clear EAX
        mov   ax,code          ;get gdata segment address
        shl   eax,4            ;shift 4 bits left
```

```
        lea     esi,pos1            ;get offset address of pos1
        add     eax,esi            ;get linear base address of
                                   ;pos1
        mov     dr1,eax            ;set debug register #1

;STEP 9.2: set DR7

        mov     eax,0ch            ;instruction breakpoint
        mov     dr7,eax            ;set debug control register

;STEP 9.3: clear DR6

        xor     eax,eax            ;clear debug status register
        mov     dr6,eax

;STEP 10,11,12,13: set GDTR,IDTR,LDTR and switch to
;                  protected mode

        build_dtr   gdt,idt,pgdt,pidt,gdt_limit,idt_limit
        build_dt    gdt,gdt_phys_tab,gdt_tab_size
        cli
        goto_prot   pgdt,pidt,CODE_selec,stk0_selec,
                    stk0_limit,GDATA_selec

;STEP 14: display message in protected mode

                                   ;clear the screen first
        mov     ax,video_selec     ;get video segment selector
        mov     es,ax              ;put in ES
        mov     cx,4000h           ;screen size
        xor     di,di              ;screen starting address
        mov     ah,attribute
        mov     al,space           ;fill space and attribute
        rep     stosw              ;fill it

        mov     si,offset in_protected  ;get protected mode
                                        ;message address
        mov     di,320             ;get display address
        call    disp_it            ;call display procedure

;STEP 15: set load TSS to TR

        mov     ax,task0_TSS_selec      ;get TSS selector for
                                        ;current task
        ltr     ax                 ;load into task register

;STEP 15.1: execute instruction in pos1

pos1:
        mov     ax,bx

;STEP 16: switch back to real-address mode

        int     20                 ;return to real-address mode

;STEP 17: Interrupt Service Routine
```

```
int_entry:              ;entry point for interrupt service routine
        REPT   INTNO
        call   disp            ;call the display message procedure
        iret
        ENDM

;STEP 18: get interrupt number and display it

disp:
        pop    ax               ;get return address from stack
        sub    ax,offset int_entry      ;get offset from the
                                        ;interrupt entry
        shr    ax,TWO           ;divide by 4 to get interrupt number
        push   ax
        mov    si,offset int_num ;get ASCII code address
        mov    cx,TWO            ;convert to 2 ASCII code
        call   htoa              ;call convert procedure
        mov    si,offset int_msg ;get interrupt message address
        mov    di,5*160          ;get display address
        call   disp_it           ;call display procedure
        pop    ax

;STEP 18.1: check if debug exception then display dr6

        cmp    ax,1             ;debug exceptions ?
        jne    goto_real
        call   dump             ;dump DR6 content
        xor    eax,eax          ;clear eax
        mov    dr6,eax          ;put in DR6
        mov    dr7,eax          ;put in DR7
        mov    dr1,eax          ;put in DR1

;STEP 19: Return to real-address mode

goto_real:
        cli                     ;disable interrupt
        mov    ax,dmy_selec     ;dummy selector
        mov    es,ax
        mov    ds,ax
        mov    fs,ax
        mov    gs,ax
        mov    ss,ax

        mov    eax,cr0          ;load the content of CR0
        and    eax,not prot_enable      ;disable protected mode
        mov    cr0,eax          ;restore the content of CR0

        db     0eah             ;far jump to flush instruction queue
        dw     offset next_instruction ;ip
        dw     code                     ;cs

;STEP 20: execute in real-address mode, and set DS,SS and SP

next_instruction:
        mov    ax,Gdata         ;get data segment address
        mov    ds,ax            ;set to DS register
        mov    ax,stk0          ;get stack segment address
```

```
       mov   ss,ax                  ;set to SS register
       mov   sp,offset stk0_limit   ;set stack pointer

;STEP 21: set IDTR to DOS interrupt table

       lidt  [pold]                 ;reset interrupt vector table
       sti                          ;enable interrupt

;STEP 22: terminate this process

       mov   ax,4c00h                  ;terminate process
       int   21h                    ;DOS system call
main   endp
code   ends
       end   main
```

Program: DBRT.ASM

This program switches from task0 to task1 by using the *CALL* to a TSS descriptor instruction. The T (trap) bit defined in the TSS of the new task is set to 1 (Figure 8.6), which causes the i386/i486 processor to generate task-switch trap after the task switching. The breakpoint is located at the first instruction of the new task.

```
TSS1   dd   0                                ;back link
       dd   task1_esp0,task1_ss0             ;esp0,ss0
       dd   task1_esp1,task1_ss1             ;esp1,ss1
       dd   task1_esp2,task1_ss2             ;esp2,ss2
       dd   0                                ;cr3
       dd   task1_eip,task1_eflags           ;eip and eflags
       dd   task1_eax,task1_ecx,task1_edx,task1_ebx
                                             ;eax,ecx,ebx,edx
       dd   task1_esp,task1_ebp,task1_esi,task1_edi
                                             ;esp,ebp,esi,edi
       dd   task1_es,task1_cs,task1_ss,task1_ds
                                             ;es,cs,ss,ds
       dd   task1_fs,task1_gs                ;fs,gs
       dd   task1_ldt                        ;ldt
       dw   1                                ;trap bit
```

Figure 8.6 Set Trap Bit in TSS

Step 1.1: Define the TSS and code segment selector and descriptor for task1.

Step 4.1: Define the segment descriptor and segment address mapping for task1.

Step 7.1: Define the TSS for task1. Notice that the trap bit is set to 1.

Step 15.1: Switch to task1 by calling the task1 TSS selector.

Step 23: Define code segment for task1. The task-switch trap is generated before the execution of the first instruction.

File: DBRT.ASM

```
.386p
include struct
include macro1
include macro2

INTNO        equ   21      ;interrupt vector number
DSCPSIZE     equ   8       ;size of descriptor
INTSIZE      equ   4       ;size of interrupt service routine
TWO          equ   2       ;
prot_enable  equ   01h     ;protected mode enable bit in CR0
attribute    equ   07h     ;display character attribute
space        equ   20h     ;ASCII code for space

;STEP 1: Global Descriptor Table

GDT    segment       para  public use16 'GDT'
gdt_tab              label qword
null_selec  equ   $-gdt_tab            ;null selector
   dscp      <,,,,,>        ;first one must be a null descriptor

code_selec  equ   $-gdt_tab    ;task0 code segment selector
dscp  <0ffffh,,,09ah,,>               ;descriptor for task0

task0_TSS_selec    equ   $-gdt_tab   ;task0 TSS selector
   dscp        <task0_TSS_limit,,,089h,,>    ;descriptor

stk0_selec  equ   $-gdt_tab           ;level 0 stack segment
                                      ;selector
   dscp       <stk0_limit,,,92h,,>    ;descriptor with
                                      ;privilege level 0
stk1_selec  equ   $-gdt_tab or 1      ;level 1 stack
                                      ;segment selector
   dscp       <stk1_limit,,,0b2h,,>   ;descriptor with
                                      ;privilege level 1
stk2_selec  equ   $-gdt_tab  or 2     ;level 2 stack
                                      ;segment selector
   dscp       <stk2_limit,,,0d2h,,>   ;descriptor with
                                      ;privilege level 2
dmy_selec   equ   $-gdt_tab           ;dummy segment selector
   dscp       <0ffffh,,,92h,,>        ;dummy segment descriptor

video_selec equ   $-gdt_tab or 3      ;video segment selector
   dscp       <0ffffh,8000h,0bh,0f2h,,>     ;descriptor
gdata_selec equ   $-gdt_tab or 3      ;data segment selector
   dscp       <gdata_limit,,,0f2h,,>  ;descriptor
```

```
int_selec   equ    $-gdt_tab   ;interrupt segment selector
   dscp       <0ffffh,,,09ah,,>        ;descriptor

;STEP 1.1: selector and descriptor for task1

task1_TSS_selec    equ    $-gdt_tab or 1     ;level 1 TSS
                                      ;selector for task1
   dscp       <task1_TSS_limit,,,0a9h,,>    ;descriptor

task1_code_selec   equ    $-gdt_tab or 1     ;level 1 code
                                ;segment selector for task1
   dscp       <task1_seg_limit,,,0bah,,>    ;descriptor

GDT_limit   equ    $-gdt_tab
GDT    ends

;STEP 2: Interrupt Descriptor Table

IDT    segment para        public use16 'idt'
idt_tab equ $
       REPT   INTNO                    ;21 interrupt entries
       dscp   <,int_selec,0,0eeh,,>    ;DPL = 3
       ENDM
idt_limit   equ    $
IDT    ends

;DATA          Segment

Gdata segment      para  public use16 'Gdata'

;STEP 3: variable to save GDT/IDT limit and linear address

pGDT   label fword
       dw    GDT_limit         ;GDT limit
       dd    0                 ;GDT linear address
pIDT   label fword
       dw    IDT_limit         ;IDT limit
       dd    0                 ;IDT linear address
pold   label fword
       dw    03ffh             ;DOS IDT limit
       dd    0                 ;DOS IDT linear address

;STEP 4: table to define the mapping of descriptor to
;        segment

gdt_phys_tab        label word
       dw     task0_TSS_selec  ;task 0 TSS segment selector
       dw     task0_TSS        ;task 0 TSS segment
       dw     stk0_selec       ;stk0 segment selector
       dw     stk0             ;stk0 segment
       dw     stk1_selec       ;stk1 segment selector
       dw     stk1             ;stk1 segment
       dw     stk2_selec       ;stk2 segment selector
       dw     stk2             ;stk2 segment
       dw     dmy_selec        ;dummy segment selector
       dw     dmy              ;dummy segment
       dw     code_selec       ;code segment selector
```

```
        dw      code                ;code segment
        dw      gdata_selec         ;data segment selector for
        dw      gdata               ;data segment
        dw      int_selec           ;interrupt segment selector
        dw      code                ;code segment

;STEP 4.1: selector and segment for task1

        dw      task1_TSS_selec     ;task 1 TSS segment selector
        dw      task1_TSS           ;task 1 TSS segment
        dw      task1_code_selec    ;task 1 code segment selector
        dw      task1_seg           ;task 1 code segment
gdt_tab_size        equ     ($ - gdt_phys_tab) / 4

;STEP 5:     message definition area

in_protected    db      'in protected mode ',0
int_msg         db      'interrupt '
int_num         dw      ?
                db      'H',0
Gdata_limit equ     $
Gdata ends


;STEP 6: Stack Segment for privilege level 0,1,2

stk0    segment     para  public use16 'stk0'
        db      100h  dup(0)
stk0_limit  equ     $
stk0  ends

stk1    segment     para  public use16 'stk1'
        db      100h  dup(0)
stk1_limit  equ     $
stk1  ends

stk2    segment     para  public use16 'stk2'
        db      100h  dup(0)
stk2_limit  equ     $
stk2  ends


;STEP 7: Task State Segment for task 0

task0_TSS    segment        para  public use16 'task0'
TSS_stack    stk0_selec,stk0_limit,stk1_selec,
             stk1_limit,stk2_selec,stk2_limit
TSS_cr3      0                       ;cr3
TSS_regs     0,0,0,0,0,0,0,0,0,stk0_limit
TSS_seg      gdata_selec,code_selec,stk0_selec,
             gdata_selec,gdata_selec,gdata_selec
             dd      0               ;LDT field
             dw      0               ;task trap flag
             dw      68h             ;I/O base
task0_TSS_limit    equ     $
task0_TSS    ends


;STEP 7.1: Task State Segment for task 1
```

```
task1_TSS    segment      para  public use16 'task0'
TSS_stack    stk0_selec,stk0_limit,stk1_selec,
             stk1_limit, stk2_selec,stk2_limit
TSS_cr3      0                    ;cr3
TSS_regs     task1_entry,2,0,0,0,0,0,0,0,stk1_limit
TSS_seg      gdata_selec,task1_code_selec,stk1_selec,
             gdata_selec,gdata_selec,gdata_selec
             dd    0              ;LDT field
             dw    1              ;turn on task trap flag
             dw    68h            ;I/O base
task1_TSS_limit   equ   $
task1_TSS    ends

;STEP 8: Dummy Segment

dmy    segment      para  public use16 'dmy'
       db    128    dup(0)
dmy    ends

;CODE Segment

code   segment      para  public use16 'code'
       assume       cs:code,ds:gdata
main   proc  far
       mov   ax,gdata
       mov   ds,ax

;STEP 9:     initialize IDT

       mov   ax,IDT             ;get IDT segment address
       mov   es,ax              ;put in ES
       mov   di,offset idt_tab  ;get IDT offset address
       mov   ax,offset int_entry    ;get interrupt service
                                     ;routine address
       mov   cx,INTNO           ;get interrupt number
fillidt:
       mov   es:[di],ax         ;put entry address in IDT
       add   di,DSCPSIZE        ;adjust address in IDT
       add   ax,INTSIZE         ;adjust interrupt service
                                ;routine address. The size of
                                ;each routine is defined in
                                ;INTSIZE
       loop  fillidt            ;keep filling

;STEP 10,11,12,13: set GDTR,IDTR,LDTR and switch to
;                  protected mode

       build_dtr   gdt,idt,pgdt,pidt,gdt_limit,idt_limit
       build_dt    gdt,gdt_phys_tab,gdt_tab_size
       cli
       goto_prot   pgdt,pidt,code_selec,stk0_selec,
                   stk0_limit,GDATA_selec


;STEP 14: display message in protected mode
                        ;clear the screen first
       mov   ax,video_selec    ;get video segment selector
```

["

```
        mov     eax,cr0             ;load the content of CR0
        and     eax,not prot_enable     ;disable protected mode
        mov     cr0,eax             ;restore the content of CR0

        db      0eah                ;far jump to flush instruction queue
        dw      offset next_instruction
        dw      code
```

;STEP 20: execute in real-address mode, and set DS,SS and SP

```
next_instruction:
        mov     ax,Gdata            ;get data segment address
        mov     ds,ax               ;set to DS register
        mov     ax,stk0             ;get stack segment address
        mov     ss,ax               ;set to SS register
        mov     sp,offset stk0_limit    ;set stack pointer
```

;STEP 21: set IDTR to DOS interrupt table

```
        lidt    [pold]              ;reset interrupt vector table
        sti                         ;enable interrupt
```

;STEP 22: terminate this process

```
        mov     ax,4c00h            ;terminate process
        int     21h                 ;DOS system call
main    endp
code    ends
```

;STEP 23: Task 1 Code Segment

```
task1_seg           segment     para  public use16 'task1_seg'
        assume      cs:task1_seg, ds:gdata
task1_entry proc    near
            ret
task1_entry endp
task1_seg_limit     equ     $
task1_seg   ends
        end     main
```

8.4 Summary

This chapter has discussed how to use the debug registers to set the instruction-breakpoint fault and data-breakpoint trap during program debugging. There are four debug address registers (DR0-DR3), which can hold four breakpoint linear addresses. The debug control register (DR7) controls the type (data or instruction), length (0 to 4 bytes), enabling, and disabling of the breakpoint. The debug status register (DR6) shows the status which generated the debug trap exception (breakpoint trap, single step trap, or task-switch trap). A task-switch trap is generated by setting the task trap bit in the new task's task state segment (TSS).

CHAPTER 9

INPUT/OUTPUT

Many peripheral devices can be connected to the i386/i486 machine. The communications between these devices and the i386/i486 are through I/O addresses. The I/O address can carry data, present the status of the peripheral devices, or control the peripheral devices. This chapter discusses the I/O addresses (I/O port address and memory I/O address) and the I/O port protection mechanism (I/O privilege level protection and I/O permission bit map protection) provided by the i386/i486 processor.

9.1 I/O Addressing

The i386/i486 processor provides two ways to refer to the I/O address. One is through the I/O instruction to access data from the I/O port address. For example, instruction *IN AL, 20H* reads data from the I/O port address *20H* and puts the data in the AL register. The other way is through the memory I/O address which has the same characteristics as the physical memory address. For example, physical address *B8000h - B9000h* is the memory I/O address that belongs to the video device, and it can be accessed by any instruction which can reference the memory address space.

The i386/i486 processor can transfer data which is 8, 16, or 32 bits to an I/O port address. But since Intel reserved the I/O port address from *0F8H* to *0FFH*, it is better not to assign an I/O port to these addresses. The memory I/O address usually is supported by the I/O devices which appear as a physical memory address in the system. The memory I/O address can be accessed through the full instruction set and the full complement of addressing modes.

The i386/i486 memory protection (segmentation and paging) can also apply to the memory I/O address. For the I/O port address, the i386/i486 processor provides two other protection mechanisms: I/O privilege level protection and I/O permission bit map protection.

145

9.2 I/O Privilege Level Protection

When any I/O instruction is executed, the i386/i486 processor compares the IOPL (input/output privilege level) defined in the EFLAGS register (bit position 11 and 12) with the CPL. If the CPL value is smaller or equal to the IOPL, the I/O instruction is executed. If it is not, the i386/i486 processor does further checks through the I/O permission bit map associated with the TSS of the current task. The instructions which cause the i386/i486 processor to do the I/O privilege level checking are *IN, INS, OUT, OUTS, CLI,* and *STI.* Since these instructions cause the i386/i486 to compare the value of the CPL and the IOPL, they are "I/O sensitive" instructions.

You can change the value of IOPL with the *POPF* instruction when CPL equals 0. Any attempt to change IOPL from a lower privilege level task (CPL > 0) does not generate an exception because the i386/i486 processor does not change the IOPL.

9.3 I/O Permission Bit Map Protection

The I/O permission bit map is associated with the TSS. It specifies the access permission for each I/O port address. Each bit in the I/O permission bit map sequentially corresponds to an I/O port address. For example, bit *20h* in the bit map corresponds to the I/O port address *20h.* When an I/O instruction does not pass the I/O privilege level checking, the i386/i486 processor checks the bit corresponding to this I/O port address from the TSS I/O permission bit map. If the bit is cleared(= 0), the I/O operation can proceed; otherwise, a general protection exception is generated.

The I/O permission bit map does not have to present all the I/O port addresses. The size of I/O permission bit map is variable. You only need to reserve the space which is necessary for the I/O bit map checking. The I/O port address bits which are not spanned in the I/O permission bit map means its corresponding I/O port addresses are I/O denied. If all the I/O addresses are I/O denied when executing the I/O instructions, there is no need to define the I/O permission bit map in the TSS because the default value of not spanned I/O bits is 1 (I/O denied).

In the v86 mode, there are different instructions which are sensitive to the IOPL: *CLI, STI, PUSHF, POPF, INT n,* and *IRET.* The CPL value of v86 mode task is 3. If the IOPL has more privilege level than 3 any of these instructions generates a general protection exception. When any I/O instruction tries to access data from an I/O port address in the v86 mode, the i386/i486 processor skips the I/O privilege level checking (it is not necessary) but directly checks the I/O permission bit map.

9.4 Sample Program

The following program shows the I/O port address protection through the use of the I/O permission bit map defined in the TSS. The program first fails in the I/O privilege level checking due to the condition CPL > IOPL (CPL has lower privilege than IOPL). Then the i386/i486 processor checks the I/O permission bit map from the TSS of the current task.

Program: IOPL.ASM

The task first sets the IOPL in the EFLAGS register equal to 0 then changes itself to a lower privilege level (see *trans.asm*). When this program tries to access data from an I/O port address, it generates exception 13 because the I/O permission bit map is set to the default state (I/O denied).

Step 7: The I/O permission bit map base address is the same as the TSS segment limit. It means no I/O permission bit map is defined. All the bits are treated set.

Step 8.1: Make sure the IOPL equals 0.

Step 15.3: Try to access data from I/O port address *20h* through the I/O instruction *IN*. This instruction generates an exception.

File: IOPL.ASM

```
.386p
include struct
include macro1
include macro2

INTNO        equ    21     ;interrupt vector number
DSCPSIZE     equ    8      ;size of descriptor
INTSIZE      equ    4      ;size of interrupt service routine
TWO          equ    2      ;
prot_enable  equ    01h    ;protected mode enable bit in CR0
attribute    equ    07h    ;display character attribute
space        equ    20h    ;ASCII code for space

;STEP 1: Global Descriptor Table

GDT    segment        para  public use16 'GDT'
gdt_tab              label qword
null_selec  equ     $-gdt_tab            ;null selector
   dscp         <,,,,,>       ;first one must be a null descriptor

code_selec  equ    $-gdt_tab   ;task 0 code segment selector
dscp  <0ffffh,,,09ah,,>                  ;descriptor

task0_TSS_selec    equ    $-gdt_tab    ;task 0 TSS selector
   dscp       <task0_TSS_limit,,,089h,,>     ;TSS descriptor
```

```
stk0_selec   equ    $-gdt_tab              ;level 0 stack segment
                                           ;selector
   dscp        <stk0_limit,,,92h,,>        ;descriptor with
                                           ;privilege level 0
stk1_selec   equ    $-gdt_tab or 1         ;level 1 stack
                                           ;segment selector
   dscp        <stk1_limit,,,0b2h,,>       ;descriptor with
                                           ;privilege level 1
stk2_selec   equ    $-gdt_tab  or 2        ;level 2 stack
                                           ;segment selector
   dscp        <stk2_limit,,,0d2h,,>       ;descriptor with
                                           ;privilege level 2
dmy_selec    equ    $-gdt_tab              ;dummy segment selector
   dscp        <0ffffh,,,92h,,>            ;dummy segment descriptor

video_selec  equ    $-gdt_tab or 3    ;video segment selector
   dscp        <0ffffh,8000h,0bh,0f2h,,>      ;descriptor

gdata_selec  equ    $-gdt_tab or 3    ;data segment selector
   dscp        <gdata_limit,,,0f2h,,>         ;descriptor

int_selec    equ    $-gdt_tab    ;interrupt segment selector
   dscp        <0ffffh,,,09ah,,>       ;descriptor

;STEP 1.1: privilege level 2 code segment

task0_code2_selec equ   $-gdt_tab or 2     ;level 2 code
                            ;segment selector for task 1
   dscp        <0ffffh,,,0dah,,>          ;descriptor with
                                          ;privilege level 2

GDT_limit    equ    $-gdt_tab
GDT    ends

;STEP 2: Interrupt Descriptor Table

IDT    segment para       public use16 'idt'
idt_tab equ $
       REPT   INTNO                       ;21 interrupt entries
       dscp <,int_selec,0,0eeh,,>   ;DPL = 3
       ENDM
idt_limit    equ    $
IDT    ends

;DATA       Segment

Gdata segment      para   public use16 'Gdata'

;STEP 3: variable to save GDT/IDT limit and linear address

pGDT  label fword
      dw    GDT_limit          ;GDT limit
      dd    0                  ;GDT linear address
pIDT  label fword
      dw    IDT_limit          ;IDT limit
      dd    0                  ;IDT linear address
pold  label fword
```

```
        dw      03ffh                   ;DOS IDT limit
        dd      0                       ;DOS IDT linear address

;STEP 4: table to define the mapping of descriptor to
;        segment

gdt_phys_tab            label word
        dw      task0_TSS_selec ;task 0 TSS segment selector
        dw      task0_TSS       ;task 0 TSS segment
        dw      stk0_selec      ;stk0 segment selector
        dw      stk0            ;stk0 segment
        dw      stk1_selec      ;stk1 segment selector
        dw      stk1            ;stk1 segment
        dw      stk2_selec      ;stk2 segment selector
        dw      stk2            ;stk2 segment
        dw      dmy_selec       ;dummy segment selector
        dw      dmy             ;dummy segment
        dw      code_selec      ;code segment selector
        dw      code            ;code segment
        dw      gdata_selec     ;data segment selector
        dw      gdata           ;data segment
        dw      int_selec       ;interrupt segment selector
        dw      code            ;code segment

;STEP 4.1: selector and segment for level 2 segment

        dw      task0_code2_selec
        dw      code
gdt_tab_size            equ     ($ - gdt_phys_tab) / 4

;STEP 5: message definition area

in_protected    db      'in protected mode ',0
int_msg         db      'interrupt '
int_num         dw      ?
                db      'H',0

;STEP 5.1: message definition area for task switch

level_msg       db      'change task to privilege level 2',0
Gdata_limit equ    $
Gdata ends

;STEP 6: Stack Segment for privilege level 0,1,2

stk0  segment   para  public use16 'stk0'
        db      100h  dup(0)
stk0_limit equ    $
stk0  ends

stk1  segment   para  public use16 'stk1'
        db      100h  dup(0)
stk1_limit equ    $
stk1  ends

stk2  segment   para  public use16 'stk2'
        db      100h  dup(0)
```

```
stk2_limit  equ    $
stk2   ends


;STEP 7: Task State Segment for task 0

task0_TSS    segment      para  public use16 'task0'
TSS_stack    stk0_selec,stk0_limit,stk1_selec,
             stk1_limit,stk2_selec,stk2_limit
TSS_cr3      0                      ;cr3
TSS_regs     0,0,0,0,0,0,0,0,0,stk0_limit
TSS_seg      gdata_selec,code_selec,stk0_selec,
             gdata_selec,gdata_selec,gdata_selec
             dd    0              ;LDT field
             dw    0              ;task trap flag
             dw    68h            ;I/O base address
task0_TSS_limit   equ    $
task0_TSS    ends


;STEP 8: Dummy Segment

dmy    segment      para  public use16 'dmy'
       db    128    dup(0)
dmy    ends



;CODE Segment

code   segment      para  public use16 'code'
       assume       cs:code,ds:gdata
main   proc far
       mov    ax,gdata
       mov    ds,ax

;STEP 8.1: Change IOPL value to 0

       pushf                    ;push flag to stack
       pop    ax                ;pop flag to ax
       and    ax,0cfffh         ;IOPL = 0
       push   ax                ;push ax to stack
       popf                     ;pop to flag

;STEP 9: initialize IDT

       mov    ax,IDT            ;get IDT segment address
       mov    es,ax             ;put in ES
       mov    di,offset idt_tab ;get IDT offset address
       mov    ax,offset int_entry    ;get interrupt service
                                     ;routine address
       mov    cx,INTNO          ;get interrupt number
fillidt:
       mov    es:[di],ax        ;put entry address in IDT
       add    di,DSCPSIZE       ;adjust address in IDT
       add    ax,INTSIZE        ;adjust interrupt service
                                ;routine address, the size of
                                ;each routine is defined in
                                ;INTSIZE
```

```
        loop    fillidt             ;keep filling

;STEP 10,11,12,13: set GDTR,IDTR,LDTR and switch to
;                      protected mode

        build_dtr   gdt,idt,pgdt,pidt,gdt_limit,idt_limit
        build_dt    gdt,gdt_phys_tab,gdt_tab_size
        cli
        goto_prot   pgdt,pidt,CODE_selec,stk0_selec,
                    stk0_limit,GDATA_selec

;STEP 14: display message in protected mode
                                ;clear the screen first
        mov     ax,video_selec      ;get video segment selector
        mov     es,ax               ;put in ES
        mov     cx,4000h            ;screen size
        xor     di,di               ;screen starting address
        mov     ah,attribute
        mov     al,space            ;fill space and attribute
        rep     stosw               ;fill it

        mov     si,offset in_protected  ;get protected mode
                                    ;message address
        mov     di,320              ;get display address
        call    disp_it             ;call display procedure

;STEP 15: set load TSS to TR

        mov     ax,task0_TSS_selec      ;get TSS selector for
                                    ;current task
        ltr     ax                  ;load into task register

;STEP 15.1: change privilege level from 0 to 2

        xor     eax,eax             ;clear eax
        mov     ax,stk2_selec       ;get ss with level 2
        push    eax                 ;push ss
        xor     eax,eax             ;clear eax
        mov     ax,offset stk2_limit  ;get sp with level 2
        push    eax                 ;push sp
        xor     eax,eax             ;clear eax
        mov     ax,task0_code2_selec  ;get cs with level 2
        push    eax                 ;push cs
        mov     eax,offset level    ;get ip
        push    eax                 ;push ip
        db      66h                 ;32-bit operand size
        retf                        ;return far

;STEP 15.2: display message after changing level

level:
        mov     si,offset level_msg  ;get message address
        mov     di,4*160            ;get display address
        call    disp_it             ;call display

;STEP 15.3: access I/O address spaces
```

```
        in     al,20h

;STEP 16: switch back to real-address mode

        int    20                              ;interrupt 20

;STEP 17: Interrupt Service Routine

int_entry:            ;entry point for interrupt service routine
        REPT   INTNO
        call   disp          ;call the display message procedure
        iret
        ENDM

;STEP 18: get interrupt number and display it

disp:
        pop    ax                   ;get return address from stack
        sub    ax,offset int_entry    ;get offset from the
                                      ;interrupt entry
        shr    ax,TWO                 ;divide by 4 to get
                                      ;interrupt number
        mov    si,offset int_num      ;get ASCII code address
        mov    cx,TWO                 ;convert to 2 ASCII code
        call   htoa            ;call convert procedure
        mov    si,offset int_msg ;get interrupt message address
        mov    di,6*160          ;get display address
        call   disp_it          ;call display procedure

;STEP 19: Return to real-address mode

        cli                     ;disable interrupt
        mov    ax,dmy_selec     ;get dummy selector
        mov    es,ax            ;put in ES
        mov    ds,ax            ;put in DS
        mov    fs,ax            ;put in FS
        mov    gs,ax            ;put in GS
        mov    ss,ax            ;put in SS

        mov    eax,cr0          ;load the content of CR0
        and    eax,not prot_enable      ;disable protected mode
        mov    cr0,eax          ;restore the content of CR0

        db     0eah          ;far jump to flush instruction queue
        dw     offset next_instruction ;ip
        dw     code             ;cs

;STEP 20: execute in real-address mode, and set DS,SS and SP

next_instruction:
        mov    ax,Gdata         ;get data segment address
        mov    ds,ax            ;set to DS register
        mov    ax,stk0          ;get stack segment address
        mov    ss,ax            ;set to SS register
        mov    sp,offset stk0_limit    ;set stack pointer

;STEP 21: set IDTR to DOS interrupt table
```

```
        lidt   [pold]                ;reset interrupt vector table
        sti                          ;enable interrupt

;STEP 22: terminate this process

        mov    ax,4c00h              ;terminate process
        int    21h                   ;DOS system call
main    endp
code    ends
        end    main
```

In the program above, if you change the definition of the I/O permission bit map as follows, it won't generate an exception.

```
;STEP 7: Task State Segment for task 0

task0_TSS     segment      para  public use16 'task0'
TSS_stack     stk0_selec,stk0_limit,stk1_selec,
              stk1_limit,stk2_selec,stk2_limit
TSS_cr3       0                 ;cr3
TSS_regs      0,0,0,0,0,0,0,0,0,stk0_limit
TSS_seg       gdata_selec,code_selec,stk0_selec,
              gdata_selec,gdata_selec,gdata_selec
              dd    0             ;LDT field
              dw    0             ;task trap flag
              dw    68h           ;I/O base address
              db    3  dup(0)     ;I/O permission bit map for
                               ;first three bytes (24 I/O address)
task0_TSS_limit    equ    $
task0_TSS     ends
```

9.5 Summary

There are two kinds of I/O addresses supported by the i386/i486 processor, I/O port address and memory I/O address.

For I/O port address, the i386/i486 processor provides two protection mechanisms: I/O privilege level (IOPL) protection and I/O permission bit map protection. The value of IOPL is defined in the IOPL field in the EFLAGS register, and the I/O permission bit map is defined in the TSS. The i386/i486 processor checks IOPL and CPL when executing an I/O instruction. If CPL < = IOPL, the I/O instruction can be executed without further checks; otherwise, the i386/i486 processor checks the I/O permission bit map. The i386/i486 processor generates a general protection fault if the I/O permission bit map defined "I/O deny" for this I/O port address. Otherwise, it executes this I/O instruction. The i386/i486 memory protection can also apply to the I/O memory address.

CHAPTER 10

EXCEPTIONS AND INTERRUPTS

Exceptions and interrupts are special control-transfer methods which can alter the normal execution of a program. Exceptions and interrupts transfer the execution control to a task or procedure called a handler. This chapter discusses the differences between exceptions and interrupts, the interrupts and exceptions vector, and the exception types in the i386/i486 processor.

10.1 Differences Between Exceptions and Interrupts

An interrupt is invoked by a hardware signal and can occur at any time during the execution of a program. The interrupt handler processes the interrupt signal when the handler gets control. For example, when you press a key from the keyboard, a keyboard interrupt signal is generated. The i386/i486 processor then transfers control to the keyboard interrupt handler, which processes the keystroke. The i386/i486 processor receives interrupt signals in two ways:

- Maskable interrupts: The maskable interrupts can be enabled and disabled by the IF bit in the EFLAGS register. If the IF bit is cleared, maskable interrupts will not occur.

- Nonmaskable interrupts: There is no way to stop nonmaskable interrupts.

An exception is generated by the i386/i486 processor during the execution of an instruction, such as a software interrupt exception (*INT n*) or fault exception (general protection exception). There are two situations that cause the i386/i486 processor to generate exceptions. One is when the i386/i486 processor detects faults, traps, and aborts during the execution of an instruction. The other is programmed exceptions, which means the instruction directly triggers the exceptions. The instructions which can trigger the exceptions directly are *INTO, INT 3, INT n*, and *BOUND*.

10.2 Vectors

The i386/i486 processor assigns a number to each type of interrupts and exceptions, which can be used as a vector index to the handler. In the i386/i486 processor architecture, the NMI (nonmaskable) interrupts and the exceptions range from 0 to 31. Vectors from 32 to 255 can be used by the maskable interrupts. The maskable interrupts vectors should be determined by the system. During the i386/i486 processor interrupt-acknowledge cycle, the external interrupt controller should initialize the vector corresponding to the supported hardware interrupts. Table 10.1 shows the exceptions and interrupts vectors assigned by the i386/i486 processor.

Vector Number	Description	Error Code
0	Divide Error	No
1	Debug Exception	No
2	NMI Interrupt	No
3	Instruction Breakpoint	No
4	INTO-detected Overflow	No
5	BOUND Range Exceeded	No
6	Invalid Opcode	No
7	Coprocessor Not Available	No
8	Double Fault	Yes
9	Coprocessor Segment Overrun	No
10	Invalid TSS	Yes
11	Segment Not Present	Yes
12	Stack Fault	Yes
13	General Protection	Yes
14	Page Fault	Yes
15	Reserved	-
16	Coprocessor Error	No
17-31	Reserved	-
32-255	Maskable Interrupt	-

Table 10.1 Exception and Interrupt Vectors

10.3 IDT Descriptors

As mentioned before, an interrupt or exception vector indexes the appropriate service handler. When the i386/i486 processor receives the vector number, it indexes the interrupt descriptor table (IDT) to get the address of the handler routine relative to the vector number and then transfers control to that handler. The base address of the IDT should be put into the IDTR register because the i386/i486 processor depends on the IDTR to get the IDT linear base address.

There are big differences between handling the IDT in the real-address mode and the protected mode. In the real-address mode, every entry of the IDT is four bytes long. It contains the starting segment and the offset address of the handler routine. In the protected mode, every entry of the IDT is an 8-byte descriptor. These descriptors define the handler routine, just like any other descriptor does. Because the i386/i486 processor provides only 256 interrupt vectors, there is no need for the IDT to contain more than 256 entries.

Unlike the GDT, only three kinds of descriptors can be defined in the IDT:

- Interrupt Gate descriptor

- Trap Gate descriptor

- Task Gate descriptor

The format of these descriptors is discussed in Chapter 1.

An interrupt clears the IF bit in the EFLAGS register when entering the handler routine through an interrupt gate. This can prevent other maskable interrupts occurring during the execution of the current interrupt handler. After the current handler finishes execution, the *IRET* instruction restores the IF bit in the EFLAGS register before returning control to the interrupted instruction. When the interrupt handler is entered through a trap gate, it does not clear the IF bit. An interrupt through a task gate causes a task switch and has the same behavior as the task switch described in Chapter 7. It depends on the operating system to determine which kind of descriptor to define in the IDT.

10.4 Handler Protection

The i386/i486 processor does not allow an interrupt or exception to transfer control to a handler in a less privileged segment. Any violation causes a general protection exception. Because both the CPL and the interrupts or exceptions are unpredictable during program execution, there are two ways to avoid this violation. One is to put the handler in the code segment with privilege level 0, since privilege level 0 is the highest privilege and can be transferred by interrupts or exceptions from any privilege level. The other way is to put the handler in a conforming code segment.

When invoking an exception or interrupt handler changes the privilege level, the i386/i486 processor, according to the current TSS, changes the stack according to the handler's privilege level and pushes the old SS and ESP to the new stack before pushing the CS, EIP and EFLAGS register. Figure 10.1 shows the stack frame format after entering the handler.

No Privilege Level Change

OLD EFLAGS
OLD CS
OLD EIP
ERROR CODE

Privilege Level Change

OLD SS
OLD ESP
OLD EFLAGS
OLD CS
OLD EIP
ERROR CODE

Figure 10.1 Stack Frame After Entering Handler Routine

10.5 Error Code

When an exception relates to a specific segment, the processor pushes an error code into the stack before entering the exception handler. The error code format is shown in Figure 10.2.

```
31              16 15         3 2 1 0
| Reserved      | Selector Index |TI| I |EXT |
```

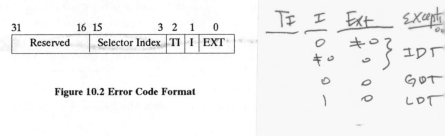

Figure 10.2 Error Code Format

The *EXT* field indicates that an external event related to the program caused the exception. When this bit is set, the selector index field contains the external interrupt number.

The *I* field indicates that the exception relates to the IDT. The selector index field contains the descriptor entry address in the IDT which caused the exception.

When both the *EXT* and *I* bit are not set, the exception relates to the segment defined in the GDT or LDT. If the *TI* bit is set, the selector index field contains the descriptor entry address in the GDT which caused the exception. Otherwise, it contains the descriptor entry address in the LDT which caused the exception.

The error code for a page fault exception has a totally different meaning and format. The format is shown in Figure 10.3.

Figure 10.3 Page Fault Error Code Format

The *U/S* field indicates that a page fault exception is generated when the processor is executing in supervisor level or user level. If set to 1, it indicates the supervisor level, else the user level.

The *W/R* field indicates that the page fault exception is generated by a read operation or write operation from the page. If it is set, it means the write operation, else the read operation.

The *P* field indicates that the page fault exception is caused by a page-level protection violation or a "page not present" violation. If it is set, it means the page-level protection violation, else the "page not present" violation.

The error code is pushed as a double word to maintain the stack alignment.

10.6 Sample Program

Some sample programs in the previous chapters demonstrated how to generate exceptions. The following program shows an exception example different from that of the previous chapters.

Program: DOUBLE.ASM

When the i386/i486 processor cannot handle two serially generated exceptions, it generates a double fault exception (exception 8). The following program defines the "segment not present" segment as program *sgnopres.asm* does. In addition, the interrupt gate descriptor resides in the IDT for this segment not present exception is also "not present." (see Figure 10.4) This causes a double fault exception. This program also prints out the contents of the stack frame after entering the double fault handler. Because this program does not involve privilege level change, only error code, CS, EIP, and EFLAGS are held in the stack.

```
int_11      dw      offset1     ;handler offset (0..15)
            dw      int_code    ;handler code segment selector
            db      0           ;reserved
            db      0eh         ;not present Interrupt Gate
            dw      offset2     ;handler offset (16..31)
```

Figure 10.4 Not Present Interrupt Gate

Step 2: The Interrupt gate descriptor of interrupt 11, "present bit," is cleared.

Step 5.1: Define data area in which to display messages.

Step 15.1: This instruction causes a double fault exception.

Step 18.2: Inside the exception handler, call procedure to dump the stack frame.

Procedure *error_dump* gets data from the stack segment and prints it out on the screen.

File: DOUBLE.ASM

```
.386p
include struct
include macro1
include macro2

INTNO         equ   21    ;interrupt vector number
DSCPSIZE      equ   8     ;size of descriptor
INTSIZE       equ   4     ;size of interrupt service routine
TWO           equ   2     ;
prot_enable   equ   01h   ;protected mode enable bit in CR0
attribute     equ   07h   ;display character attribute
space         equ   20h   ;ASCII code for space

;STEP 1: Global Descriptor Table

GDT    segment       para  public use16 'GDT'
gdt_tab              label qword
null_selec  equ   $-gdt_tab            ;null selector
  dscp      <,,,,,>      ;first one must be a null descriptor

code_selec  equ   $-gdt_tab            ;code segment selector
  dscp      <0ffffh,,,09ah,,>          ;descriptor

task0_TSS_selec    equ    $-gdt_tab    ;TSS selector
  dscp      <task0_TSS_limit,,,089h,,>    ;TSS descriptor

stk0_selec  equ   $-gdt_tab            ;level 0 stack segment
                                       ;selector
  dscp      <stk0_limit,,,92h,,>       ;descriptor with
                                       ;privilege level 0
stk1_selec  equ   $-gdt_tab or 1       ;level 1 stack
                                       ;segment selector
  dscp      <stk1_limit,,,0b2h,,>      ;descriptor with
                                       ;privilege level 1
stk2_selec  equ   $-gdt_tab or 2       ;level 2 stack
                                       ;segment selector
  dscp      <stk2_limit,,,0d2h,,>      ;descriptor with
                                       ;privilege level 2
dmy_selec   equ   $-gdt_tab            ;dummy segment selector
  dscp      <0ffffh,,,92h,,>           ;dummy segment descriptor
```

```
video_selec equ   $-gdt_tab              ;video segment selector
  dscp        <0ffffh,8000h,0bh,0f2h,,>     ;descriptor

gdata_selec equ   $-gdt_tab              ;data segment selector
  dscp        <gdata_limit,,,0f2h,,>  ;data segment descriptor

int_selec   equ   $-gdt_tab    ;interrupt segment selector
  dscp        <0ffffh,,,09ah,,>          ;descriptor

;STEP 1.1: define segment not present descriptor in GDT

notp_selec  equ   $-gdt_tab              ;selector
  dscp        <0ffffh,,,072h,,>          ;descriptor with segment
                                         ;not present

GDT_limit   equ   $-gdt_tab
GDT   ends

;STEP 2: Interrupt Descriptor Table

IDT   segment para       public use16       'idt'
idt_tab equ $
      REPT  11             ;interrupt entries from 0 to 10
      dscp  <,int_selec,0,0eeh,,>   ;DPL = 3
      ENDM
      dscp  <,int_selec,0,03eh,,>   ;interrupt 11 entries
                            ;with segment not present
      REPT  10             ;interrupt entries from 12 to 20
      dscp  <,int_selec,0,0eeh,,>   ;DPL = 3
      ENDM
idt_limit   equ   $
IDT   ends

;DATA        Segment

Gdata segment      para  public use16'Gdata'


;STEP 3: variable to save GDT/IDT limit and linear address

pGDT  label fword
      dw    GDT_limit   ;GDT limit
      dd    0           ;GDT linear address
pIDT  label fword
      dw    IDT_limit   ;IDT limit
      dd    0           ;IDT linear address
pold  label fword
      dw    03ffh       ;DOS IDT limit
      dd    0           ;DOS IDT linear address

;STEP 4: table to define the mapping of descriptor to seg-
ment

gdt_phys_tab       label word
      dw    task0_TSS_selec   ;TSS segment selector
      dw    task0_TSS         ;TSS segment
      dw    stk0_selec        ;stk0 segment selector
```

```
        dw      stk0                    ;stk0 segment
        dw      stk1_selec              ;stk1 segment selector
        dw      stk1                    ;stk1 segment
        dw      stk2_selec              ;stk2 segment selector
        dw      stk2                    ;stk2 segment
        dw      dmy_selec               ;dummy segment selector
        dw      dmy                     ;dummy segment
        dw      code_selec              ;code segment selector
        dw      code                    ;code segment
        dw      gdata_selec             ;data segment selector
        dw      gdata                   ;data segment
        dw      int_selec               ;interrupt segment selector
        dw      code                    ;code segment
gdt_tab_size        equ     ($ - gdt_phys_tab) / 4  ;

;STEP 5: message definition area

in_protected        db      'in protected mode ',0
int_msg             db      'interrupt '
int_num             dw      ?
                    db      'H',0

;STEP 5.1: Data area for displaying message

error_msg           db      'Error code: '
error_off           db      9 dup(0)
csip_msg            db      'cs:ip :      '
cseg                db      8 dup(0)
                    db      ':'
ip_off              db      9 dup(0)
flg_msg             db      'flags    : '
flg                 db      9 dup(0)
Gdata_limit equ     $
Gdata ends

;STEP 6: Stack Segment for privilege level 0,1,2

stk0  segment       para  public use16 'stk0'
      db      100h  dup(0)
stk0_limit          equ     $
stk0  ends

stk1  segment       para  public use16 'stk1'
      db      100h  dup(0)
stk1_limit          equ     $
stk1  ends

stk2  segment       para  public use16 'stk2'
      db      100h  dup(0)
stk2_limit          equ     $
stk2  ends

;STEP 7: Task State Segment

task0_TSS   segment     para  public use16 'task0'
TSS_stack   stk0_selec,stk0_limit,stk1_selec,
            stk1_limit,stk2_selec,stk2_limit
```

```
TSS_cr3      0                 ;cr3
TSS_regs     0,0,0,0,0,0,0,0,0,stk0_limit
TSS_seg      gdata_selec,code_selec,stk0_selec,
             gdata_selec,gdata_selec,gdata_selec
             dd    0                ;LDT field
             dw    0                ;task trap flag
             dw    68h              ;I/O base
task0_TSS_limit    equ    $
task0_TSS    ends

;STEP 8: Dummy Segment

dmy    segment     para public use16 'dmy'
       db    128    dup(0)
dmy    ends

;CODE Segment

code   segment     para public use16 'code'
       assume      cs:code,ds:gdata
main   proc  far
       mov   ax,gdata
       mov   ds,ax

;STEP 9: initialize IDT

       mov   ax,IDT              ;get IDT segment address
       mov   es,ax               ;put in ES
       mov   di,offset idt_tab   ;get IDT offset address
       mov   ax,offset int_entry    ;get interrupt service
                                     ;routine address
       mov   cx,INTNO            ;get interrupt number
fillidt:
       mov   es:[di],ax          ;put entry address in IDT
       add   di,DSCPSIZE         ;adjust address in IDT
       add   ax,INTSIZE          ;adjust interrupt service
                                 ;routine address. The size of
                                 ;each routine is defined in
                                 ;INTSIZE
       loop  fillidt      ;keep filling

;STEP 10,11,12,13: set linear address for descriptor in
;   GDT, GDTR,IDTR and LDTR, then switch to protected mode

       build_dtr   gdt,idt,pgdt,pidt,gdt_limit,idt_limit
       build_dt    gdt,gdt_phys_tab,gdt_tab_size
       cli
       goto_prot   pgdt,pidt,code_selec,stk0_selec,
                   stk0_limit,GDATA_selec

;STEP 14: display message in protected mode

                                 ;clear the screen first
       mov   ax,video_selec      ;get video segment selector
       mov   es,ax               ;put in ES
       mov   cx,4000h            ;screen size
       xor   di,di               ;screen starting address
```

```
        mov    ah,attribute
        mov    al,space           ;fill space and attribute
        rep    stosw              ;fill it

        mov    si,offset in_protected  ;get protected mode
                                       ;message address
        mov    di,320             ;get display address
        call   disp_it            ;call display procedure

;STEP 15: load TSS to TR

        mov    ax,task0_TSS_selec      ;get TSS selector for
                                       ;current task
        ltr    ax                 ;load into task register

;STEP 15.1: try to load the selector with segment not
;           present

        mov    ax,notp_selec      ;get the selector
        mov    es,ax              ;move into ES

;STEP 16: switch back to real-address mode

        int    20                 ;interrupt 20

;STEP 17: Interrupt Service Routine

int_entry:          ;entry point for interrupt service routine
        REPT   INTNO
        call   disp        ;call the display message procedure
        iret
        ENDM

;STEP 18: get interrupt number and display it

disp:
        mov    ax,gdata_selec
        mov    ds,ax
        pop    ax                 ;get return address from stack
        sub    ax,offset int_entry     ;get offset from the
                                       ;interrupt entry
        shr    ax,TWO             ;divide by 4 to get interrupt
                                  ;number
        mov    si,offset int_num  ;get ASCII code address
        mov    cx,TWO             ;convert to 2 ASCII code
        call   htoa               ;call convert procedure
        mov    si,offset int_msg  ;get interrupt message address
        mov    di,5*160           ;get display address
        call   disp_it            ;call display procedure

;STEP 18.1: call procedure to dump the stack frame

        call   error_dump

;STEP 19: Return to real-address mode

        cli                       ;disable interrupt
```

```
        mov    ax,dmy_selec       ;dummy selector
        mov    es,ax              ;reset segment register
        mov    ds,ax
        mov    fs,ax
        mov    gs,ax
        mov    ss,ax

        mov    eax,cr0            ;load the content of CR0
        and    eax,not prot_enable    ;disable protected mode
        mov    cr0,eax            ;restore the content of CR0

        db     0eah               ;far jump to flush instruction
                                  ;queue
        dw     offset next_instruction
        dw     code
```

;STEP 20: execute in real-address mode, and set DS,SS and SP

```
next_instruction:
        mov    ax,Gdata           ;get data segment address
        mov    ds,ax              ;set to DS register
        mov    ax,stk0            ;get stack segment address
        mov    ss,ax              ;set to SS register
        mov    sp,offset stk0_limit    ;set stack pointer
```

;STEP 21: set IDTR to DOS interrupt table

```
        lidt   [pold]             ;reset interrupt vector table
        sti                       ;enable interrupt
```

;STEP 22: terminate this process

```
        mov    ax,4c00h           ;terminate process
        int    21h                ;DOS system call
main    endp
```

```
;Procedure: error_dump
;This procedure dumps the contents of the stack frame
;when enter exception handler

error_dump    proc    near
        mov    esi,offset error_off    ;get data area offset
        mov    eax,dword ptr [esp][0+2];get first data in stack
        mov    cx,8               ;convert to ASCII value
        call   htoa
        mov    esi,offset error_msg    ;display the data
        mov    edi,9*80
        call   disp_it

        mov    esi,offset ip_off  ;get data area offset
        mov    eax,dword ptr [esp][4+2] ;get second data in stack
        mov    cx,8               ;convert to ASCII value
        call   htoa
        mov    esi,offset cseg    ;get data area offset
        mov    eax,dword ptr [esp][8+2] ;get third data in stack
        mov    cx,8               ;convert to ASCII value
```

```
        call  htoa
        mov   esi,offset csip_msg      ;display the data
        mov   edi,11*80
        call  disp_it

        mov   esi,offset flg           ;get data area offset
        mov   eax,dword ptr [esp][12+2] ;get fourth data in stack
        mov   cx,8                      ;convert to ASCII value
        call  htoa
        mov   esi,offset flg_msg       ;display the data
        mov   edi,13*80
        call  disp_it
        ret
error_dump  endp
code  ends
        end   main
```

10.8 Summary

Exceptions and interrupts are other ways to transfer control during program execution. An interrupt is a signal from hardware which can occur at any time during program execution. An exception is generated when faults, traps, aborts, or a programmed exception is found during instruction execution. The i386/i486 processor transfers control to the handler routine based on the vectors defined in the IDT when interrupts or exceptions occur.

SECTION IV

VIRTUAL-8086 MODE

CHAPTER 11

V86 MODE PROGRAMMING

We noted earlier that the v86 mode is a 8086/88 mode emulated by the i386/i486 processor with the protected mode features. So it is possible to have paging, multitasking, and the protection mechanism supported in the v86 mode. A v86 mode task can be thought of as the 8086 program running in a i386/i486 machine under the control of a software interface which resides in the protected mode. The software interface supporting the v86 mode task is called a v86 monitor.

11.1 V86 Mode Environment

The v86 mode is enabled when the VM bit defined in the EFLAGS register is set to 1. The VM bit can be set only by executing the *IRET* instruction at privilege level 0 and by the task switch instruction in the protected mode. You need to set the VM bit in the EFLAGS image on the stack or on the TSS, then use the *IRET* and the task switch instructions to enter the v86 mode. The instruction *POPF* cannot affect the VM bit in the EFLAGS register.

The i386/i486 sets the CPL (current privilege level) value for all the tasks in the v86 mode to 3 (user level in paging system). Any operation that violates the privilege level checking causes an exception.

The paging mechanism can also apply to the v86 mode. The linear address generated in the v86 mode can be up to 21 bits, (from *0:0 to 0ffffh:0ffffh*) because the i386/i486 processor does not wrap around when the linear address is over 1 megabyte. The processor takes this 21-bit linear address and, through the page mapping, translates it to a 32-bit physical address. Additionally, task switch reloads the CR3 (PDBR) register from TSS, so that each v86 mode task can use a different page mapping scheme to map pages to different locations or the same locations. This allows the v86 mode tasks to use separate spaces to protect each other or use the same spaces to share data or code (such as system functions).

11.2 Enter and Leave V86 Mode

To run the v86 mode task in the i386/i486 machine, a v86 monitor must exist in the system to provide the interface services. Basically, the v86 mode monitor consists of initialization and exception-handling procedures. The v86 monitor must be at privilege level 0 in the protected mode, and control should be issued to a v86 mode task by the v86 monitor. After control transfers to the v86 mode task, there is no way for the v86 mode monitor to regain control except through exceptions. When an exception is generated in a v86 mode task, it enters the exception routine provided by the v86 mode monitor. Since the v86 mode monitor is executed in the protected mode, the VM bit is cleared by the i386/i486 processor when control is passed to the exception routine. At this point the v86 mode monitor can start services that depend on the system needs.

Task switch is one way to enter the v86 mode by using the *IRET* instruction or the task switch instruction. Since the new task is a v86 mode task, the value stored in the TSS is different from that in the protected mode. The VM bit must be set to 1 in the EFLAGS field, and the segment fields should contain the segment address value instead of the segment selector. If you use the *IRET* instruction to return to the v86 mode task, the NT bit in the EFLAGS register must be set and the back link field of the current TSS must link to the TSS segment selector of the v86 mode task.

11.3 Exceptions and Interrupts in V86 Mode

When exceptions or interrupts occur in the v86 mode, the way for transferring control to the handler is the same as in the protected mode. This is because the v86 mode is under control of the protected mode. The i386/i486 gets the descriptor entry from the IDT and then dispatches to the handler.

There is one restriction for the v86 mode exception and interrupt handler. The code segment descriptor definition for the handler must be a nonconforming, privilege level 0 segment. If the handler is entered through a task gate, there is no such restriction.

When entering the handler in the v86 mode, other than through the task gate, the stack is altered. The i386/i486 processor pushes more data into the stack which can be used by the handler routine. Figure 11.1 shows the stack frame format after entering the interrupt handler from the v86 mode.

The handler must check whether the exceptions or the interrupts occurred in the protected mode or the v86 mode. If it occurred in the v86 mode, the interrupt handler can pass control to the v86 monitor and let the v86 monitor handle it. The v86 monitor can either do the service by itself or emulate the 8086/88 program's interrupt handler.

OLD GS
OLD FS
OLD DS
OLD ES
OLD SS
OLD ESP
OLD EFLAGS
OLD CS
OLD EIP
ERROR CODE

Figure 11.1 Stack Frame After Entering Handler in the V86 Mode

11.4 Sample Programs

The following sample programs use task switch to make a program execute in the v86 mode and show how to enable and use paging in the v86 mode.

Program: v86.asm

This program is a simple v86 mode monitor program. It switches to a v86 mode task from the protected mode and executes in the v86 mode just as in the real-address mode, DOS environment. Since the DOS system in the real-address mode supports many system functions (such as interrupt 20h), this must be handled by the v86 mode monitor to support these functions. The method used in this program sets the DPL for all the interrupt gates to 0. When software interrupt is issued in the v86 mode with privilege level 3, it causes general protection fault (exception 13). The v86 interrupt handler can reflect this v86 mode software interrupt to the DOS interrupt function and get it executed in the v86 mode. To return to the protected mode from the v86 mode, this program sets instruction *INT 1* as a key to go back to the protected mode.

Step 0: Define some EQU value. This program provides 256 interrupts.

Step 0.1: Define EQU address in the TSS.

Step 1.1: Define segment selector and descriptor for the v86 mode task.

Step 2: Define IDT. Make sure that the descriptor privilege level (DPL) is 0.

Step 4.1: Define mapping for the v86 mode task descriptor and segment.

Step 5.1: Define messages and variables for the v86 mode task.

Step 6.1: Define stack segment for the v86 mode task.

Step 7.1: Define the TSS for the v86 mode task. Make sure that the v86 mode bit and interrupt enable bit are turned on and the IOPL equals 3 in the EFLAGS field. Also the CS,IP,SS,SP are set to the appropriate values for the v86 mode task.

Step 15.1: Switch to the v86 mode task by jumping to the TSS descriptor of the v86 mode task.

Step 15.2: Display message after return from the v86 mode task.

Step 16: Go back to the real-address mode.

Step 16.1: Define EQU value for SP0. When interrupt occurs in the v86 mode, the i386/i486 processor pushes the contents of segment registers and error code (if any) in the stack of privilege level 0.

Step 17.1: The interrupt routines are executed in the protected mode, so DS contains the data segment selector in the protected mode. Save the return address for later use and pop the error code if any.

Step 17.2: Get interrupt number and check if it is general protection fault.

Step 17.3: Interrupt is not issued by the software interrupt. Get the return IP from stack and jump to *setint*.

Step 17.4: The v86 monitor has to make sure the exception 13 is invoked by the software interrupt, so get the CS:IP of the v86 mode task from the stack and check the instruction code. Since the CS:IP is in the real-address mode format and now is executed in the protected mode, the CS:IP needs to be converted to 32-bit linear address and the code in CS:IP can only be accessed through the descriptor.

Step 17.5: If it is an interrupt instruction then get the interrupt number. Notice that DS:SI now points to the instruction following *INT xx*.

Step 17.6: If instruction is *INT 1*, go back to the protected mode.

Step 17.7: Get SS:SPof the v86 mode task and convert it to 32-bit linear address and put it in the working descriptor. Push FLAG, the v86 mode task code segment, and IP for next instruction into the v86 mode task stack segment.

Step 17.8: Get the interrupt vector from the DOS interrupt table and clear the interrupt and trap bit in flag value. Next, replace the CS, IP, FLAG value in the stack that belongs to the interrupt handler. By using *IRET*, the program returns to the DOS interrupt routine and executes in the v86 mode. Because the address of the next instruction has been pushed into the stack of the v86 mode task, when the interrupt routine is finished with *IRET,* it returns to the next instruction address and continues execution.

Step 17.9: Unexpected interrupt 13 occurred, so return to the protected mode.

Step 17.10: Switch back to the protected mode by jumping to the TSS descriptor of task0.

Step 23: Define the v86 mode task code segment.

Step 24: Set data segment and display message by calling the DOS function call.

Step 25: Get a key from console by calling the DOS function call.

Step 26: Use *INT 1* to go back to the protected mode.

File: V86.ASM

```
.386p
include struct
include macro1
include macro2

;STEP 0: define equ

INTNO         equ   256            ;interrupt vector number
DSCPSIZE      equ   8              ;size of descriptor
INTSIZE       equ   4           ;size of interrupt service routine
TWO           equ   2              ;
prot_enable   equ   01h     ;protected mode enable bit in CR0
attribute     equ   07h            ;display character attribute
space         equ   20h            ;ASCII code for space

;STEP 0.1: Define equ address in TSS

EIP_TSS           equ   20h        ;EIP offset in TSS
ESP_TSS           equ   38h        ;ESP offset in TSS
CS_TSS            equ   4ch        ;CS offset in TSS
SS_TSS            equ   50h        ;SS offset in TSS
CR3_TSS           equ   1ch        ;CR3 offset in TSS

;STEP 1: Global Descriptor Table

GDT     segment       para  public use16 'GDT'
gdt_tab               label qword
null_selec  equ   $-gdt_tab            ;null selector
   dscp       <,,,,,>       ;first one must be a null dscriptor

code_selec  equ   $-gdt_tab          ;code segment selector
   dscp       <0ffffh,,,09ah,,>      ;code segment descriptor
```

```
task0_TSS_selec    equ    $-gdt_tab      ;task 0 TSS selector
   dscp         <task0_TSS_limit,,,089h,,>      ;TSS descriptor

stk0_selec    equ    $-gdt_tab            ;level 0 stack
                                          ;segment selector
   dscp         <stk0_limit,,,92h,,>      ;descriptor with
                                          ;privilege level 0
stk1_selec    equ    $-gdt_tab or 1       ;level 1 stack segment
                                          ;selector
   dscp         <stk1_limit,,,0b2h,,>     ;descriptor with
                                          ;privilege level 1
stk2_selec    equ    $-gdt_tab or 2       ;level 2 stack
                                          ;segment selector
   dscp         <stk2_limit,,,0d2h,,>     ;descriptor with
                                          ;privilege level 2
dmy_selec     equ    $-gdt_tab            ;dummy segment selector
   dscp         <0ffffh,,,92h,,>          ;dummy segment descriptor

video_selec   equ    $-gdt_tab or 3       ;video segment selector
   dscp         <0ffffh,8000h,0bh,0f2h,,>      ;descriptor

gdata_selec   equ    $-gdt_tab            ;data segment selector
   dscp         <gdata_limit,,,0f2h,,>         ;descriptor

int_selec     equ    $-gdt_tab ;interrupt segment selector
   dscp         <0ffffh,,,09ah,,>         ;descriptor

;STEP 1.1: Define selector/descriptor for v86 mode task

dos_selec     equ    $-gdt_tab            ;dos interrupt vector
                                          ;selector
 dscp <0ffffh,0,0,092h,0fh,0>             ;descriptor

task1_TSS_selec    equ    $-gdt_tab or 3     ;level 3 TSS
                                             ;selector
   dscp         <task1_TSS_limit,,,0e9h,,>      ;descriptor

stack0_selec       equ    $-gdt_tab    ;stack segment selector
   dscp         <stack0_limit,,,092h,,>        ;descriptor

gdata1_selec       equ    $-gdt_tab          ;working selector
gdata1        dscp   <0ffffh,0,0,0f2h,0,0>     ;working descriptor

gdt_selec     equ    $-gdt_tab            ;GDT segment selector
   dscp         <gdt_limit,,,0f2h,,>      ;GDT segment descriptor

GDT_limit     equ    $-gdt_tab
GDT    ends

;STEP 2: Interrupt Descriptor Table

IDT    segment para        public use16 'idt'
idt_tab        equ    $
       REPT   INTNO                       ;256 interrupts
       dscp   <0,int_selec,0,08eh,,>  ;DPL = 0
       ENDM
idt_limit      equ    $
```

```
IDT     ends

;DATA          Segment

Gdata segment       para  public use16 'Gdata'

;STEP 3: variable to save GDT/IDT limit and linear address

pGDT   label fword
       dw    GDT_limit           ;GDT limit
       dd    0                   ;GDT linear address
pIDT   label fword
       dw    IDT_limit           ;IDT limit
       dd    0                   ;IDT linear address
pold   label fword
       dw    03ffh               ;DOS IDT limit
       dd    0                   ;DOS IDT linear address

;STEP 4: table to define the mapping of descriptor to
;        segment

gdt_phys_tab        label word
       dw    task0_TSS_selec     ;task 0 TSS segment selector
       dw    task0_TSS           ;task 0 TSS segment
       dw    stk0_selec          ;stk0 segment selector
       dw    stk0                ;stk0 segment
       dw    stk1_selec          ;stk1 segment selector
       dw    stk1                ;stk1 segment
       dw    stk2_selec          ;stk2 segment selector
       dw    stk2                ;stk2 segment
       dw    dmy_selec           ;dummy segment selector
       dw    dmy                 ;dummy segment
       dw    code_selec          ;code segment selector
       dw    code                ;code segment
       dw    gdata_selec         ;gdata segment selector
       dw    gdata               ;gdata segment
       dw    int_selec           ;int segment selector
       dw    code                ;code segment

;STEP 4.1: Define mapping for v86 task descriptor to segment

       dw    stack0_selec        ;stack0 segment selector
       dw    stack0              ;stack0 segment
       dw    task1_TSS_selec     ;task 1 TSS segment selector
       dw    task1_TSS           ;task 1 TSS segment
       dw    gdt_selec           ;GDT segment selector
       dw    gdt                 ;gdt segment
gdt_tab_size        equ   ($ - gdt_phys_tab) / 4

;STEP 5: message definition area

in_protected        db    'in protected mode ',0

;STEP 5.1: v86 mode task message define area

task1_msg   db    'switch to v86 mode',0
success     db    'now in v86 mode task 1 !!!',0dh,0ah
```

```
                db      'press any key to go back to '
                db      'protected mode',0dh,0ah,'$'
error           db      'error !',0
retmsg          db      'return to protected mode',0
stopmsg         db      'stop',0
intnum          db      ?
retaddr         dw      ?
err1            dw      0
err2            dw      0
Gdata_limit equ     $
Gdata ends


;STEP 6: Stack Segment for privilege level 0,1,2

stk0   segment      para  public use16 'stk0'
       db      100h  dup(0)
stk0_limit equ     $
stk0  ends

stk1   segment      para  public use16 'stk1'
       db      100h  dup(0)
stk1_limit equ     $
stk1  ends

stk2   segment      para  public use16 'stk2'
       db      100h  dup(0)
stk2_limit equ     $
stk2  ends

;STEP 6.1: Stack Segment for v86 mode task

stack0       segment      para  public use16 'stack0'
       db      100h  dup(0)
stack0_limit        equ     $
stack0       ends

;STEP 7: Task State Segment for task0

task0_TSS    segment      para public use16 'task0'
TSS_stack    stk0_selec,stk0_limit,stk1_selec,
             stk1_limit,stk2_selec,stk2_limit
TSS_cr3      0                 ;cr3
TSS_regs     0,0,0,0,0,0,0,0,0,stk0_limit
TSS_seg      gdata_selec,code_selec,stk0_selec,
             gdata_selec,gdata_selec,gdata_selec
             dd      0        ;LDT field
             dw      0                ;task trap flag
             dw      68h              ;I/O base
task0_TSS_limit equ     $
task0_TSS   ends

;STEP 7.1: Task State Segment for v86 mode task

task1_TSS    segment      para public use16 'task1'
TSS_stack    stk0_selec,stk0_limit,stk1_selec,
             stk1_limit,stk2_selec,stk2_limit
```

```
TSS_cr3      0                      ;cr3
TSS_regs     entry,23202h,0,0,0,0,stack0_limit,0,0,0
TSS_seg      0,task1_seg,stack0,0,0,0
             dd     0               ;LDT field
             dw     0               ;task trap flag
             dw     68h             ;I/O base
             dw     100h  dup(0)        ;I/O bit maps
task1_TSS_limit    equ    $
task1_TSS    ends

;STEP 8: Dummy Segment

dmy      segment       para  public use16 'dmy'
         db     128    dup(0)
dmy      ends

;CODE Segment

code     segment       para  public use16 'code'
         assume        cs:code
main     proc   far
         assume        ds:gdata
         mov    ax,gdata          ;get gdata segment address
         mov    ds,ax             ;put in DS

;STEP 9: The following code initialize IDT

         mov    ax,IDT            ;get IDT segment address
         mov    es,ax             ;put in ES
         mov    di,offset idt_tab       ;get IDT offset address
         mov    ax,offset int_entry     ;get interrupt service
                                        ;routine address
         mov    cx,INTNO          ;get interrupt numbers
fillidt:
         mov    es:[di],ax        ;put entry address in IDT
         add    di,DSCPSIZE       ;adjust address in IDT
         add    ax,INTSIZE        ;get next interrupt service
                                  ;routine address
         loop   fillidt           ;till end of IDT

;STEP 10,11,12,13: set GDTR,IDTR,LDTR and switch to
;protected mode

         build_dtr    gdt,idt,pgdt,pidt,gdt_limit,idt_limit
         build_dt     gdt,gdt_phys_tab,gdt_tab_size
         cli
         goto_prot    pgdt,pidt,CODE_selec,stack0_selec,
                      stack0_limit,GDATA_selec

;STEP 14: display message in protected mode
                                  ;clear the screen first
         mov    ax,video_selec    ;get video segment selector
         mov    es,ax             ;put in ES
         mov    cx,4000h          ;counter
         xor    di,di             ;offset = 0
         mov    ah,attribute      ;ah has the character attribute
         mov    al,space          ;al has the space character
```

```
        rep     stosw                   ;write to the screen

        mov     si,offset in_protected  ;get message address
        mov     di,6*160                ;get display position
        call    disp_it                 ;display it
```

;STEP 15: set load TSS to TR

```
        mov     ax,task0_TSS_selec      ;get task0 TSS selector
        ltr     ax                      ;put in current task register
```
;STEP 15.1: switch to v86 mode task

```
        jmpf    task1_TSS_selec     ;switch to task1 (v86 mode
                                    ;task)
```
;STEP 15.2: display message after return from v86 task

```
        mov     si,offset retmsg        ;get message address
        mov     di,8*160                ;get display address
        call    disp_it                 ;display it
```

;STEP 16: go back real-address mode

```
        jmp     goto_real
```

;STEP 16.1: define sp equ value

```
spcheck         equ   offset stk0_limit - size stkdef - 4
                ;value of sp when enter interrupt service
                ;routine including error code
```

;STEP 17: interrupt service routines

```
int_entry:              ;entry for interrupt service routines
        REPT    INTNO           ;256 contiguous routines
        call    intchk          ;call check procedure (push return
                                ;address in stack)
        iret                    ;interrupt return
        ENDM
```

;STEP 17.1: change DS segment address, get interrupt return
;   address and pop error code if any

```
intchk:
        push    eax                 ;save EAX
        mov     ax,gdata_selec      ;get data segment selector
        mov     ds,ax               ;put in DS
        pop     eax                 ;restore EAX
        pop     retaddr             ;get return address from stack and sa
        cmp     sp,spcheck          ;is error code come in with
                                    ;interrupt ?
        jne     contint             ;don't handle it if not
        pop     err1                ;get rid of error code
        pop     err2                ;it is not needed
```

;STEP 17.2 get interrupt number

```
contint:
```

```
        pusha                       ;save all registers
        mov     ax,retaddr          ;get return address value
        sub     ax,offset int_entry     ;get the offset of
                            ;return address from the entry
                            ;of the interrupt service routine
        shr     ax,2  ;divide by 4 to get the interrupt number
cont13:
        cmp     ax,13           ;is it interrupt 13 ?
        je      int_13          ;yes, go handle it

;STEP 17.3: get return ip from stack

        mov     cx,stk0_selec       ;no, get stk0 segment selector
        mov     es,cx               ;put in ES
        mov     bx,sp               ;get stack pointer
        add     bx,16               ;adjust it (remember pusha)
        mov     si,es:[bx].oldeip   ;get return ip for this interrupt
        jmp     setint              ;ax has the interrupt number

;STEP 17.4: get cs:ip for v86 mode task, and check the
;instruction caused interrupt 13. If it is instruction
;int XX then handle it. Otherwise, jump to stop.

int_13:
        mov     ax,stk0_selec       ;get stk0 segment selector
        mov     es,ax               ;put in ES
        mov     bx,sp               ;get stack pointer
        add     bx,16               ;adjust it (remember pusha)
        mov     ax,es:[bx].oldcs    ;get code segment for v86 task
        mov     ch,ah               ;convert it to linear address
        shl     ax,4                ;AX has the low 16 bits
        shr     ch,4                ;CH has the high 4 bits
        assume          ds:gdt
        mov     dx,gdt_selec        ;get GDT segment selector
        mov     ds,dx               ;put in DS
        mov     gdata1.d_base1,ax   ;set working descriptor linear
                            ;base address to the code
        mov     gdata1.d_base2,ch   ;segment of v86 mode task
        mov     ax,gdata1_selec     ;get v86 mode task code
                            ;segment selector
        mov     ds,ax               ;put in DS
        mov     si,es:[bx].oldeip   ;get ip for v86 task
                    ;(ip = address where interrupt occurred)
        cld                         ;clear direction flag
        lodsb                       ;load one byte from v86 code segment
        cmp     al,0cdh             ;is this interrupt caused by INT
                            ;instruction ?
        jne     stop                ;no, then stop

;STEP 17.5: get the interrupt number

procint:
        lodsb                       ;get interrupt number to al

;STEP 17.6: if instruction = int 1 then go back to
; protected mode
```

```
        cmp     al,1                    ;is it INT 1 instruction ?
        je      int_1           ;yes, go return to protected mode
```

```
;STEP 17.7: get v86 mode task stack, push return cs:ip
;and flag in it
```

```
setint:
        mov     cx,es:[bx].oldss    ;get v86 mode task stack segment
        mov     dh,ch               ;convert it to linear address
        shl     cx,4                ;CX has the low 16 bits
        shr     dh,4                ;DH has the high 4 bits
        mov     di,gdt_selec        ;get GDT segment selector
        mov     ds,di               ;put in DS
        mov     gdata1.d_base1,cx   ;set working descriptor
                                    ;linear address point
        mov     gdata1.d_base2,dh   ;to the stack segment of v86
                                    ;mode task
        mov     dx,gdata1_selec     ;get stack segment selector
                                    ;for v86 mode task
        mov     ds,dx               ;put in DS
        mov     di,es:[bx].oldsp    ;get v86 mode task stack pointer
        sub     di,6                ;adjust it (for CS,IP,FLAG)
        mov     es:[bx].oldsp,di    ;restore v86 mode task stack
                                    ;pointer
        mov     [di],si             ;put return ip in stack
        mov     dx,es:[bx].oldcs    ;get return cs
        mov     word ptr [di+2],dx      ;put in stack
        mov     dx,es:[bx].oldflg       ;get return flag
        mov     word ptr [di+4],dx      ;put in stack
        and     dx,0fcffh           ;clear interrupt and trap flag
```

```
;STEP 17.8: get the interrupt cs:ip from DOS interrupt
;table. push this cs:ip and flag in stk0, then ;IRET.
```

```
        mov     cx,dos_selec        ;get DOS interrupt vector
                                    ;table selector
        mov     ds,cx               ;put in DS
        xor     ah,ah               ;clear ah
        shl     ax,2                ;int number multiple by 4
        xor     si,si               ;clear si
        add     si,ax               ;get DOS interrupt vector index
        mov     ax,[si]             ;get interrupt vector offset
        mov     cx,[si+2]           ;get interrupt vector segment
        mov     es:[bx].oldcs,cx    ;put interrupt vector cs in
stk0    mov     es:[bx].oldeip,ax   ;put interrupt vector ip in stk0
        mov     es:[bx].oldflg,dx   ;put flag in stk0
        popa                        ;pop all registers
        db      66h                 ;go to DOS interrupt service
                                    ;routine
        iret                        ;in v86 mode
```

```
;STEP 17.9: stop ! something wrong
```

```
stop:
        mov     dx,gdata_selec      ;get gdata segment selector
        mov     ds,dx               ;put in DS
```

```
        mov   si,offset stopmsg  ;get message address
        mov   di,13*160          ;get display position
        call  disp_it            ;display the message

;STEP 17.10: procedure to return to task 0 in protected mode

int_1:
        popa                     ;pop all the registers
        jmpf  task0_TSS_selec    ;switch back to task 0 in
                                 ;protected mode
;STEP 19: Return to real-address mode

goto_real:
        mov   ax,gdata_selec     ;get data segment descriptor
        mov   ds,ax              ;put in DS

        cli                      ;clear interrupt

        mov   ax,dmy_selec       ;get dummy selector
        mov   es,ax              ;put in ES
        mov   ds,ax              ;put in DS
        mov   fs,ax              ;put in FS
        mov   gs,ax              ;put in GS
        mov   ss,ax              ;put in SS

        mov   eax,cr0            ;load CR0
        and   eax,not prot_enable    ;disable protected
                                     ;mode bit
        mov   cr0,eax            ;restore CR0

        db    0eah               ;far jump to flush instruction queue
        dw    offset next_instruction ;ip
        dw    code               ;cs

;STEP 20: execute in real-address mode, and set DS,SS and SP

next_instruction:
        assume      ds:gdata
        mov   ax,Gdata           ;get data segment
        mov   ds,ax              ;put in DS

        mov   ax,stack0          ;get stack segment
        mov   ss,ax              ;put in SS
        mov   sp,offset stack0_limit ;set stack pointer

;STEP 21: set IDTR to DOS interrupt table

        lidt  [pold] ;set IDTR to dos interrupt vector table
        sti                      ;enable interrupt

;STEP 22: terminate this process

        mov   ax,4c00h    ;DOS terminate process function
        int   21h         ;call it to return to DOS prompt
main    endp
code    ends
```

```
;STEP 23: v86 mode task code segment

task1_seg      segment      para  public use16 'task1_seg'
      assume       cs:task1_seg, ds:gdata
task_entry proc  near
entry:
      mov   ax,gdata           ;get gdata segment address
      mov   ds,ax              ;put in DS


;STEP 24: call DOS function to display message

      mov   dx,offset success ;get message address
      mov   ah,9              ;write string to console
      int   21h              ;DOS function call,

;STEP 25: call DOS function to get a key from console

      mov   ah,1              ;get a key from console
      int   21h              ;DOS function call

;STEP 26: go back to protected mode

      int   1                 ;go back to task 0 in protected mode
task_entry   endp
task1_seg_limit   equ   $
task1_seg    ends
      end   main
```

Program: v86p.asm

This program copies everything that resides below the 1 megabyte address to above the 1 megabyte address, then switches to a v86 mode task residing above the 1 megabyte address by using the paging mechanism. (The steps of this program follows the steps in program *v86.asm*.)

Step 0.1: Define EQU for paging.

Step 1.1: Define the segment selector and descriptor for the v86 mode task and address above 1 megabyte.

Step 4.1: Define mapping for the segment of the v86 mode task and descriptor.

Step 5.1: Message and variable definition.

Step 7.1: Define the TSS for the v86 mode task. Note that CS was defined to page 90h.

Step 7.2: Define page table segment.

Step 7.3: Reserve 4 K area to align page table address.

Step 7.4: Define page table entry and make sure that the entry address is above the 1 megabyte address.

Step 7.5: Define page table size.

Step 7.6: Define page directory.

Step 7.7: Variable to save page table address.

Step 9.1: Call procedure *setup_pgtbl* and then set PDBR.

Step 9.2: Set up PDBR (CR3) field in the TSS for the v86 mode task.

Step 14.1: Copy data from linear address 0 to address 100000h.

Step 14.2: Copy the TSS of the v86 mode task to address 180000h.

Step 14.3: Copy the v86 mode task code segment to 190000h.

Step 15.0: Enable memory paging.

Step 15.1: Switch to the v86 mode task residing above 1 megabyte address.

Step 19.1: Disable memory paging.

Step 23: The data segment used in the v86 mode task is the same as the code segment.

File: V86P.ASM

```
.386p
include struct
include macro1
include macro2

INTNO        equ    256     ;interrupt vector number
DSCPSIZE     equ    8       ;size of descriptor
INTSIZE      equ    4       ;size of interrupt service routine
TWO          equ    2       ;
prot_enable  equ    01h     ;
attribute    equ    07h     ;
space        equ    20h     ;

;STEP 0.1: define equ for paging

pg_present   equ    01h
pg_enable    equ    80000000h
pte_mask     equ    07h
```

```
pdbr_offset equ    1000h        ;4k
CR3_TSS     equ    1ch          ;CR3 offset in TSS

;STEP 1: Global Descriptor Table

GDT    segment    para  public       use16 'GDT'
gdt_tab           label qword
null_selec  equ    $-gdt_tab                 ;NULL selector
       dscp   <,,,,,>       ;first one must be a NULL dscriptor

idt_selec   equ    $-gdt_tab         ;IDT segment selector
       dscp       <,,,92h,,>         ;descriptor

code_selec  equ    $-gdt_tab         ;code segment selector
       dscp   <0ffffh,,,09ah,,>      ;descriptor

task0_TSS_selec   equ   $-gdt_tab    ;task 0 TSS selector
       dscp   <task0_TSS_limit,,,089h,,>   ;TSS descriptor

stk0_selec  equ    $-gdt_tab         ;level 0 stack segment
                                     ;selector
       dscp   <stk0_limit,,,92h,,>   ;descriptor with
                                     ;privilege level 0
stk1_selec  equ    $-gdt_tab or 1    ;level 1 stack
                                     ;segment selector
       dscp   <stk1_limit,,,0b2h,,>  ;descriptor with
                                     ;privilege level 1
stk2_selec  equ    $-gdt_tab  or 2   ;level 2 stack
                                     ;segment selector
       dscp   <stk2_limit,,,0d2h,,>  ;descriptor with
                                     ;privilege level 2
dmy_selec   equ    $-gdt_tab         ;dummy segment selector
       dscp   <0ffffh,,,92h,,>       ;dummy segment descriptor

video_selec equ    $-gdt_tab or 3    ;video segment selector
       dscp   <0ffffh,8000h,0bh,0f2h,,>     ;descriptor

gdata_selec equ    $-gdt_tab         ;data segment selector
       dscp   <0ffffh,,,0f2h,,>      ;data segment descriptor

int_selec   equ    $-gdt_tab    ;interrupt segment selector
       dscp   <0ffffh,,,09ah,,>      ;descriptor

;STEP 1.1: Define selector/descriptor for v86 mode task

stack0_selec          equ   $-gdt_tab    ;v86 task stack segment
       dscp           <stack0_limit,,,092h,,> ;descriptor

task1_TSS_selec       equ   $-gdt_tab or 3   ;task 1 TSS selector
                                     ;(above 1M)
       dscp   <task1_TSS_limit,0,08h,0e9h,,> ;TSS descriptor

task1_OTSS_selec equ       $-gdt_tab    ;task 1 TSS selector
                                     ;(below 1M)
       dscp   <task1_TSS_limit,,,0f2h,,>     ;TSS descriptor

task1_seg_selec       equ   $-gdt_tab    ;task 1 segment selector
```

```
        dscp  <0ffffh,,,0f2h,,>        ;task 1 segment descriptor

dos_selec   equ   $-gdt_tab            ;DOS interrupt vector
                                       ;table selector
        dscp  <0ffffh,0,0,092h,0fh,0>  ;descriptor

gdata1_selec     equ   $-gdt_tab       ;working segment selector
gdata1      dscp  <0ffffh,0,0,0f2h,0,0>   ;descriptor

gdt_selec   equ   $-gdt_tab            ;GDT segment selector
        dscp  <gdt_limit,,,0f2h,,>     ;GDT segment descriptor

gdata3_selec     equ   $-gdt_tab       ;selector for base linear
        dscp  <0ffffh,0,18h,0f2h,0fh,0>  ;address at 00180000h

gdata4_selec     equ   $-gdt_tab       ;selector for base linear
        dscp  <0ffffh,0,19h,0f2h,0fh,0>  ;address at 00190000h

gdata5_selec     equ   $-gdt_tab       ;selector for base linear
        dscp  <0ffffh,0,0,0f2h,0fh,>   ;address at 0

gdata6_selec     equ   $-gdt_tab       ;selector for base linear
        dscp  <0ffffh,0,10h,0f2h,0fh,> ;address at 100000h
GDT_limit   equ   $-gdt_tab
GDT    ends

;STEP 2: Interrupt Descriptor Table

IDT    segment para      public use16      'idt'
idt_tab         equ   $
        REPT  INTNO                    ;256 interrupts
        dscp  <,int_selec,0,08eh,,>    ;DPL = 0
        ENDM
idt_limit       equ   $
IDT    ends

;DATA       Segment

gdata segment      para  public 'data' use16
;STEP 3: variable to save GDT/IDT limit and linear address.

pGDT   label fword
        dw    GDT_limit                ;GDT limit
        dd    0                        ;GDT linear address
pIDT   label fword
        dw    IDT_limit                ;IDT limit
        dd    0                        ;IDT linear address
pold   label fword
        dw    03ffh                    ;DOS IDT limit
        dd    0                        ;DOS IDT linear address

;STEP 4: table to define the mapping of descriptor to
;segment

gdt_phys_tab         label word
        dw    idt_selec                ;IDT segment selector
        dw    idt                      ;IDT segment
```

```
            dw      task0_TSS_selec    ;task 0 TSS segment selector
            dw      task0_TSS          ;task 0 TSS segment
            dw      stk0_selec         ;stk0 segment selector
            dw      stk0               ;stk0 segment
            dw      stk1_selec         ;stk1 segment selector
            dw      stk1               ;stk1 segment
            dw      stk2_selec         ;stk2 segment selector
            dw      stk2               ;stk2 segment
            dw      dmy_selec          ;dummy segment selector
            dw      dmy                ;dummy segment
            dw      code_selec         ;code segment selector
            dw      code               ;code segment
            dw      gdata_selec        ;gdata segment selector
            dw      gdata              ;gdata segment
            dw      int_selec          ;interrupt segment selector
            dw      code               ;code segment

;STEP 4.1: Define mapping for v86 task descriptor to segment

            dw      stack0_selec       ;stack0 segment selector
            dw      stack0             ;stack0 segment
            dw      task1_OTSS_selec   ;task 1 TSS segment selector
                                       ;(below 1M)
            dw      task1_TSS          ;task 1 TSS segment (below 1M)
            dw      task1_seg_selec    ;task 1 code segment selector
                                       ;(below 1M)
            dw      task1_seg          ;task 1 code segment (below 1M)
            dw      gdt_selec          ;gdt segment selector
            dw      gdt                ;gdt segment
gdt_tab_size        equ     ($ - gdt_phys_tab) / 4

;STEP 5: message definition area

in_protected        db      'in protected mode ',0

;STEP 5.1: v86 mode task message definition area

error       db      'error !',0
returnmsg   db      'switch back to protected mode',0
stopmsg     db      'stop',0
intnum      db      ?
retaddr     dw      ?
err1        dw      0
err2        dw      0
pdbr        dd      ?
Gdata_limit equ     $
Gdata_ends

;STEP 6: Stack Segment for privilege level 0,1,2

stk0  segment       para  public use16       'stk0'
      db    100h    dup(0)
stk0_limit equ      $
stk0_ends

stk1  segment       para  public use16       'stk1'
      db    100h    dup(0)
```

```
stk1_limit    equ    $
stk1  ends

stk2  segment       para   public        use16  'stk2'
      db    100h  dup(0)
stk2_limit    equ    $
stk2  ends

;STEP 6.1: Stack Segment for v86 mode task

stack0        segment       para   public        use16  'stack0'
      db    100h  dup(0)
stack0_limit          equ    $
stack0        ends
;STEP 7: Task State Segment for task 0

task0_TSS     segment       para   public use16         'task0'
TSS_stack     stk0_selec,stk0_limit,stk1_selec,
              stk1_limit,stk2_selec,stk2_limit
TSS_cr3       0                     ;cr3
TSS_regs      0,0,0,0,0,0,0,0,0,stk0_limit
TSS_seg       gdata_selec,code_selec,stk0_selec,
              gdata_selec,gdata_selec,gdata_selec
              dd     0                     ;LDT field
              dw     0                     ;task trap flag
              dw     68h                   ;I/O base
              db     100h  dup(0ffh)       ;I/O bit maps
task0_TSS_limit     equ    $
task0_TSS     ends

;STEP 7.1: Task State Segment for v86 mode task

task1_TSS     segment       para   public use16         'task1'
TSS_stack     stk0_selec,stk0_limit,stk1_selec,
              stk1_limit,stk2_selec,stk2_limit
TSS_cr3       0                     ;cr3
TSS_regs      entry,23202h,0,0,0,0,stack0_limit,0,0,0
TSS_seg       0,9000h,stack0,0,0,0
              dd     0                     ;LDT field
              dw     0                     ;task trap flag
              dw     68h                   ;I/O base
              dw     100h  dup(0)          ;I/O bit maps
task1_TSS_limit     equ    $
task1_TSS     ends

;STEP 7.2: page segment

pagetbl       segment para public 'pagetbl' use16

;STEP 7.3: reserve 4K area to adjust page table address

      db    4096  dup(0)

;STEP 7.4: define page table entry

tmp_ptbl      label byte
      rept   256
```

```
        dd      (($-tmp_ptbl)/4*1000h + pte_mask + 100000h)
        endm

;STEP 7.5: page table size

page_tbl_size       equ    ($-tmp_ptbl)/4

;STEP 7.6: page directory

        org     tmp_ptbl+pdbr_offset    ;2000h
        dd      ?                       ;first entry for page directory

;STEP 7.7: working area to save page table address

ptbl_addr    dw    ?
pagetbl_limit       equ    $
pagetbl      ends

;STEP 8: Dummy Segment

dmy     segment      para  public use16      'dmy'
        db      128    dup(0)
dmy     ends

;CODE Segment

code    segment      para  public use16      'code'
        assume       cs:code
main    proc  far
        assume       ds:gdata
        mov    ax,gdata              ;get gdata segment address
        mov    ds,ax                 ;put in DS

;STEP 9: The following code initialize IDT

        mov    ax,IDT                ;get IDT segment address
        mov    es,ax                 ;put in ES
        mov    di,offset idt_tab     ;get IDT offset address
        mov    ax,offset int_entry       ;get interrupt service
                                         ;routine address
        mov    cx,INTNO              ;get interrupt numbers
fillidt:
        mov    es:[di],ax            ;put entry address in IDT
        add    di,DSCPSIZE           ;adjust address in IDT
        add    ax,INTSIZE            ;get next interrupt service
                                     ;routine address
        loop   fillidt              ;till end of IDT
;STEP 9.1: set up page table

        call   setup_pgtbl           ;set up page directory and
                                     ;page table
        mov    eax,pdbr              ;get pdbr address
        mov    cr3,eax               ;put in CR3

;STEP 9.2: set PDBR

        mov    bx,task1_TSS          ;get task1 TSS segment address
```

```
        mov   es,bx                 ;put in ES
        mov   es:[CR3_TSS],eax      ;set pdbr address for task 1

;STEP 10,11,12,13: set GDTR,IDTR,LDTR and switch to
;protected mode

        build_dtr   gdt,idt,pgdt,pidt,gdt_limit,idt_limit
        build_dt    gdt,gdt_phys_tab,gdt_tab_size
        cli
        goto_prot   pgdt,pidt,CODE_selec,stack0_selec,
                    stack0_limit,GDATA_selec

;STEP 14: display message in protected mode
                                    ;clear the screen first
        mov   ax,video_selec        ;get video segment selector
        mov   es,ax                 ;put in ES
        mov   cx,4000h              ;counter
        xor   di,di                 ;offset = 0
        mov   ah,attribute          ;ah has the character attribute
        mov   al,space              ;al has the space character
        rep   stosw                 ;write to the screen

        mov   si,offset in_protected ;get message address
        mov   di,6*160              ;get display position
        call  disp_it               ;display it

;STEP 14.1: copy data from 0 - 1 M to above 1 M

        push  ds                    ;save DS
        cld                         ;clear direction flag
        mov   ax,gdata5_selec       ;get selector for linear
                                    ;address = 0
        mov   ds,ax                 ;put in DS
        mov   ax,gdata6_selec       ;get selector for linear
                                    ;address = 100000h
        mov   es,ax                 ;put in ES
        xor   esi,esi               ;esi = 0
        xor   edi,edi               ;edi = 0
        mov   ecx,0fffffh           ;counter = 1 M
        db    66h                   ;operand size is 32 bits
        db    67h                   ;addressing size is 32 bits
        rep   movsb                 ;copy it

;STEP 14.2: copy task 1 TSS to linear address 180000h

        mov   ax,task1_OTSS_selec      ;get task 1 TSS selector
                                       ;(below 1 M)
        mov   ds,ax                 ;put in DS
        mov   ax,gdata3_selec       ;get selector for linear
                                    ;address = 180000h
        mov   es,ax                 ;put in ES
        xor   si,si                 ;si = 0
        xor   di,di                 ;di = 0
        mov   cx,offset task1_TSS_limit   ;counter = task 1
                                          ;TSS size
        rep   movsb                 ;copy it
```

```
;STEP 14.3: copy task1 code segment to linear address
;190000h

        mov     ax,task1_seg_selec ;get task1 segment selector
        mov     ds,ax               ;put in DS
        mov     ax,gdata4_selec     ;get selector for linear
                                    ;address = 190000h
        mov     es,ax               ;put in ES
        xor     si,si               ;si = 0
        xor     di,di               ;di = 0
        mov     cx,offset task1_seg_limit       ;counter = task 1
                                                ;code size
        rep     movsb               ;copy it
        pop     ds                  ;restore DS

;STEP 15: set load TSS to TR

        mov     ax,task0_TSS_selec      ;get task0 TSS selector
        ltr     ax                  ;put in current task register

;STEP 15.0: enable memory paging

        mov     eax,cr0             ;load CR0
        or      eax,pg_enable       ;enable paging
        mov     cr0,eax             ;restore CR0

;STEP 15.1: switch to task1 (v86 mode)

        jmpf    task1_TSS_selec     ;jump to task1 TSS selector

;STEP 15.2: display message after return from v86 task

        mov     si,offset returnmsg     ;get message address
        mov     di,8*160                ;get display position
        call    disp_it                 ;display it

;STEP 16: go back real-address mode

        jmp     goto_real

;STEP 16.1: define sp equ value

spcheck         equ     offset stk0_limit - size stkdef - 4
        ;value of sp when enter interrupt service
        ;routine with error code

;STEP 17: interrupt service routines

int_entry:              ;entry for interrupt service routines
        REPT    INTNO           ;256 contiguous routines
        call    intchk          ;call check procedure (it will push
                                ;return address in stack)
        iret                    ;interrupt return
        ENDM

;STEP 17.1: change DS segment address, get interrupt return
;address and pop error code if any
```

```
intchk:
        push    eax                     ;save EAX
        mov     ax,gdata_selec          ;get data segment selector
        mov     ds,ax                   ;put in DS
        pop     eax                     ;restore EAX
        pop     retaddr                 ;get return address from stack
                                        ;and save it
        cmp     sp,spcheck              ;is error code come in with
                                        ;interrupt ?
        jne     contint                 ;don't handle it if not
        pop     err1                    ;get rid of error code
        pop     err2                    ;it is not needed

;STEP 17.2 get interrupt number

contint:
        pusha                           ;save all registers
        mov     ax,retaddr              ;get return address value
        sub     ax,offset int_entry     ;get the offset of
                                        ;return address from the entry
                                        ;of the interrupt service routine
        shr     ax,2                    ;divide by 4 to get the interrupt
                                        ;number
cont13:
        cmp     ax,13                   ;is it interrupt 13 ?
        je      int_13                  ;yes, go handle it

;STEP 17.3: get return ip from stack

        mov     cx,stk0_selec           ;no, get stk0 segment selector
        mov     es,cx                   ;put in ES
        mov     bx,sp                   ;get stack pointer
        add     bx,16                   ;adjust it (remember pusha)
        mov     si,es:[bx].oldeip       ;get ip for v86 task
        jmp     setint                  ;ax has the interrupt number

;STEP 17.4: get cs:ip for v86 mode task, and check the
;instruction caused interrupt 13. If it is int XX
;instruction then handle it. Otherwise, jump to stop.

int_13:
        mov     ax,stk0_selec           ;get stk0 segment selector
        mov     es,ax                   ;put in ES
        mov     bx,sp                   ;get stack pointer
        add     bx,16                   ;adjust it (remember pusha)
        mov     ax,es:[bx].oldcs        ;get code segment for v86 task
        mov     ch,ah                   ;convert it to linear address
        shl     ax,4                    ;AX has the low 16 bits
        shr     ch,4                    ;CH has the high 4 bits
        assume          ds:gdt
        mov     dx,gdt_selec            ;get GDT segment selector
        mov     ds,dx                   ;put in DS
        mov     gdata1.d_base1,ax       ;set working descriptor linear
                                        ;base address to the code
        mov     gdata1.d_base2,ch       ;segment of v86 mode task
        mov     ax,gdata1_selec         ;get v86 mode task code
                                        ;segment selector
```

```
        mov     ds,ax               ;put in data segment
        mov     si,es:[bx].oldeip   ;get ip for v86 task
                    ;ip = address where interrupt occurred
        cld                         ;clear direction flag
        lodsb                       ;load one byte from v86 code segment
        cmp     al,0cdh             ;is this interrupt caused by INT
                                    ;instruction ?
        jne     stop                ;no, then stop
```

;STEP 17.5: get the interrupt number

procint:

```
        lodsb                       ;get interrupt number value
```

;STEP 17.6: if instruction = int 1 then go back to
;protected mode

```
        cmp     al,1                ;is it INT 1 instruction ?
        je      int_1               ;yes, go return to protected mode
```

;STEP 17.7: get v86 mode task stack, push return cs:ip and
; FLAG in it

setint:
```
        mov     cx,es:[bx].oldss    ;get v86 mode task stack
                                    ;segment
        mov     dh,ch               ;convert it to linear address
        shl     cx,4                ;CX has the low 16 bits
        shr     dh,4                ;DH has the high 4 bits
        mov     di,gdt_selec        ;get GDT segment selector
        mov     ds,di               ;put in DS
        mov     gdata1.d_base1,cx   ;set working descriptor base
                                    ;linear address to the stack
        mov     gdata1.d_base2,dh   ;segment of v86 mode task

        mov     dx,gdata1_selec     ;get stack segment selector
                                    ;for the v86 mode task
        mov     ds,dx               ;put in DS
        mov     di,es:[bx].oldsp    ;get v86 mode task stack
                                    ;pointer
        sub     di,6                ;adjust it (for CS,IP,FLAG)
        mov     es:[bx].oldsp,di    ;restore v86 mode task stack
                                    ;pointer
        mov     [di],si             ;set return address after
                                    ;int nn
        mov     dx,es:[bx].oldcs    ;set return segment
        mov     word ptr [di+2],dx
        mov     dx,es:[bx].oldflg   ;set return flag
        mov     word ptr [di+4],dx
        and     dx,0fcffh           ;clear interrupt and trap flag
```

;STEP 17.8: get the interrupt cs:ip from DOS interrupt
;table. push this cs:ip and flag in stk0, then ;IRET.

```
        mov     cx,dos_selec        ;get DOS interrupt vector
                                    ;table selector
```

```
        mov    ds,cx               ;put in DS
        xor    ah,ah               ;int number multiply by 4
        shl    ax,2
        xor    si,si
        add    si,ax               ;get DOS interrupt vector index
        mov    ax,[si]             ;get interrupt vector offset
        mov    cx,[si+2]           ;get interrupt vector segment
        mov    es:[bx].oldcs,cx    ;put interrupt vector segment
                                   ;in stk0
        mov    es:[bx].oldeip,ax   ;put interrupt vector offset
                                   ;in stk0
        mov    es:[bx].oldflg,dx   ;put flag in stk0
        popa                       ;pop all registers
        db     66h                 ;go to DOS interrupt service
        iret                       ;routine in v86 mode

;STEP 17.9: stop ! something wrong

stop:
        mov    dx,gdata_selec      ;get gdata segment selector
        mov    ds,dx               ;put in DS
        mov    si,offset stopmsg   ;get message address
        mov    di,13*160           ;get display position
        call   disp_it             ;display the message

;STEP 17.10: procedure to return to task 0 in protected mode

int_1:
        mov    eax,cr0             ;load CR0 register
        and    eax,not pg_enable   ;disable paging
        mov    cr0,eax             ;store in CR0
        popa                       ;pop all the registers
        jmpf   task0_TSS_selec     ;switch back to task 0 in
                                   ;protected mode

;STEP 19: Return to real-address mode

goto_real:
        cli                        ;disable interrupt

;STEP 19.1: disable memory paging

        mov    eax,cr0             ;load CR0 register
        and    eax,not pg_enable   ;disable paging
        mov    cr0,eax             ;store in CR0

        mov    ax,dmy_selec        ;get dummy selector
        mov    es,ax               ;reset segment register
        mov    ds,ax
        mov    fs,ax
        mov    gs,ax
        mov    ss,ax

        mov    eax,cr0             ;load CR0
        and    eax,not prot_enable     ;disable protected mode
        mov    cr0,eax             ;restore CR0
```

```
        db     0eah              ;far jump to flush instruction queue
        dw     offset next_instruction ;IP for far jump
        dw     code              ;CS for far jump

;STEP 20: execute in real mode, set DS,SS and SP

next_instruction:
        assume        ds:gdata
        mov    ax,gdata          ;get gdata segment address
        mov    ds,ax             ;put in DS
        mov    ax,stack0         ;get stack0 segment address
        mov    ss,ax             ;put in SS
        mov    sp,offset stack0_limit  ;set SP

;STEP 21: set IDTR to DOS interrupt table

        lidt   [pold]            ;load DOS interrupt vector
                                 ;table base address to IDTR
        sti                      ;enable interrupt

;STEP 22: terminate this program

        mov    ax,4c00h          ;call DOS terminate process
        int    21h               ;function and return to DOS prompt
main    endp

;procedure: disp_it
;display string in protected mode
;input: ds:si - string address, the end of the string must
;be 0

disp_it       proc  near
        mov    ax,video_selec    ;get video segment selector
        mov    es,ax             ;put in ES
        mov    ah,attribute      ;display attribute
disp_it1:
        lodsb                    ;get display character
        stosw                    ;put it in screen
        cmp    al,0              ;end of display character ?
        jne    disp_it1          ;no, continue
        ret                      ;yes, return
disp_it       endp

;procedure:setup_pgtbl
;align the predefined page table to page boundary. set the
;first entry of page directory table to this aligned page
;table. The page directory table will be set below the page
;table.

setup_pgtbl proc   near
        push   ds                ;save DS
        push   es                ;save ES
        assume        ds:pagetbl
        mov    ax,pagetbl        ;get page table segment address
        mov    ds,ax             ;put in DS
        mov    es,ax             ;put in ES
        mov    cx,page_tbl_size  ;get page table size
```

```
        mov     bx,ax           ;bx has page table segment address
        and     bx,00ffh        ;bx is in 4K range (segment)
        xor     edi,edi
        mov     di,100h         ;di has 4K size (segment)
        sub     di,bx           ;address for 4K boundary,
                                ;also page table address
        shl     di,4            ;convert to offset
        mov     ptbl_addr,di    ;save page table address
        push    di              ;save it
        mov     si,offset tmp_ptbl      ;get predefined page
                                        ;table address
        rep     movsd           ;move it to the page boundary
                                ;address
        pop     di              ;restore di
;set pdbr & pdir
        xor     ebx,ebx
        mov     bx,ax           ;get page table segment address
        shl     ebx,4           ;convert to 20-bit address
        add     ebx,edi         ;page table linear base address
        or      bl,pte_mask     ;user level,read-write,present
        mov     dword ptr [di].pdbr_offset,ebx      ;put in page
                                        ;directory table
        add     ebx,offset pdbr_offset  ;page directory base
                                        ;address
        push    ds
        assume          ds:gdata
        mov     ax,gdata        ;get gdata segment
        mov     ds,ax           ;put in DS
        and     ebx,0fffff000h  ;PDBR
        mov     pdbr,ebx        ;save page directory address
        pop     ds
        assume          ds:pagetbl
        mov     bx,ptbl_addr    ;get page table address
        add     bx,0b8h shl 2   ;get entry b8h (1 entry has
                                ;4 bytes)
        mov     dword ptr [bx][pg_stat],0b8007h ;map to 0b8000h
        pop     es              ;restore ES
        pop     ds              ;restore DS
        ret
setup_pgtbl endp
code    ends

;STEP 23: v86 mode task code segment

task1_seg       segment         para    public  use16 'task1_seg'
        assume          cs:task1_seg,ds:task1_seg
task_entry proc   near
entry:
        push    cs              ;CS = DS
        pop     ds

;STEP 24: call DOS function to display message

        mov     dx,offset task1msg      ;get message address
        mov     ah,9            ;call DOS int 21h function
        int     21h             ;to display the message
```

```
;STEP 25: call DOS function to get a key from console

        mov     ah,1               ;call DOS int 21h function
        int     21h                ;to get a key from console

;STEP 26: go back to protected mode

        int     1      ;switch back to task 0 in protected mode
task_entry  endp

;STEP 27: define message

task1msg    db      'now in v86 mode task 1',0dh,0ah
        db      'press any key to return to protected mode'
        db      0dh,0ah,'$'
task1_seg_limit     equ     $
task1_seg   ends
        end     main
```

11.5 Summary

The v86 mode is an 8086/88 emulation mode under control of the protected mode. Before entering the v86 mode, a software interface called the v86 monitor must exist in the protected mode. This v86 monitor is responsible for initializing the v86 task environment, emulating the v86 I/O instructions, and handling the v86 interrupts or exceptions. The processor can enter the v86 mode by enabling the VM bit in the EFLAGS register. There are two ways to do this:

- A task switch by loading the image of the EFLAGS register from the new task's TSS.

- An *IRET* instruction by loading the EFLAGS register from the stack.

SECTION V

APPENDICES

APPENDIX A
Sample i486 Programs

The sample programs in this appendix show how to use two i486 functions: the cache memory function and the alignment check function.

Program: CACHE.ASM

The i486 processor internal cache memory is available in all operation modes. To use internal cache memory, enable the cache and write-through bit in CR0 register. The following sample program shows general protection fault exception generated by the wrong setting of CD and NW bits in the protected mode.

Step 15.1: Set CD bit to 0 and NW bit to 1 in CR0 register. This causes interrupt 13– general protection fault.

File: CACHE.ASM

```
.386p
include struct
include macro1

INTNO       equ    21        ;interrupt vector number
DSCPSIZE    equ    8         ;size of descriptor
INTSIZE     equ    4         ;size of interrupt service
                            ;routine
TWO         equ    2         ;
prot_enable equ    01h       ;protected mode enable bit in
                            ;CR0
attribute   equ    07h       ;display character attribute
space       equ    20h       ;ASCII code for space

;STEP 1: Global Descriptor Table

GDT    segment       para  public use16 'GDT'
gdt_tab       label qword
null_selec  equ    $-gdt_tab            ;null selector
   dscp       <,,,,,>       ;first one must be a null descriptor

code_selec  equ    $-gdt_tab            ;code segment selector
   dscp       <0ffffh,,,09ah,,>         ;descriptor

task0_TSS_selec   equ   $-gdt_tab   ;TSS selector
   dscp       <task0_TSS_limit,,,089h,,>   ;descriptor

stk0_selec  equ    $-gdt_tab         ;level 0 stack segment
                                    ;selector
   dscp       <stk0_limit,,,92h,,>   ;descriptor with
                                    ;privilege level 0
stk1_selec  equ    $-gdt_tab or 1    ;level 1 stack
                                    ;segment selector
```

```
   dscp          <stk1_limit,,,0b2h,,>    ;descriptor with
                                          ;privilege level 1
stk2_selec  equ    $-gdt_tab or 2         ;level 2 stack
                                          ;segment selector
   dscp          <stk2_limit,,,0d2h,,>    ;descriptor with
                                          ;privilege level 2
dmy_selec   equ    $-gdt_tab              ;dummy segment selector
   dscp          <0ffffh,,,92h,,>         ;dummy segment descriptor

video_selec equ    $-gdt_tab or 3         ;video segment selector
   dscp          <0ffffh,8000h,0bh,0f2h,,>       ;descriptor

gdata_selec equ    $-gdt_tab              ;data segment selector
   dscp          <gdata_limit,,,0f2h,,>           ;descriptor

int_selec   equ    $-gdt_tab ;interrupt segment selector
   dscp          <0ffffh,,,09ah,,>        ;descriptor
gdt_limit   equ    $-gdt_tab
GDT    ends

;STEP 2: Interrupt Descriptor Table

IDT    segment para        public use16 'idt'
idt_tab equ $
       REPT   INTNO                       ;21 interrupt entries
       dscp   <,int_selec,0,0eeh,,>    ;DPL = 3
       ENDM
idt_limit    equ    $
IDT    ends

;DATA         Segment

Gdata segment        para   public use16 'Gdata'

;STEP 3: variable to save GDT/IDT limit and linear address.

pGDT          label fword
pGDT_limit dw     ?                ;GDT limit
pGDT_addr  dd     ?                ;GDT segment linear address
pIDT          label fword
pIDT_limit dw     ?                ;IDT limit
pIDT_addr  dd     ?                ;IDT segment linear address

pold          label fword
dIDT_limit dw     03ffh            ;DOS IDT limit
dIDT_addr  dd     0        ;DOS IDT segment linear address

;STEP 4: table to define the mapping of descriptor to
;segment

gdt_phys_tab         label word
       dw     task0_TSS_selec   ;TSS segment selector
       dw     task0_TSS         ;TSS segment
       dw     stk0_selec        ;stk0 segment selector
       dw     stk0              ;stk0 segment
       dw     stk1_selec        ;stk1 segment selector
       dw     stk1              ;stk1 segment
```

```
        dw      stk2_selec        ;stk2 segment selector
        dw      stk2              ;stk2 segment
        dw      dmy_selec         ;dummy segment selector
        dw      dmy               ;dummy segment
        dw      code_selec        ;code segment selector
        dw      code              ;code segment
        dw      gdata_selec       ;data segment selector
        dw      gdata             ;data segment
        dw      int_selec         ;interrupt segment selector
        dw      code              ;code segment
gdt_tab_size        equ   ($ - gdt_phys_tab) / 4
        ;entry numbers in above table

;STEP 5: message definition area

in_protected        db    'in protected mode ',0
int_msg             db    'interrupt '
int_num             dw    ?
                    db    'H',0
Gdata_limit equ     $
Gdata ends


;STEP 6: Stack Segment for privilege level 0,1,2

stk0   segment      para  public use16 'stk0'
        db    100h  dup(0)
stk0_limit equ      $
stk0   ends

stk1   segment      para  public use16 'stk1'
        db    100h  dup(0)
stk1_limit equ      $
stk1   ends

stk2   segment      para  public use16 'stk2'
        db    100h  dup(0)
stk2_limit equ      $
stk2   ends


;STEP 7: Task State Segment

task0_TSS    segment       para   public use16 'task0'
TSS_stack    stk0_selec,stk0_limit,stk1_selec,
             stk1_limit,stk2_selec,stk2_limit
TSS_cr3      0                       ;cr3
TSS_regs     0,0,0,0,0,0,0,0,0,stk0_limit
TSS_seg      gdata_selec,code_selec,stk0_selec,
             gdata_selec,gdata_selec,gdata_selec
             dd    0                 ;LDT field
             dw    0                 ;task trap flag
             dw    68h               ;I/O base
task0_TSS_limit     equ    $
task0_TSS    ends
```

```
;STEP 8: Dummy Segment

dmy     segment      para  public use16 'dmy'
        db      128    dup(0)
dmy     ends

;CODE Segment

code    segment      para  public use16 'code'
        assume       cs:code,ds:gdata
main    proc far
        mov     ax,gdata            ;get gdata segment address
        mov     ds,ax               ;put in DS

;STEP 9: The following code will initial IDT

        mov     ax,IDT              ;get IDT segment address
        mov     es,ax               ;put in ES
        mov     di,offset idt_tab   ;get IDT offset address
        mov     ax,offset int_entry     ;get interrupt service
                                        ;routine address
        mov     cx,INTNO            ;get interrupt number
fillidt:
        mov     es:[di],ax          ;put entry address in IDT
        add     di,DSCPSIZE         ;adjust address in IDT
        add     ax,INTSIZE          ;adjust interrupt service
                                    ;routine address, the size of
                                    ;each routine is defined in
                                    ;INTSIZE
        loop    fillidt             ;keep filling

;STEP 10:   get GDT/IDT limit and linear address

        mov     ax,offset gdt_limit     ;get GDT segment limit
        mov     pGDT_limit,ax       ;put in pGDT_limit
        xor     eax,eax             ;clear eax
        mov     ax,GDT              ;get GDT segment address
        shl     eax,4               ;convert to 32-bit linear
                                    ;address
        mov     pGDT_addr,eax       ;put in pGDT_addr

        mov     ax,offset idt_limit     ;get IDT segment limit
        mov     pIDT_limit,ax       ;put in pGDT_limit
        xor     eax,eax             ;clear eax
        mov     ax,idt              ;get IDT segment address
        shl     eax,4               ;convert to 32-bit linear
                                    ;address
        mov     pIDT_addr,eax       ;put in pIDT_addr

;STEP 11: base on gdt_phys_tab to set linear base address
;for each corresponding descriptor

        mov     ax,GDT              ;get gdt segment address
        mov     es,ax               ;put in ES
        mov     si,offset gdt_phys_tab  ;get address of
                                        ;gdt_phys_tab
        mov     cx,gdt_tab_size     ;get gdt_phys_tab size
```

```
bdt1:
        lodsw                           ;get descriptor number
        mov     bx,ax                   ;put in BX
        and     bx,0fff8h               ;mask off TI bit and RPL
        lodsw                   ;get corresponding segment address
                                        ;for the above descriptor
        push    ax                      ;save it
        shl     ax,4                    ;get lower 4 bytes offset
        mov     es:[bx][d_base1],ax     ;save it in descriptor
                                                ;base1
        pop     ax                      ;restore segment address
        shr     ax,12                   ;get the highest byte
        mov     es:[bx][d_base2],al     ;save it in descriptor
                                                ;base2
        loop    bdt1                    ;continue

;STEP 12: switch to protected mode

        cli                             ;clear interrupt
        lgdt    [pGDT]                  ;load GDT address and limit
                                        ;into GDTR
        lidt    [pIDT]                  ;load IDT address and limit
                                        ;into IDTR
        mov     eax,cr0                 ;get cr0 register
        or      al,prot_enable          ;set protected mode enable
        mov     cr0,eax                 ;restore cr0

        jmp     dword ptr cs:[enter_prot]       ;far jump to flush
                                                ;instruction queue
enter_prot:
        dw      offset now_in_prot      ;EIP
        dw      code_selec              ;code segment selector

;STEP 13: execute in protected mode. Set
;LDTR,SS,SP,DS,ES,FS,GS

now_in_prot:
        xor     ax,ax                   ;clear ax
        lldt    ax                      ;load NULL selector to LDTR

        mov     ax,stk0_selec           ;get stack segment selector
        mov     ss,ax                   ;put in SS
        mov     sp,offset stk0_limit    ;set stack pointer

        mov     ax,gdata_selec          ;get data segment selector
        mov     ds,ax                   ;put in DS
        mov     es,ax                   ;put in ES
        mov     fs,ax                   ;put in FS
        mov     gs,ax                   ;put in GS

;STEP 14: display message in protected mode
                                        ;clear the screen first
        mov     ax,video_selec          ;get video segment selector
        mov     es,ax                   ;put in ES
        mov     cx,4000h                ;buffer size to clear
        xor     di,di                   ;screen starting address
        mov     ah,attribute            ;character attribute
```

```
        mov    al,space                ;space
        rep    stosw                   ;fill it
        mov    si,offset in_protected  ;get protected mode
                                       ;message address
        mov    di,320                  ;get display address
        call   disp_it                 ;call display procedure

;STEP 15: load TSS to TR

        mov    ax,task0_TSS_selec      ;get TSS selector for
                                       ;current task
        ltr    ax                      ;load into task register

;STEP 15.1: enable write through but disable cache

        mov    eax,cr0                 ;get CR0 value
        or     eax,20000000h           ;enable write-through
        mov    cr0,eax                 ;restore CR0 value

;STEP 16: switch back to real mode

        int    20                      ;interrupt 20

;STEP 17: Interrupt Service Routine

int_entry:          ;entry point for interrupt service routine
        REPT   INTNO
        call   disp         ;call the display message procedure
        iret
        ENDM

;STEP 18: get interrupt number and display it

disp:
        pop    ax                   ;get return address from stack
        sub    ax,offset int_entry     ;get offset from the
                                       ;interrupt entry
        shr    ax,TWO               ;divide by 4 to get interrupt
                                    ;number
        mov    si,offset int_num       ;get ASCII code address
        mov    cx,TWO               ;convert to 2 ASCII code
        call   htoa                 ;call convert procedure
        mov    si,offset int_msg    ;get interrupt message address
        mov    di,5*160             ;get display address
        call   disp_it              ;call display procedure

;STEP 19: Return to real mode

        cli                         ;disable interrupt

        mov    ax,dmy_selec         ;dummy selector
        mov    es,ax                ;reset segment registers
        mov    ds,ax
        mov    fs,ax
        mov    gs,ax
        mov    ss,ax
```

```
          mov    eax,cr0             ;load the content of CR0
          and    eax,not prot_enable      ;disable protected mode
          mov    cr0,eax             ;restore the content of CR0
          db     0eah           ;far jump to flush instruction queue
          dw     offset next_instruction ;EIP
          dw     code                    ;CS
```

;STEP 20: execute in real mode, set DS,SS and SP.

```
next_instruction:
          mov    ax,Gdata            ;get data segment address
          mov    ds,ax               ;put in DS
          mov    ax,stk0             ;get stack segment address
          mov    ss,ax               ;put in SS
          mov    sp,offset stk0_limit     ;set stack pointer
```

;STEP 21: set IDTR to DOS interrupt table

```
          lidt   [pold]         ;load DOS interrupt vector
                                ;table to IDTR register
          sti                   ;enable interrupt
```

;STEP 22: terminate this process

```
          mov    ax,4c00h    ;DOS function terminate process
          int    21h         ;DOS function call
main      endp
code      ends
          end    main
```

Program: ALIGN.ASM

The following program enables alignment check and alignment mask in a privilege level 3 task. It generates an alignment fault exception—exception 17 when the program tries to access data from a misaligned address.

Step 15.1: Enable alignment mask bit in CR0 register.

Step 15.4: Enable alignment check bit in EFLAGS register.

Step 15.5: Try to access misaligned data. This causes an alignment fault.

File: ALIGN.ASM

```
.386p
include struct
include macro1
include macro2

INTNO      equ    21    ;interrupt vector number
DSCPSIZE   equ    8     ;size of descriptor
INTSIZE    equ    4     ;size of interrupt service routine
TWO        equ    2     ;
```

```
prot_enable equ    01h    ;protected mode enable bit in CR0
attribute   equ    07h    ;display character attribute
space       equ    20h    ;ASCII code for space
;STEP 1: Global Descriptor Table

GDT    segment       para  public use16 'GDT'
gdt_tab              label qword
null_selec           equ   $-gdt_tab    ;null selector
   dscp     <,,,,,>        ;first one must be a null descriptor

code_selec equ  $-gdt_tab    ;task 0 code segment selector
   dscp     <0ffffh,,,09ah,,>         ;descriptor

task0_TSS_selec    equ   $-gdt_tab    ;task 0 TSS selector
   dscp      <task0_TSS_limit,,,089h,,>    ;TSS descriptor

stk0_selec  equ   $-gdt_tab              ;level 0 stack segment
                                         ;selector
   dscp     <stk0_limit,,,92h,,>         ;descriptor with
                                         ;privilege level 0
stk1_selec  equ   $-gdt_tab or 1         ;level 1 stack
                                         ;segment selector
   dscp     <stk1_limit,,,0b2h,,>        ;descriptor with
                                         ;privilege level 1
stk2_selec  equ   $-gdt_tab or 2         ;level 2 stack
                                         ;segment selector
   dscp     <stk2_limit,,,0d2h,,>        ;descriptor with
                                         ;privilege level 2
stk3_selec  equ   $-gdt_tab  or 3        ;level 3 stack
                                         ;segment selector
   dscp     <stk3_limit,,,0f2h,,>        ;descriptor with
                                         ;privilege level 3
dmy_selec   equ   $-gdt_tab              ;dummy segment selector
   dscp     <0ffffh,,,92h,,>             ;dummy segment descriptor

video_selec equ   $-gdt_tab or 3    ;video segment selector
   dscp      <ffffh,8000h,0bh,0f2h,,>       ;descriptor

gdata_selec equ   $-gdt_tab or 3    ;data segment selector
   dscp      <gdata_limit,,,0f2h,,>  ;data segment descriptor

int_selec   equ   $-gdt_tab    ;interrupt segment selector
   dscp     <0ffffh,,,09ah,,>         ;descriptor

;STEP 1.1: privilege level 3 code segment

task0_code3_selec equ    $-gdt_tab or 3    ;level 3 code
                                           ;segment selector
   dscp     <0ffffh,,,0fah,,>        ;descriptor with
                                     ;privilege level 3
GDT_limit   equ   $-gdt_tab
GDT   ends

;STEP 2: Interrupt Descriptor Table

IDT   segment para       public use16 'idt'
idt_tab equ $
```

```
        REPT   INTNO                         ;21 interrupt entries
        dscp   ,int_selec,0,0eeh,,    ;DPL = 3
        ENDM
idt_limit    equ    $
IDT   ends

;DATA         Segment

Gdata segment       para   public use16 'Gdata'

;STEP 3: variable to save GDT/IDT limit and linear address.

pGDT  label fword
        dw     GDT_limit              ;GDT limit
        dd     0                      ;GDT linear address
pIDT  label fword
        dw     IDT_limit              ;IDT limit
        dd     0                      ;IDT linear address
pold  label fword
        dw     03ffh                  ;DOS IDT limit
        dd     0                      ;DOS IDT linear address

;STEP 4: table to define the mapping of descriptor to
;segment

gdt_phys_tab        label word
        dw     task0_TSS_selec        ;task 0 TSS segment selector
        dw     task0_TSS              ;task 0 TSS segment
        dw     stk0_selec             ;stk0 segment selector
        dw     stk0                   ;stk0 segment
        dw     stk1_selec             ;stk1 segment selector
        dw     stk1                   ;stk1 segment
        dw     stk2_selec             ;stk2 segment selector
        dw     stk2                   ;stk2 segment
        dw     stk3_selec             ;stk3 segment selector
        dw     stk3                   ;stk3 segment
        dw     dmy_selec              ;dummy segment selector
        dw     dmy                    ;dummy segment
        dw     code_selec             ;code segment selector
        dw     code                   ;code segment
        dw     gdata_selec            ;data segment selector for
        dw     gdata                  ;data segment
        dw     int_selec              ;interrupt segment selector
        dw     code                   ;code segment

;STEP 4.1: selector and segment for level 3 segment

        dw     task0_code3_selec
        dw     code
gdt_tab_size        equ    ($ - gdt_phys_tab) / 4

;STEP 5: message definition area

in_protected        db     'in protected mode ',0
int_msg             db     'interrupt '
int_num             dw     ?
                    db     'H',0
```

```
;STEP 5.1: message definition area for task switch

level_msg    db      'change task to privilege level 3',0

;STEP 5.2 define data that is not on dword boundary

             db      ?
data1        dd      ?         ;unalignment address
Gdata_limit equ     $
Gdata ends

;STEP 6: Stack Segment for privilege level 0,1,2,3

stk0   segment        para  public use16 'stk0'
       db      100h   dup(0)
stk0_limit             equ    $
stk0  ends

stk1   segment        para  public use16 'stk1'
       db      100h   dup(0)
stk1_limit             equ    $
stk1  ends

stk2   segment        para  public use16 'stk2'
       db      100h   dup(0)
stk2_limit             equ    $
stk2  ends

stk3   segment        para  public use16 'stk3'
       db      100h   dup(0)
stk3_limit             equ    $
stk3  ends

;STEP 7: Task State Segment for task 0

task0_TSS    segment       para  public use16 'task0'
TSS_stack    stk0_selec,stk0_limit,stk1_selec,
             stk1_limit,stk2_selec,stk2_limit
TSS_cr3      0                       ;cr3
TSS_regs     0,0,0,0,0,0,0,0,0,stk0_limit
TSS_seg      gdata_selec,code_selec,stk0_selec,
             gdata_selec,gdata_selec,gdata_selec
             dd      0               ;LDT field
             dw      0               ;task trap flag
             dw      68h             ;I/O base
task0_TSS_limit    equ    $
task0_TSS    ends

;STEP 8: Dummy Segment

dmy    segment        para  public use16 'dmy'
       db   128   dup(0)
dmy    ends
```

```
;CODE Segment

code    segment     para  public use16 'code'
        assume      cs:code,ds:gdata
main    proc  far
        mov   ax,gdata
        mov   ds,ax

;STEP 9: The following code will initial IDT

        mov   ax,IDT                    ;get IDT segment address
        mov   es,ax                     ;put in ES
        mov   di,offset idt_tab         ;get IDT offset address
        mov   ax,offset int_entry       ;get interrupt service
                                        ;routine address
        mov   cx,INTNO                  ;get interrupt number
fillidt:
        mov   es:[di],ax        ;put entry address in IDT
        add   di,DSCPSIZE       ;adjust address in IDT
        add   ax,INTSIZE        ;adjust interrupt service
                               ;routine address, the size of
                               ;each routine is defined in
                               ;INTSIZE
        loop  fillidt          ;keep filling

;STEP 10,11,12,13: set GDTR,IDTR,LDTR and switch to
;protected mode

        build_dtr  gdt,idt,pgdt,pidt,gdt_limit,idt_limit
        build_dt   gdt,gdt_phys_tab,gdt_tab_size
        cli
        goto_prot  pgdt,pidt,CODE_selec,stk0_selec,
                   stk0_limit,GDATA_selec

;STEP 14: display message in protected mode

                               ;clear the screen first
        mov   ax,video_selec   ;get video segment selector
        mov   es,ax            ;put in ES
        mov   cx,4000h         ;screen size
        xor   di,di            ;screen starting address
        mov   ah,attribute
        mov   al,space         ;fill space and attribute
        rep   stosw            ;fill it

        mov   si,offset in_protected  ;get protected mode
                                      ;message address
        mov   di,320           ;get display address
        call  disp_it          ;call display procedure

;STEP 15: set load TSS to TR

        mov   ax,task0_TSS_selec       ;get TSS selector for
                                       ;current task
        ltr   ax                       ;load into task register
```

```
;STEP 15.1: enable alignment mask bit in CR0

        mov     eax,cr0
        or      eax,00040000h        ;enable alignment mask bit
        mov     cr0,eax

;STEP 15.2: change privilege level from 0 to 3

        xor     eax,eax              ;clear eax
        mov     ax,stk3_selec        ;get ss with level 2
        push    eax                  ;push ss
        xor     eax,eax              ;clear eax
        mov     ax,offset stk3_limit      ;get sp with level 2
        push    eax                  ;push sp
        xor     eax,eax              ;clear eax
        mov     ax,task0_code3_selec     ;get cs with level 2
        push    eax                  ;push cs
        mov     eax,offset level     ;get ip
        push    eax                  ;push ip
        db      66h                  ;32 bit operand size
        retf                         ;return far

;STEP 15.3: display message after change level

level:
        mov     si,offset level_msg        ;get message address
        mov     di,4*160             ;get display address
        call    disp_it              ;call display

;STEP 15.4: enable alignment checking bit in EFLAGS

        pushfd                       ;push eflags value into stack
        pop     eax                  ;pop to EAX register
        or      eax,00040000h        ;enable alignment checking bit
        push    eax                  ;push EAX value to stack
        popfd                        ;pop value to eflags

;STEP 15.5: try to access an unalignment data

        mov     eax,data1

;STEP 16: switch back to real-address mode

        int     20                   ;interrupt 20

;STEP 17: Interrupt Service Routine

int_entry:              ;entry point for interrupt service routine
        REPT    INTNO
        call    disp         ;call the display message procedure
        iret
        ENDM

;STEP 18: get interrupt number and display it

disp:
        pop     ax               ;get return address from stack
```

```
        sub     ax,offset int_entry     ;get offset from the
                                        ;interrupt entry
        shr     ax,TWO                  ;divide by 4 to get
                                        ;interrupt number
        mov     si,offset int_num       ;get ascii code address
        mov     cx,TWO                  ;convert to 2 ascii code
        call    htoa                    ;call convert procedure
        mov     si,offset int_msg       ;get interrupt message address
        mov     di,6*160                ;get display address
        call    disp_it                 ;call display procedure

;STEP 19: Return to real-address mode

        cli                             ;disable interrupt
        mov     ax,dmy_selec            ;get dummy selector
        mov     es,ax                   ;put in ES
        mov     ds,ax                   ;put in DS
        mov     fs,ax                   ;put in FS
        mov     gs,ax                   ;put in GS
        mov     ss,ax                   ;put in SS

        mov     eax,cr0                 ;load the content of CR0
        and     eax,not prot_enable     ;disable protected mode
        mov     cr0,eax                 ;restore the content of CR0

        db      0eah                    ;far jump to flush instruction
                                        ;queue
        dw      offset next_instruction ;ip
        dw      code                    ;cs

;STEP 20: execute in real mode, set DS,SS and SP

next_instruction:
        mov     ax,Gdata                ;get data segment address
        mov     ds,ax                   ;set to DS register
        mov     ax,stk0                 ;get stack segment address
        mov     ss,ax                   ;set to SS register
        mov     sp,offset stk0_limit    ;set stack pointer

;STEP 21: set IDTR to DOS interrupt table

        lidt    [pold]                  ;reset interrupt vector table
        sti                             ;enable interrupt

;STEP 22: terminate this process

        mov     ax,4c00h                ;terminate process
        int     21h                     ;DOS system call
main    endp
        end     main
```

APPENDIX B

The i386/i486 Instruction Set

Mnemonic Description

AAA	ASCII Adjust after Addition
AAD	ASCII Adjust AX before Division
AAM	ASCII Adjust AX after Multiply
AAS	ASCII Adjust AL after Subtraction
ADC	Add with Carry
ADD	Add
AND	Logical AND
ARPL	Adjust RPL Field of Selector
BOUND	Check Array Index against Bounds
BSF	Bit Scan Forward
BSR	Bit Scan Reverse
BT	Bit Test
BTC	Bit Test and Complement
BTR	Bit Test and Reset
BTS	Bit Test and Set
CALL	Call Procedure
CBW	Convert Byte to Word
CDQ	Convert Double Word to Quadword
CLC	Clear Carry Flag
CLD	Clear Direction Flag
CLI	Clear Interrupt Flag
CLTS	Clear Task-Switching Flag in CR0
CMC	Complement Carry Flag
CMP	Compare Two Operands
CMPSB	Compare String Byte Operand
CMPSW	Compare String Word Operand
CMPSD	Compare String Double Word Operand
CWD	Convert Word to Double Word
CWDE	Convert Word to Double Word with Sign Extended
DAA	Decimal Adjust AL after Addition
DAS	Decimal Adjust AL after Subtraction
DEC	Decrement by 1
DIV	Unsigned Divide
ENTER	Make Stack Frame for Procedure Parameters
HLT	Halt
IDIV	Signed Divide
IMUL	Signed Multiply
IN	Input from Port
INC	Increment by 1
INSB	Input from Port to Byte String
INSW	Input from Port to Word String
INSD	Input from Port to Double Word String
INT	Call to Interrupt Procedure
INTO	Call to Interrupt 4 (Overflow) Procedure
IRET	16-bit Interrupt Return
IRETD	32-bit Interrupt Return
JA	Jump if Above
JAE	Jump if Above or Equal

JB	Jump if Below
JBE	Jump if Below or Equal
JC	Jump if Carry
JCXZ	Jump if CX Register is 0
JECXZ	Jump if ECX Register is 0
JE	Jump if Equal
JG	Jump if Greater
JGE	Jump if Greater or Equal
JL	Jump if Less
JLE	Jump if Less or Equal
JNA	Jump if not Above
JNAE	Jump if not Above or Equal
JNB	Jump if not Below
JNBE	Jump if not Below or Equal
JNC	Jump if not Carry
JNE	Jump if not Equal
JNG	Jump if not Greater
JNGE	Jump if not Greater or Equal
JNL	Jump if not Less
JNLE	Jump if not Less or Equal
JNO	Jump if not Overflow
JNP	Jump if not Parity
JNS	Jump if not Sign
JNZ	Jump if not Zero
JO	Jump if Overflow
JP	Jump if Parity
JPE	Jump if Parity Even
JPO	Jump if Parity Odd
JS	Jump if Sign
JZ	Jump if Zero
JMP	Jump
LAHF	Load Flags into AH Register
LAR	Load Access Rights Byte
LDS	Load DS Segment Register with Pointer
LEA	Load Effective Address
LEAVE	High Level Procedure Exit
LES	Load ES Segment Register with Pointer
LFS	Load FS Segment Register with Pointer
LGDT	Load Global Descriptor Table Register
LGS	Load GS Segment Register with Pointer
LIDT	Load Interrupt Descriptor Table Register
LLDT	Load Local Descriptor Table Register
LMSW	Load Machine Status Word
LOCK	Assert LOCK# Signal Prefix
LODSB	Load String Byte Operand
LODSW	Load String Word Operand
LODSD	Load String Double Word Operand
LOOP	Loop
LOOPE	Loop if Equal
LOOPNE	Loop if not Equal
LOOPNZ	Loop if not Zero

LOOPZ	Loop if Zero
LSL	Load Segment Limit
LSS	Load SS Segment Register with Pointer
LTR	Load Task Register
MOV	Move Data
MOVSB	Move Data from Byte String to Byte String
MOVSW	Move Data from Word String to Word String
MOVSD	Move Data from DWord Stirng to DWord String
MOVSX	Move with Sign-Extend
MOVZX	Move with Zero-Extend
MUL	Unsigned Multiplication of AL or AX
NEG	Two's Complement Negation
NOP	No Operation
NOT	One's Complement Negation
OR	Logical Inclusive OR
OUT	Output to Port
OUTSB	Output String Byte to Port
OUTSW	Output String Word to Port
OUTSD	Output String Double Word to Port
POP	Pop a Word from the Stack
POPA	Pop 16-bit All General Registers
POPAD	Pop 32-bit All General Register
POPF	Pop Stack Into FLAGS
POPFD	Pop Stack Into EFLAGS
PUSH	Push Operand onto the Stack
PUSHA	Push 16-bit All General Registers
PUSHAD	Push 32-bit All General Registers
PUSHF	Push FLAGS Register onto the Stack
PUSHFD	Push EFLAGS Register onto the Stack
RCL	Rotate Left with Carry
RCR	Rotate Right with Carry
REP	Repeat Following String Operation
REPE	Repeat Following String Operation if Equal
REPZ	Repeat Following String Operation if Zero
REPNE	Repeat Following String Operation if not Equal
REPNZ	Repeat Following String Operation if not Zero
RET	Return form Procedure
ROL	Rotate Left
ROR	Rotate Right
SAHF	Store AH into Flags
SAL	Arithmetic Shift Left
SAR	Arithmetic Shift Right
SHL	Shift Left
SHR	Shift Right
SBB	Integer Subtraction with Borrow
SCASB	Compare String Byte
SCASW	Compare String Word
SCASD	Compare String Double Word
SETA	Set Byte if Above
SETAE	Set Byte if Above or Equal
SETB	Set Byte if Below

SETBE	Set Byte if Below of Equal
SETC	Set Byte if Carry
SETE	Set Byte if Equal
SETG	Set Byte if Greater
SETGE	Set Byte if Greater or Equal
SETL	Set Byte if Less
SETLE	Set Byte if Less or Equal
SETNA	Set Byte if not Above
SETNAE	Set Byte if not Above or Equal
SETNB	Set Byte if not Below
SETNBE	Set Byte if not Below or Equal
SETNC	Set Byte if not Carry
SETNE	Set Byre if not Equal
SETNG	Set Byte if not Greater
SETNGE	Set Byte if not Greater or Equal
SETNL	Set Byte if not Less
SETNLE	Set Byte if not Less or Equal
SETNO	Set Byte if not Overflow
SETNP	Set Byte if not Parity
SETNS	Set Byte if not Sign
SETNZ	Set Byte if not Zero
SETO	Set Byte if Overflow
SETP	Set Byte if Parity
SETPE	Set Byte if Parity Even
SETPO	Set Byte if Parity Odd
SETS	Set Byte if Sign
SETZ	Set Byte if Zero
SGDT	Store Global Descriptor Table Register
SHLD	Double Precision Shift Left
SHRD	Double Precision Shift Right
SIDT	Store Interrupt Descriptor Table Register
SLDT	Store Local Descriptor Table Register
SMSW	Store Machine Status Word
STC	Set Carry Flag
STD	Set Direction Flag
STI	Set Interrupt Flag
STOSB	Store String Byte Data
STOSW	Store String Word Data
STOSD	Store String Double Word Data
STR	Store Task Register
SUB	Integer Subtraction
TEST	Logical Compare
VERR	Verify a Segment for Reading
VERW	Verify a Segment for Writing
WAIT	Wait until BUSY# Pin is Inactive
XCHG	Exchange Operand
XLAT/XLATB	Table Look-up Translation
XOR	Logical Exclusive OR

APPENDIX C

Assembler and Linker

The assembler and linker used for compilation of the programs in this book is the Microsoft Assembler Version 5.1 and the Microsft Linker Version 5.1. Following is a batch file example which can assemble and link an assembly program.

File: ASM.BAT

```
    masm %1;

    link %1;
```

When the assembly program is ready, you can type "asm filename" from the command line and get the object file and execution file. To execute the program, you can type the name of the execution file from the command line.

GLOSSARY

Breakpoint: The address of memory location which is held by the debug register to support debugging. The i386/i486 processor generates an exception when memory access is made to the breakpoint.

Cache: A small, high-speed memory that holds the data that the processor may need soon.

Cache fill: An operation that loads a block of data from main memory into the cache line.

Call Gate: A gate descriptor used for control transfers from lower privilege level to higher privilege level within a task.

Conforming code segment: A code segment that executes at the privilege level of the calling procedure. When control is transferred to a conforming code segment, the CPL does not change.

Coprocessor: An auxiliary processor which has a specific interface and extension instruction set of a processor.

Current Privilege Level (CPL): The privilege level of the task currently under execution in the system. The CPL value is defined in the lowest two bits of the CS segment register.

Debug registers: Six registers used to specify breakpoint and control debugging.

Descriptor Privilege Level (DPL): A field in the segment descriptor that defines the privilege level value for this segment.

Exceptions: A special control transfer method that can alter the normal execution of a program. There are two ways to generate an exception. One is when the i386/i486 processor detects faults, traps, and aborts during instruction execution. The other is a programmed exception.

Global Descriptor Table (GDT): An array of 8-byte segment descriptors for programs running in the protected mode.

Interrupts: A special control transfer method that can alter the normal execution of a program. An interrupt is invoked by a hardware signal and can occur at any time during the execution of a program.

Interrupt Descriptor Table (IDT): An array of 8-byte gate descriptors that can point out the address of up to 256 interrupt service routines. Three kinds of descriptors can be defined in the IDT: Task Gate Descriptor, Trap Gate Descriptor, and Interrupt Gate Descriptor.

Interrupt Gate: A gate descriptor that should be defined in the Interrupt Descriptor Table (IDT) to invoke an interrupt handler.

Local Descriptor Table (LDT): An array of 8-byte segment descriptors for one task. This table allows each task to have its own code and data segment.

Multiprocessing: A system that supports more than one processor.

Multitasking: A management method controlled by the operating system to let several tasks share one processor.

Page Directory Table: The first-level page table used to map to the second-level page table.

Page Directory Base Register (PDBR): A register that holds the physical base address of the page directory table. It is also called the CR3 register.

Page: A fixed memory block. In the i386/i486 processor, one page occupies four kilobytes of memory.

Paging: One of the memory management mechanisms supported by the i386/i486 processor. Paging can be used to simulate a large memory by using pages in conjunction with disk storage.

Privilege Level: A number defined by the i386/i486 processor to present the degree of protection. There are four privilege levels, numbered from 0 to 3, for each task.

Protected mode: The original operation mode of the i386/i486 processor. The full 32-bit architecture, multitasking, paging, and debugging are available in this mode.

Real-address mode: An 8086/8088 processor emulation operation provided by the i386/i486 processor. The features of the protected mode are not available in this mode.

Requested Privilege Level (RPL): The privilege level given by any procedure to access a segment. The RPL value is defined in the lowest two bits of any segment selector.

Segment descriptor: An 8-byte data entry defined in the segment descriptor table. It includes the definition of the base address, size, type, attribute, and protection information for a segment.

Segment selector: A 16-bit offset value relative to the descriptor table (GDT or LDT). It specifies which descriptor table (GDT or LDT) is used and the requested privilege level in the three least significant bits.

Segmentation: One of the memory management mechanisms supported by the i386/i486 processor. It provides multiple independent, variable-sized, and protected address spaces (called segments) to the program. The segment information such as base address, size, and type must be defined in the segment descriptor table before the segment can be accessed.

Supervisor level: The privilege level when paging is enabled. A task is running in the supervisor level if the CPL of this task equals 0, 1, or 2.

Task State Segment (TSS): A system data structure used to store the machine state of one task during a task switch.

Task Switch: Change execution from one task to another task. The change is not only transfer control. It exchanges the context of machine state for both tasks.

Translation Look-aside Buffer (TLB): The on-chip cache used to store the most recently used page table entries when paging is enabled.

Trap Gate: A gate descriptor that should be defined in the Interrupt Descriptor Table (IDT) to invoke an interrupt handler. The difference between Interrupt Gate and Trap Gate is the effect on an IF flag. The Interrupt Gate clears the IF flag during the service of a handler, while a Trap Gate leaves the IF flag unchanged.

User level: The privilege level when paging is enabled. A task is running in the user level if the CPL of this task equals 3.

V86 monitor: A software interface residing in the protected mode to initialize and handle exceptions for a v86 task.

V86 mode: An 8086/8088 processor emulation under the control of the protected mode.

Write-through: A kind of caching that updates both cache memory and main memory during a write operation.

INDEX